Experiencing Poetry

Titles in the series:

Experiencing Poetry

A Guidebook to Psychopoetics

WILLIE VAN PEER AND ANNA CHESNOKOVA

BLOOMSBURY ACADEMIC
LONDON • NEW YORK • OXFORD • NEW DELHI • SYDNEY

BLOOMSBURY ACADEMIC
Bloomsbury Publishing Plc
50 Bedford Square, London, WC1B 3DP, UK
1385 Broadway, New York, NY 10018, USA
29 Earlsfort Terrace, Dublin 2, Ireland

BLOOMSBURY, BLOOMSBURY ACADEMIC and the Diana logo
are trademarks of Bloomsbury Publishing Plc

First published in Great Britain 2023

ISBN: HB: 978-1-3502-4801-4
         PB: 978-1-3502-4802-1
         ePDF: 978-1-3502-4804-5
         eBook: 978-1-3502-4803-8

Series: Bloomsbury Advances in Stylistics

Typeset by Integra Software Services Pvt. Ltd.
Printed and bound in Great Britain

To find out more about our authors and books visit www.bloomsbury.com
and sign up for our newsletters.

Contents

Figures

Preface

The title of this book has the word *psychopoetics* in it, and you may wonder what it means. Does the book deal with psychology? Or with poetry? Or with both of them? *Psychopoetics*, then, in our view, is the study of poetic *experiences*, of what goes through you when you are confronted with poetic texts. In fact, it is not a new word, but an existing one. Some literary studies have used it before, albeit in a different sense.[1] Such references to *psychopoetics* were rather scattered and unsystematic. They largely remained on the level of *nullius in verba*—'words' (*verba*), in which however, there is 'nothing' (*nullius*). This phrase, *nullius in verba*, is the motto of the British Royal Society—and functioned as a guideline for researchers, opening up the scientific revolution of the seventeenth century. But that happened mainly in the natural sciences. When it comes to understanding mankind—presumably one of the central tasks of the Humanities, things often remain stuck in *verba*. The remedy to it, we believe, is *gnothi seauton* (Greek for 'know thyself,' one of the Delphic maxims). And one of the best ways to get to know ourselves is through independent research about human (including psychological) experiences—the approach this book relies on. If it is not independent, it is most likely to be skewed by researchers' prejudices, making it unreliable.

In this book, we will use the term 'psychopoetics' for the study of literary content, form, and its concomitant personal experience, with the aim to come up with an *evidence-based* approach to the study of literature—not *nullius in verba*, but trying to find *validation* for the claims we uphold. We propose that it is extremely fruitful to look at poetry from a psychological point of view. That means looking not just at poetic texts *per se*, but also at the kind of subjective processes readers go through, as well as examining their effects on the lives of individuals and groups. This has always been part of the traditional study of poetry, but not as a form of systematic exploration. It was mostly *assumed* that texts exerted some influence, but scholars never went so far as to methodically investigate whether their claims could be factually substantiated. That is precisely what we intend to do in this book: expose claims about the psychological workings of poetry to serious and methodical tests as well as instruct our readers on how to apply and interpret such tests.

Psychopoetics, as we understand it, is indeed connected to psychology, or rather to the study of psychological aspects of language, or psycholinguistics—the area of research for which the term was coined in the 1940s and came into wider use with the publication in 1954 of Osgood and Sebeok's *Psycholinguistics: A Survey of Theory and Research Problems*. And since poetry exists *in* language, a good deal of our work will hinge on the insights and methods of psycholinguistics.

Over the past decades, there have been developments in literary studies that also undertook a shift toward the psychological end of reading literature. These are usually subsumed under the label of 'cognitive poetics.' The field has produced quite a number of interesting publications, such as Brone and Vandaele (2009), Freeman (2020), Gavins and Steen (2003), Semino and Culpeper (2002), Stockwell (2020), and Tsur (2008). While this approach has undeniably contributed to a higher awareness of how literary texts are understood, it differs from what the present book aims at. The reason is clear enough from the label by which this approach goes: it is 'cognitive,' i.e., geared at processes of comprehension and interpretation. The present book, however, aims at *experiencing* poetry, which is a much broader category, especially encompassing emotional experiences, which are hardly envisaged by the cognitive program.

There are other differences with more traditional introductions to poetics. One is that we will not look at literature in English only, but will also involve texts in other languages: German, Greek, Italian, Japanese, Latin, Mande, Portuguese, Russian, Spanish, and Sumerian—to name just a few.

Why are we doing this, you may ask. There are two main reasons for this choice. First, we write this book for an international audience, while the bulk of introductory books on literary theory only treat English texts (thus being monocultural). And although English is no doubt the global language for academic and scientific communication, we believe there is value in also drawing attention to the multiplicity and variety of cultural expressions. An even more pregnant reason is that different cultures handle poetic issues in different ways. Just one example to think about—*qua* population Iceland equals Luxembourg (the Grand-Duché) as a country, but no writers or works of note have emerged in the latter country, while Iceland has produced a plethora of sagas in the past and continues to produce internationally renowned authors today. Psychopoetics, in our view, is the study of poetry *generally*. So we cannot confine ourselves to one language only. Limiting ourselves to English examples would severely reduce the richness of poetic traditions and thus neglect themes, structures, and affects that are common in the world of poetry at large. Comparisons between various poetic traditions deepen our grasp of psychopoetics.

Additionally, we believe that a valid *psychopoetics* needs not only an *intercultural*, but also a *historical* perspective. Without this combination, no validity in any poetic theory can be established. Unfortunately, most books on literary theory predominantly look at texts from the eighteenth century onward only (hence being a-historical).

Furthermore, apart from being multicultural and historical, our general orientation of psychopoetics is *evidence-based* and *reader-focused* in nature. A certain degree of speculation is inevitable and even necessary in thinking about poetry, but the hallmark of research lies in submitting such speculations to rigorous inquiry. The general attitude in literary studies is that they actually stop at the speculative stage, so that their comments remain hanging in the air. In this book we seriously attempt to find out whether there is good (i.e., methodologically reliable) evidence for our hypotheses. For readers interested in such a research program, we wholeheartedly recommend the volume by Kuiken and Jacobs (2021), which contains illuminating chapters on methods and theoretical foundations, plus numerous examples of concrete research carried out. It is a real treasure trove for anyone wishing to know about readers' *real* experiences of literature, and how to explore them.

But what do we mean by 'poetic'? We may find children at play 'poetic.' Or we may be impressed by a spectacular sunset and call this 'poetic.' We agree with such notions, as they are everyday expressions of the poetic nature of things in everyday life. But in this book we will limit ourselves to the use of 'poetic' in relation to poetry—either in its written (or printed) form or as performed orally for an audience.

With this in mind, we wish you a captivating journey of discovery in the little known land of psychopoetics.

Further reading

Dissanayake, E. (1992), *Homo Aestheticus. Where Art Comes from and Why.* Seattle and London: University of Washington Press.

Freeman, M. H. (2020), *The Poem as Icon: A Study in Aesthetic Cognition.* Oxford: Oxford University Press.

Greene, R. and S. Cushman, (eds) (2012), *The Princeton Encyclopedia of Poetry and Poetics.* Princeton: Princeton University Press.

Harley, T. A. (2014), *The Psychology of Language. From Data to Theory.* 4th edn, Hove: Taylor & Francis.

Miall, D. S. (2006), *Literary Reading. Empirical and Theoretical Studies.* New York: Peter Lang.

Foreword

During the summer of 2021, I attended the online meeting of the Empirical Study of Literature conference hosted by the University of Liverpool. Due to mistaken timing on my part, I found myself, by myself in a Zoom room waiting to give a keynote on the processes of poetry writing and personal insight. To my delight, Willie van Peer, an old and dear acquaintance, in fact one of the few researchers whose own work had facilitated and shown the way for my own dissertation utilizing empirical studies of poetry, appeared on the screen before me. After a brief interaction of catching up, he asked me if I would be willing to read and comment on the book that is before you now. I agreed and following my commentary Willie and his co-author, Anna Chesnokova, asked me if I was willing to write a foreword for the book. As you can see, I agreed to this request.

So first, in line with the voice and aims of this book, let me share my own experiences of reading this book. How refreshing is it to read a book that talks to you directly and does not hide behind third person prose? How invigorating is it to read a book which enacts before you the points it is trying to make rather than just telling you the outcome? My first impression of this book was just the way it was written, with the focus on speaking directly to the reader, and taking the reader through the analytical processes that are being described. Clearly this approach is intentional, with the aim of allowing readers less versed in the variety of empirical methods exemplified here to have a point of access. This is similar to how my own first graduate courses in psycholinguistics were taught, with an emphasis on experiencing the methodologies being taught and not just working through the described findings. The use of voice and form in the writing of this book make it an inviting choice for allowing a variety of readers from the diversity of disciplines to enter into the field of empirical studies of poetics. Hopefully many new types of readers may, as I did many years ago, through this new work of van Peer and Chesnokova, find a point of entry into a field that they might not have known was a possibility.

This book develops the concept of psychopoetics and applies this to a range of poetic forms. While the term is not new in itself, it is new in the way the term is understood and applied here. The concept of psychopoetics could be summarized as the psycholingusitics of poetics, an attempt to systematically explore the ways in which literary texts interact with human readers. There is, of course, a history for this and a collection of researchers who have been interested and active with this research agenda. The Empirical Study of Literature (IGEL) professional community, for example, regularly brings together researchers involved in this research and the journal the *Scientific Study of Literature*, of which van Peer was the first editor, disseminates scholarship of this kind. And yet, the empirical study of literature is often felt to be strange and distant by other literary scholars, and the world of literary text and creative writing is often felt to be out of the norm for empirical researchers in psychology. Perhaps the concept of psychopoetics as manifest in this book can offer a solution to the sense of strangeness felt by some in the field of literary and psychological studies.

The agenda of enlarging the population of empirical literary researchers is also clear in the choice of discussed materials. The authors are right when they point out the bias toward monocultural texts in many literary studies, empirical or otherwise. The application of empirical approaches to world literature materials is a welcome departure from nationalist emphases of many past studies. Shouldn't a psychopoetics be on a level above the individual language group and address the processes of poetics themselves? Importantly, this also potentially facilitates the inclusion of a wider range of researchers from a broader set of countries. Once again, this book may serve as a point of entry for this broader world of researchers.

I have spoken of the value of the book as a point of entry. But this is not to be confused with simplicity. One of the joys of reading this book is the combination of quality literary text, stylistic analysis, and empirical research all presented in a single progression. The complexity of psychopoetics is that it brings together different disciplinary analytical approaches. This is clear in the construction of the term itself and enacted throughout this book. While I can see some arguing whether a new usage of the term 'psychopoetics' is necessary, my own perspective as a long-term empirical researcher of poetry, is that if this concept brings new people into the field and at the same time offers a clear integration of the disciplines, then this is a valuable contribution. It is clear to me that the underpinning aims of this book are similar to those that van Peer has had throughout his career, to propose and exemplify a systematic, data-driven approach to the reading of a wide range of literary texts with the aim of promoting and facilitating new studies and inviting new researchers into the arena of psycholinguistic studies of poetics. I hope that you as the reader of this book enjoy it as much as I have done.

David I. Hanauer
Editor: *Scientific Study of Literature*
Professor of Applied Linguistics, English Department, Indiana University of Pennsylvania

Acknowledgments

This book has been long in the making. The challenge was to both open up a new field of research, the psychological experiences of poetry, and at the same time develop the field to newcomers, both students and educators.

We are thankful to all our colleagues who helped us make this book better by reading earlier versions of the manuscript. Our special gratitude goes to Marisa Bortolussi Dixon, Brian Boyd, Mimi Debruyn, Nigel Fabb, David Hanauer, Max Louwerse, and Paul Sopčák, who generously sent us detailed comments to both individual chapters and the whole volume.

We are also indebted to Margaret H. Freeman, Akiko Hirose, Alberto Martínez, Ursula Offerman and Elisa Soster, for giving us their valuable advice on particular issues.

Greatly appreciated was Becky Holland and Laura Gallon's skillful assistance in guiding us through the publication process.

The authors and publishers are grateful to the following for permission granted to reproduce copyright material in this book:

- The heirs of Joaquim Frederico de Brito, for reprinting the lyrics of the song 'Loucura';

- Taylor and Francis (Books) Limited, for reprinting Fig. 3.1 from *Stylistics and Psychology* by W. van Peer;

- Carcanet Press Limited and Farrar Straus and Giroux, for reprinting 'A Song' by J. Brodsky;

- Liveright Publishing Corporation, for reprinting 'Anyone Lived in a Pretty How Town' and the opening lines from 'Yes Is a Pleasant Country' by E. E. Cummings;

- The British Museum, for reprinting the Flood Tablet of the *Epic of Gilgamesh*;

- John Wiley & Sons, Inc., for reprinting Fig. 9.4 from *Power. The Inner Experience* by D. C. McClelland;

- Martino Fine Books, for reprinting Fig. 5.1 from *The Achieving Society* by D. C. McClelland;

- The Staatliche Antikensammlung and Glyptothek in Munich, for reprinting the picture of Sappho;

- The *American Economic Journal: Applied Economics*, for reprinting Fig. 3 from the article 'Soap Operas and Fertility: Evidence from Brazil' by E. La Ferrara et al.

1

Poetry Is Structure

Keywords

psychopoetics	*meter*
prototype	*foot*
stanza	*figurative language*
verse	*ballad*
rhyme	*Lied*
rhyme scheme	*high and low culture*

Psychopoetics is a combination of psychology and poetics. Presumably the word 'psychology' needs no further elucidation. It is the (wide-ranging) study of human mental processes: cognition, emotion, attitudes, and behavior. This is also the sense in which we will use the term in this book.

But what is 'poetics'? In general, it deals with literature in theoretical terms: what *is* literature, what are its forms and manifestations, how did it evolve historically and in different cultures? More specifically (and this is the meaning in which it is used here), it is the theory of poetry. Psychopoetics, then, is the study of the psychological experience of literature and, more specifically, of poetry in its various aspects and meanings.

But what is 'poetry'? That may be the most difficult of the terms to define, because there is no strict definition—all efforts at defining it point to tendencies that may be present to a greater or lesser extent. Characteristics that are often mentioned are:

1 shortness, though some of the most famous poems, such as the *Iliad* or the *Divina Commedia* are extraordinarily long;

2 formal qualities (such as meter, rhyme, alliteration or verse, and stanza forms)—but many poems do not contain any of them;

3 density of meaning, through figurative language such as metaphor, allegory, or symbolism—though some very beautiful poems are also very simple;

4 an emphasis on subjective emotional aspects—but some poems relate stories.

Instead of looking for a conclusive definition, it may be more fruitful to think of poetry in terms of *prototypes*. Let us give you an example. It may be difficult to provide an undisputed definition of a 'bird' (outside of biology, of course). Should it be able to fly? Well, yes, but some birds, like penguins, cannot. But we could say that some fowl, like robins, ducks, or falcons, are more 'prototypical' birds than ostriches or coursers. If we take this approach to poetry, we could say that the more each of the above four qualities is present in a text, the more people will be likely to deem it a poem.

Psychopoetic research can be compared to the situation in *Hamlet* (Act II, scene ii), where Polonius asks Hamlet what he is reading, to which the latter replies:

Words, words, words.

Indeed, that is what poetry is about: words. But as Shakespeare's play amply illustrates: words are not without effect. They can fool someone; they can mislead; they may even kill, as becomes clear in the play. Words in poetry often carry such powerful meanings. Because it aims at powerful emotional experiences.

Prototype poetry

We will now deal with a particular poem at length, demonstrating a number of typical characteristics, like the ones just mentioned, as they have come down to us through tradition. This will occupy some time, introducing you to some psychological experiences when confronting poetic texts.

The poem we are going to look at is one of the most famous poems written in German, by the towering figure of German literature, Johann Wolfgang von Goethe, or Goethe, as he is usually called. Wait! Do not run away: you may soon find out how close it is to present-day concerns.

Many people, especially in the English-speaking world, struggle with the pronunciation of his name, which you will hear in the short clip we will ask you to listen to. These are the first lines of the poem, read in German (the middle line) with the English translation above, and some phonetic transcription below it. The reading is not particularly appealing, but is meant to introduce the text to you. Please play it a couple of times, to familiarize yourself with the sound and the meaning of the poem before we go on: Link 1.1 on the Companion Website.

How does it sound to you? What do you make of the repetitive

Röslein, Röslein, Röslein rot?

Some people find this threefold repetition enchanting, even bewitching. Is that also your reaction? Often in our first reactions we feel attracted to something, or rather repelled. But it also happens sometimes that we change our views when we look closer: what appeared fanciful may now look trite. And what initially sounded strange and unappealing strengthens its captivation when studied closer. So let us have a closer look at the poem itself. You may have heard its title, 'Heidenröslein,' which literally means 'little rose on the heath.' That is the title of the poem, but the word does not itself turn up in the poem, though *Röslein* ('little rose', or the more old-fashioned 'briar') does—eighteen times even. The word *Heidenröslein* is not really a German word. If you look it up in a dictionary, you may not find it. And *if* it happens to be there, it will be because of this poem by Goethe. This is how it begins:

> *Sah ein Knab' ein Röslein stehn,*
>   (Once a boy a briar saw)
> *Röslein auf der Heiden.*
>   (Briar on the meadow.)
> *War so jung und morgenschön,*
>   (Was so young and beauteous,)
> *Lief er schnell, es nah zu sehn,*
>   (Quickly ran to see it near,)
> *Sah's mit vielen Freuden.*
>   (Saw't with untold fondness.)
> *Röslein, Röslein, Röslein rot,*
>   (Briar, briar, briar red,)
> *Röslein auf der Heiden.*
>   (Briar on the meadow.)

What strikes one's attention immediately is the 'white' space surrounding the lines. Or maybe it does not strike you because that is what you expect in poetry in the first place. In fact, you can often recognize poetry at a glance, precisely because of the white space to the right and left of each line. In prose, we fill the lines up to the margin. But in poetry, we leave a white space between the line and the margin, sometimes also to the right of a line, as is the case here. But there is more: we also have a white space above and below the lines. The effect of the white is that the group of lines is separated from its environment. Such a group of isolated lines in poetry is called a *stanza*, and each line is called a *verse (line)*.

Here, each verse line forms a unit in itself. While reading the lines aloud, you can make a pause after each one. That is because the line coincides with a major grammatical unit, say, a sentence or a clause. We call such lines *end-stopped*. This is clearly a pattern in this poem—which is not always the case. Sometimes meaning in a line of poetry goes over to the next line without a grammatical pause and terminal punctuation by way of *enjambment*. Now look at the last word of each line. Even if you do not know German, you will notice that some lines *rhyme*: *stehn/sehn*. And then *Heiden* and *Freuden* are, well, not a complete rhyme, but 'almost'—we call that a *half-rhyme*. There is another half-rhyme: it is between *stehn/sehn* and *schön*. But there is one line that does not rhyme at all. It is the one ending in *rot* (pronounced more or less like 'roat,' meaning the color red in German), making it stand out, on its own, separated from the rest of the poem. And it also contains the threefold repetition of *Röslein* we mentioned earlier.

When we talk about rhymes in poetry, there is a convention for representing them, called a *rhyme scheme*. It goes like this: you take the vowel and the following consonant of the first rhyme word (that is the vowel in the last word of the first line) and represent it by the symbol *A*. Whenever this vowel + the same consonant turns up at the end of a line, you repeat the *A*. (And we can use *A'* for half-rhymes.) When, by contrast, you encounter another vowel in the last word of a line, you give it the symbol *B*, etc. Let us look at an example, one of the most famous love poems in the English language, Andrew Marvell's 'To His Coy Mistress':

Had we but world enough and time,
This coyness, lady, were no crime.
We would sit down, and think which way
To walk, and pass our long love's day.

'Time' and 'crime' both rhyme, so that is *A A*. But 'way' does not rhyme with 'time,' so here we use the next letter of the alphabet, *B*, and the rhymes of verses 3–4 are *B B*. Thus the rhyme scheme of this stanza is:

A A B B.

In 'Heidenröslein' the rhyme scheme is somewhat more complex. You may check it in the German original, if you want:

A B A' A B C B.

If you look at a rhyme scheme like this, it becomes clear that rhymes form a network that intertwines the sounds and meanings of the verses. And thus it illuminates that the *C* word stands out all alone, for us to notice, again and again, focusing our attention on the color, red. Here we see the ingredients of a psychological effect: sound and meaning are woven together in such a way that they appeal to our feelings, even if you had not consciously observed it. The expectation subliminally built up by the rhyme scheme makes the penultimate line stand out, by its threefold repetition, and by its *deviation* from the expected sound pattern (we will talk more about this in Chapter 4 later).

Now let us put the serious matters away for a while and play a game. Yes, we are not joking. Games can be very informative, as participants display their genuine gut reactions—and this is exactly what we need when applying the evidence-based approach to poetry. So read the poem below and finish the last line of it with whatever word comes to your mind:

> I didn't look above my head;
> I tried to cross the street instead.
> Thank god my mother thought ahead;
> In fact, without her I'd be dead.
> So, 'Check the traffic lights!,' she said,
> 'And wait until the man turns _____'.

What was your choice then? In all probability it was 'red,' which, if you stop and think about it, makes no sense: you need a 'green' light to cross the street safely. So rhyme beats common sense and pragmatics, right?

Now another poem, and the task remains the same:

> Having pests at home is never nice.
> If you do, dispose of cheese and rice.
> That's of course, if you have seen a _____.

What was your word this time? 'Mice'? Or 'mouse'? Stop and look at the indefinite article 'a' preceding the gap. The noun to complete the line should be singular, thus 'mouse.' Is it again the rhyme that won, or grammar? Tsoukala, Vogelzang, and Tsimpli (2021) hold that '[p]honological cues can affect word selection (Rapp and Samuel 2002) and possibly override contextual constraints.' In the experiment they ran with this rhyme inhibition task, 'the inaccurate choice was spontaneously produced more frequently (43%) for texts leading to a violation of pragmatics and less frequently (17%) when it led to grammar violation.' They also predict that the effect may even be stronger in case poems are read aloud—as they were in old times, when the genre originated.

But so much for the ends of the lines, as the lines also display an internal pattern *within* themselves. When you count the number of syllables in

'Heidenröslein,' you notice an alternation of 6 and 7 syllables per line, distributed as follows: 7-6-7-7-6-7-6. Such a regularity is no accident and often occurs in poetry. There is also another regularity. Read the lines aloud one by one (also in the English version). It turns out that not all syllables are pronounced with the same *stress*. The regularity consists of a steady alternation between stressed and unstressed syllables, with the stressed syllable as the first one of each line. A common way to render this in poetics is the use of the following marks:

/ = stressed
x = unstressed.

When we apply this to 'Heidenröslein,' the pattern looks as follows:

/ x / x / x /
/ x / x / x
/ x / x / x /
/ x / x / x /
/ x / x / x
/ x / x / x /
/ x / x / x.

Such alternations have been studied for (literally) millennia by scholars, who have come up with a whole arsenal of insights, to which they gave names, or literary terms. (You will find a list of such terms in the Glossary at the end of this book.) The regularities were then systematized. The general term for such groupings of stressed/unstressed syllables (at least in a language like English) is *meter*. A group of recurrent alternations is called a *foot*. In 'Heidenröslein' the foot is the repetition of /x, that is first a stressed, then an unstressed syllable: you find a good deal of this in nursery rhymes, such as, for instance,

Peter Peter, pumpkin eater
/   x / x   /   x / x.

This kind of foot is called a *trochee*. (The corresponding adjective is *trochaic*.) So the first line of our poem has three trochees and a half, the second one three trochees, and so on. Verse lines like these are called a *trochaic trimeter*. They contain *three* trochaic feet per line, sometimes (as with the odd-numbered verse lines) with an after-beat—three trochees and a half, so to say. Such patterns of stress, *meter*, allow them to be set to music, as we shall see in an instant. This metrical structure is often, however, at odds with the stress pattern in spoken language. Check for instance, the first two lines:

Sah ein Knab' ein Röslein stehn,
Röslein auf der Heiden.

(Once a boy a briar saw,
Briar on the meadow.)

The meter is clear:

/ x / x / x /
/ x / x / x.

This structure implies that *auf* (on) in the second line would be stressed, but nobody would put a stress on that word, when saying 'briar on the meadow.' 'On' is a preposition, and prepositions, like most *function words*, do not ordinarily carry stress. Thus the spoken *rhythm* of the text builds an oscillation with the abstract rigidity of the meter. And poets play around with this pulsation between the poles of meter and rhythm. It is often precisely this interaction between meter and rhythm that underlies the pleasure of listening to this kind of poetry. Again we observe that poets play around with structures, triggering our pleasure, albeit largely unconsciously. Basho, the Japanese master of *haiku* poetry in the seventeenth century, expressed this through a *simile*: 'In my view a good poem is one in which the form of the verse and the joining of its parts seems light as a shallow river flowing over its sandy bed' (Basho 1985: 10).

Is this love?

Now, with this information in mind, let us look at the text in full—with the English translation by its side:

Sah ein Knab' ein Röslein stehn,
Röslein auf der Heiden,
War so jung und morgenschön,
Lief er schnell es nah zu sehn,
Sah's mit vielen Freuden.
Röslein, Röslein, Röslein rot,
Röslein auf der Heiden.

Once a boy a briar saw,
Briar on the meadow,
Was so young and beauteous,
Quickly ran to see it near,
Saw't with untold fondness.
Briar, briar, briar red,
Briar on the meadow.

Knabe sprach: 'Ich breche dich,
Röslein auf der Heiden.'
Röslein sprach: 'Ich steche dich,
Dass du ewig denkst an mich,
Und ich will's nicht leiden.'

Boy said: 'I'll break you,
Little briar on the heath.'
Little briar said: 'I'll prick you,
That you'll always think of me,
And, I don't want to suffer it.'

Röslein, Röslein, Röslein rot,	Briar, briar, briar red,
Röslein auf der Heiden.	Briar on the meadow.
Und der wilde Knabe brach	And the wild boy broke
's Röslein auf der Heiden;	Little briar of the heath.
Röslein wehrte sich und stach,	Little briar fought and pricked,
Half ihr doch kein Weh und Ach,	But helped her no Woe! or Ahh!,
Musste es eben leiden.	Had to suffer it quietly.
Röslein, Röslein, Röslein rot,	Briar, briar, briar red,
Röslein auf der Heiden.	Briar on the meadow.

Surprisingly, it is written in an almost childish German, with (except for *morgenschön*) only one- or two-syllable words, which may induce people to believe the text to be child-like. A boy comes along, sees a beautiful flower, a rose, and wants to cull it. The rose objects, threatens to prick him with its thorns, but eventually succumbs to the boy. Nothing more. That is indeed how many, perhaps most, people know and understand the poem. If read and understood in this way, it is indeed almost a children's story. There is nothing wrong in seeing it that way. Except that one is missing something rather crucial.

A typical trademark of poetry, namely, is the possibility of understanding the text in another, deeper, way. Flowers do not speak, nor do they normally have a will of their own. So how to understand the interaction between the rose and the boy? This may become clear when we ask ourselves: is the rose here really just a flower? Or does it stand for something else? If we see it that way, we are involved in *figurative* talk, one form of which is *metaphor*. A metaphor is a word or expression referring to something that is to be taken not literally, but figuratively. For instance, if you say of a particular politician that he is a 'fox,' you do not mean that he has a tail, or a brown furry skin—or that he goes out at night to catch chicken. Without any effort, we understand that it is some characteristics ascribed to the animal that we see in the politician. In the same way, the rose in the poem may refer not to a real flower—although the whole text makes you think so—but to a young woman. In literary tradition it is not at all unusual to use a flower as a *metaphor* for a (loved) woman. The rose is a *prototypical* example of such a flower. *The* literary example par excellence that springs to mind is, of course, Robert Burns's

> O my Luve's like a red, red rose,
>   That's newly sprung in June;
> O my Luve's like the melodie
>   That's sweetly play'd in tune.

('Melody' is, of course, another metaphor.) But now the whole idea of the Goethe poem changes dramatically: it may not be just a boy culling a flower; it may be a boy ruining a girl. And she has to suffer it quietly. The German is quite explicit: *Musste es eben leiden* (she had no choice but to suffer it). Now the poem is no longer a child's story.

There is still another, third, meaning hidden in the poem. It is that the rose stands not just for a girl, but for a young woman's virginity. Once we see this, the violence by the boy in the third stanza comes into relief. What is happening here is not just a boy culling a flower, but a forceful defloration. (Think of the word! It literally means ... 'plucking a flower.') To put it in harsh everyday terms: he rapes the girl. Remember, the boy is 'wild.' The German word *Knabe* means not only a young boy in the sense of a child, but a youth, an adolescent. The boy is thus a young adult who rapes a girl, maybe his beloved girl, or in any case has sex with her against her own will.

A historical comment is in place here. In many societies, and also in ours in the past, the loss of a young woman's virginity outside marriage meant a permanent collective eviction. It involved nothing less than social expulsion from the marriage market. She was now an outcast, a 'fallen' woman, and her prospects of living the life of a respectable lady were virtually nil. In that sense, her life was ruined. How harsh society treated female liberty in sexual matters may be seen in the fact that even consensual sex outside marriage was considered illegitimate: a woman's sexuality was bound exclusively within the confines of marriage. Any sexual activity outside marriage was considered beyond the bounds of respectability.

You may ask yourself: why would we have to see it that way, to read the rose as a girl and the poem as one about a relationship gone awry? The reason is that we have some information about the poem's history. It was written (in all probability) in 1771, while Goethe was studying (law) in Strasbourg and dedicated the poem to a young woman he was then wildly in love with. We know her name, Friederike Brion, and also part of the love story. Tumultuous it was, but short. Goethe, the ever-restless soul, ended the relationship a few months later and disappeared to Frankfurt, his home town, leaving Friederike in utter distress, since she had interpreted their trysts as a prelude to engagement and marriage. Friederike sent him a heart-wrenching letter, which deeply shocked Goethe: he had not anticipated that his departure and the separation had caused her such a deep wound. Her letter threw him off his feet, and he never forgave himself the episode. The guilt it had caused lasted his whole life. Several years later, he visited her again and was surprised how hospitable and good-heartedly he was received by all, Friederike and her family alike. Friederike never married.

We have come a long way from a love poem here. The theme is love indeed, but love turned violent. What the poem is about, basically, is not love, but frenzy. The young man physically overpowers the girl and subdues her to his sexual desires, in spite of her unwillingness to lose her virginity. We may happily think of love poems as romantic, but here that romantic idea is ruined. And the poet merely describes the cruelty, without morally commenting on it, which makes reading it even more disturbing. From the moment one realizes that this is not a children's song, the disturbance turns ghastly. And your experience of the text changes instantly to something eerie.

Music, maestro!

You may have heard about 'Heidenröslein' before—not this poem by Goethe, but as a song. Indeed, the composer Franz Schubert set it to music (in 1815). This disturbance we may experience in reading (once we have realized it is not a children's song)—is it mitigated by the music? Let us see. Before we start, however, do realize that this music may come about as unusual to you. Here the text *and* the melody play a vital role, and singers are expected to express a whole range of emotions, from tenderness to temerity, from frailty to fury, from downfall to death. So give it a chance—who knows what you may discover? Here it is, sung by Barbary Bonney, a famous American soprano: Link 1.2 on the Companion Website.

The melody is simple enough:[1] in the musical *key* of G major, known for its calm, tender and idyllic mood, with only one variation at the very end of line 3 (*morgenschön*), where it briefly turns to D major, usually reserved for a triumphant mood. (The word *morgenschön* literally means 'beautiful as the morning.') Is not the word indicating the triumphant beauty of the rose? But this key lasts only until line 5, and we return to G major in lines 6 and 7, in an almost jubilant tone, celebrating the beauty of the rose, to the very end.

At this point we may look in somewhat more detail at the structure of the poem. It is composed of three stanzas of seven lines each, totaling twenty-one lines. Each of the stanzas has a similar design: the first five verses, the *couplet*, tell a story, while the final two lines form a recurring *refrain*. The couplets form a progressive *narrative*, here from a (seemingly) innocent love encounter to a dramatic denouement at the end, while the refrain keeps reiterating the beauty of the rose. A refrain is usually independent of the narrative, highlighting a central message. We can represent this structure abstractly (similarly to the rhyme scheme) as: *A A' A''* (and so on). The structure is also called *strophic* (from 'strophe,' which is the same as a stanza) and is typical for romantic songs originating in German nineteenth-century culture, which today is still called, in English, a *Lied*, the German word for 'song' (pronounced 'leet,' plural *Lieder* pronounced like 'leeder').

The strophic structure reveals something deeper also. Remember that we talked about the *C* rhyme before, and how it stood out from the other rhymes, thereby drawing (surreptitiously) attention to itself. We can now observe that this line is part of the *refrain*:

Röslein, Röslein, Röslein rot
Röslein auf der Heiden.

Maybe you did not pay attention to it, but who *says* this? Who speaks these words? The preceding lines, in the *couplet*, are piece of a little story that is told by some narrator (a kind of poetic voice), whom we do not know. It is an invisible instance who 'presents' the events to us, but does not reveal itself. So this invisible narrator is the one who speaks in the couplets. But also in the refrain? That does not seem to be the case: the refrain is not really part of the story, but some general observation about the rose—and its beauty. This is clearly spoken by someone who is *outside* the story events. This aspect of songs is often central to their meaning, but—a meaning that is not given, but has to be in some way 'detected':

> The spoken ending is a characteristic example of 'markedness' in a song. Remember that a part of a text is 'marked' when it is different in some noticeable way from the rest. Markedness never has any particular meaning, but asks us to find a meaning, based on the text and to some extent on convention.
>
> (Nigel Fabb, personal communication)

Here we know that the meaning must relate to the brutal rape of the girl, but also to the tradition of celebrating the beauty of young women, by comparing them to flowers. The contrast between the concrete incidents of the drama that has unfolded and our obligation to search for a meaning of the refrain makes for the seriousness of the song: this is not a ditty.

If we understand the couplets to be spoken by the narrator, then we may assume that the refrain is spoken by the singer, who comments on the events that the narrator just revealed. That the comments are the same after each couplet bolsters the message: the unforgettable beauty of the little rose—in all the reverberating meanings that we have discovered.

These structures come out of folk traditions, where (professional) singers would perform them at markets or in closed circles. Classical composers (for example, Ludwig van Beethoven, Johannes Brahms, Joseph Haydn, Fanny Hensel, Liza Lehmann, Gustav Mahler, Wolfgang Amadeus Mozart, Robert Schumann, and Richard Strauss) used these structures to produce their own art songs. The most famous of such composers doubtlessly was Franz Schubert, who wrote whole cycles of *Lieder*, such as *Die schöne Müllerin* (literally 'The Beautiful Miller Girl'), *Die Winterreise* (The Winter Journey), and *Schwanengesang* (Swan Song). On the internet you can find scores of excellent video clips of these songs.

Folk traditions

This strophic structure of 'Heidenröslein' resembles that of a *ballad* in the English folk tradition (in fact, in many traditions), also developed in American ballads, the most famous of which are well known the world over, like 'The Ballad of Davy Crocket' or 'Jesse James.' Ballads are *narrative* poems: they tell a story, often a tragic one, in a poetic form. Typical for them is that the story starts *in medias res*, that is, in the middle of the action, without telling the listener what went on before, giving the story a somewhat mysterious character. Let us consider such a traditional ballad from the British Isles, in this case from Scotland. It is called 'Jock O'Hazeldean' and can be heard sung by one of the most exquisite Scottish folk singers, Dick Gaughan, Link 1.3 on the Companion Website.

And here are the lyrics:

Why weep ye by the tide, lady?
Why weep ye by the tide?
A'll wed ye tae[2] my youngest son
An ye shall be his bride.
An ye shall be his bride, lady,
Sae comely tae be seen.
But aye, she loot the tears doon fa'[3]
For Jock O'Hazeldean.

Noo let this willfu' grief be done
And dry those cheeks sae pale.
Young Frank is chief of Erthington,
And lord o' Langleydale.
His step is first in peaceful haa',[4]
His sword in battle keen.
But aye, she loot the tears doon fa'
For Jock O'Hazeldean.

A coat o' gowd[5] ye shall nae lack
Nor kaim[6] to bind your hair,
Nor mettled hound, nor managed hawk,
Nor palfrey fresh and fair.
And you, the foremost o' them aa'

Shall ride our forest queen.
But aye, she loot the tears doon fa'
For Jock O'Hazeldean.

The kirk[7] was decked at mornin' tide,
The tapers glimmerd fair.
The priest and bridegroom wait the bride
And dame and knight were there.
They searched for her in bower and haa',
The lady was nae seen.
She's o'er the border and awa'
Wi' Jock O'Hazeldean.

You notice four stanzas of eight verses each: six to each couplet, and two for the refrain, each time expressing the girl's profound attachment to her lover, Jock O'Hazeldean. The fact that the narrative starts *in medias res* may make it difficult to construct what is going on, especially at the beginning. It takes some concentration to notice that it is the father (of a boy) speaking (to the girl) in the first stanza. And he keeps talking to her in the following two stanzas, while the girl never answers him. The only thing she does is weep ('she loot the tears doon fa'—'she let the tears fall down'). By stanza four, we have become so accustomed to the father addressing her with his promises about what awaits her when she marries his son, that we may miss what happens next. The girl apparently consented to be married to the father's son, and we are now in church to celebrate the marriage. This is also typical for ballad-like poetry: the narrative moves by leaps and bounds that are neither announced nor marked. And then, also typical for the ballad, there is a dramatic and unexpected end, highlighting the central theme—in this case unrelenting love, regardless of material circumstances.

But what about the structure of the text? Apart from the first stanza, there is a regular rhyme scheme:

A B A B
C D C D

with a richness of rhyme words echoing the name of the lover, 'Hazel-dean' (lines 8, 16, 24 and 32): 'seen' (lines 6 and 30), 'keen' (line 14) and 'queen' (line 22). To make the text be set to music, a steady meter is required, as we saw before. So the foot corresponds—more or less—to (part of) a *bar* in musical notation. The alternation of syllables here is a mirror image of the *trochee* that we found in 'Heidenröslein.' Here each verse line starts with an unstressed syllable followed (more or less) by a stressed one. The pattern here is:

Why weep ye by the tide, lady?
x   /   x /   x /   x /
Why weep ye by the tide?
x   /   x /   x   /.

Such a foot (x /) is called a *iamb* in poetics, and it is one of the most frequent meters in the English language. (Tradition may play a role, but there may also be a good reason for this: many sentences in English start with a *function word*, like an article, or a personal pronoun, which takes little or no stress, followed by a stressed verb, noun, or adjective.) So the lines contain four and three feet alternatively. A line containing four iambs is called an *iambic tetrameter*, which means, simply, that there are four iambic feet in the line (*tetra* stands for 'four' in Greek).

Note, however, that the meter is an *abstract* pattern: if you listen to the music, you will notice that Dick Gaughan's rendering of these lines does not fit this abstract pattern. For instance, 'lady' cannot have final stress. But if you listen carefully, you will hear that he actually does lengthen the final syllable, making the father's begging even more emphatic. At the same time, 'ye' does get stress, although it should be unstressed according to the metrical pattern. The tension between these different structures, the poetic (metrical) and the musical (sung) one, is what gives this poem its 'live' character, and why we are often moved by it. The rich musical traditions of cultures all over the world are full of this interplay between abstract regularity and concrete rendering. This is what is usually called 'interpreting' a song: playing on the tension between prescribed patterns and their specific realization. Different singers have their own individual talents for making their listeners moved by their distinct interpretations.

Contrary to 'Heidenröslein,' there is no central metaphor in this poem: the story is simple in itself, and there is no figurative meaning we have to ascribe to the characters. We *can*, of course, if we want to. We could see in the figure of the father a pragmatic businessman, who is looking for a good match for his son. But wait—the girl is poor, she does not show any evidence of wealth, and she is weeping all the time. So a cold-hearted businessman he can hardly be. A better interpretation would be to see him as a compassionate old man, some Samaritan. The young woman, in turn, is a symbol for a stead-fast lover, who will not be lured into richness or comfort if she has to renounce her (poor) love. When we see in the persons and actions of a poem (or story) some more general pattern of characters or behavior, we are treating the text as an *allegory*. Some of the best-known allegorical texts are the *parables* that Jesus tells in the New Testament, or the mediaeval tale of *Everyman*. Allegories are often a vehicle for moral, political, or religious lessons. A famous modern example is George Orwell's *Animal Farm*, in which the animals stand for specific groups of people—the pigs, for instance, represent (in one reading) the political leaders of the former Soviet Union.

But literary authors also used the ballad scheme in their poems, such as Coleridge's 'The Rime of the Ancient Mariner,' Keats's 'La Belle Dame sans Merci' or E. A. Poe's 'Annabel Lee.' If you look at these, you will find that the 'rules' we previously discovered in 'Heidenröslein' are not to be found there in exactly the same way. Poetry *may* obey certain rules, and, in fact, it owes its very *existence* to poetic rules. No rules, no poetry. But these rules are not fixed: they are meant as schemes for general outlay. On the basis of these, poets are constantly looking for variation on those schemes. They thus build up a tension between an adherence to traditional rules and partial deviations from them, in a way that is not dissimilar from the tension between meter and rhythm that we have noticed before. As Malin (2014: 30) has noted, 'we may attend to the voice, the accompaniment, and the words, emerging and receding in independent rhythmic layers. This is the aesthetic pleasure of the "polyrhythmic" Lied.'

But let us return once more to the performance of 'Heidenröslein' by Barbara Bonney. The strophic structure of the text, with its repetitive music may lead to some monotony. Indeed, this is what you find in most performances. Even superstars like Elisabeth Schwarzkopf or Dietrich Fischer-Dieskau execute each stanza in an almost identical way, thereby in fact treating the text very unfairly, with only a slowing down in the last refrain. Not so, however, in the performance by Barbara Bonney. She follows the narrative development in the *couplets* by changing the way in which she inflects her voice, from the very beginning: how she emphasizes the *Freuden* (fondness, joy) in the first stanza. This is not prescribed in the musical score: it is *her* interpretation, to intensify the feeling for the rapture the boy feels when observing the beauty of the flower. She starts off the second stanza in a slightly faster pace and then makes the rose's defiance sound more vehement by distinctly raising her voice in *dass du ewig denkst an mich* (that you will always—in fact *eternally*—think of me). Listen how she brings to life the word *leiden* (suffer), the final word in the second couplet. Although again this is not in the score, she first executes a beautiful embellishment on the note (at 0:48) and then slows down (a *ritardando*, in musical terms) and goes into a *filato* (at 1:25): a technique a singer can use to slide into a *pianissimo* (the softest sound possible) especially on high notes, creating a sweet and elegiac mood, with her voice almost fading at the end.

She then begins the third stanza in a furious spurt, much faster than the previous stanzas, highlighting the drama which is going to unfold, but slows down sharply on *leiden* (suffer) again, and continues this extremely slow delivery in the penultimate verse (*Röslein, Röslein, Röslein rot*). In the final verse, however, she returns to an affirmative mode, reiterating the permanence of the rose's beauty.

This final line of 'Heidenröslein,' after the girl has suffered the assault, shows an interesting characteristic of the *Lied*, and maybe of classical songs in general. It re-affirms her existence, her beauty, and her presence on the plain, as if it is going to stay there forever. The song may have sounded melancholic or sad, if not violent, but the final line keeps fixed in our memory a picture of the beautiful and courageous rose (and her false lover). It has been said that such meditative lines at the end of classical songs also function as some sort of solace—that after the horror we witnessed it brings us some peace of mind, some reconciliation with the brutal world. This strategy of an appeasement is not a regular ingredient of popular music. There the emotions, be they joy or sadness, mostly remain untampered until the final words and chords.

High and low

This is a distinction that is regularly made between 'high' and 'low' culture. Mozart and Schubert are then considered 'high', while The Rolling Stones or Beyoncé is 'low'. The opposition is not limited to music, but inscribed deeply in our culture. In whatever direction we gaze, we bump into it: we find quality newspapers (high) next to the tabloid press (low), an opera house (high) next to a commercial cinema (low), or a museum with some of the world's finest pieces of art (high) next to Disneyland (low). But we do not find it in the lives of desert nomads, the Inuit or with fishermen on Polynesian islands. We are dealing here with a spatial metaphor, HIGH/LOW—where 'high' is better, of course, than 'low'. The anthropologist Ernst Gellner has argued that the distinction is based on *literacy*. The more widespread literacy is in a society, the more likely it is that one will encounter the distinction between 'the high style, founded on writing and the low, illiterate forms of ordinary folks', as Gellner (1988: 295) has it. (See also van Peer [1997] for a further discussion of the high/low opposition.)

The opposition applies to poetry, too. So 'high' poets such as Homer, Dante, Wordsworth, or E. E. Cummings are adored, while less elevated poems are considered as 'doggerel', a kind of pleasant entertainment without much profundity. But as this chapter has shown, the boundary between the two is somewhat porous, as the ballad 'Jock O'Hazeldean' illustrated: it belongs to traditional, oral, folk culture, but is nevertheless considered worthy of attention. So it is better to consider the opposition in terms of a continuum. The birthday poem you may compose for a family member may never make it into high culture, but some poems by recognized poets (like, for instance, Robert Burns) may verge on popular and hence low culture.

The products of high culture usually survive the ages, while popular products are often ephemeral. Low culture is forgotten, and high culture is preserved (in museums, archives, book editions, audio recordings, etc.). When it comes to high culture, this chapter has seen some age-old poems that are still read, and the music listened to—and often people are in awe when exposed to them. The poem 'Heidenröslein' joined two towering figures in the history of Western literature and music: Goethe and Schubert. And such works of high culture generally attract our attention and foster efforts to try to understand them at a deeper level.

At this point, you may be asking yourself why we have devoted so much time to songs while this is, presumably, a book about poetry. The reason is that poetry almost always has a song-like character, distinguishing it from narrative. Even when we have narrative poems that in fact tell a story, like in the examples we have seen, they often do so in a song-like manner. The next chapter will present you with a full-blown illustration of this. And the opposite is the case, too: songs almost necessarily employ texts that are more or less poetic; they require some regular structure of meter in order to be set to music, but also often refer to things by figurative language, such as metaphor, and exploit language possibilities that we neglect in daily speech, such as rhyme.

Why psychopoetics?

You may also be asking yourself another question: why is all this called 'psychopoetics'? Most of the things discussed in this chapter belong to the traditional field of *poetics*, the theory about poetry, its nature and characteristics. Why the 'psycho'? We have already hinted here and there that the structures described may result in emotional reactions of readers and listeners. At the end of this chapter, we must now face the question: is there any *evidence* for this view?

The question is crucial because evidence is the essence of psychopoetics: that such structures have an effect is not a wild guess. We are convinced that they are there for a reason. Most poetry lovers (and we ourselves) will agree immediately. At the same time, we want to see whether that conviction is valid, and the mere wish to do so is not enough. We all agree that the sun rises in the morning, while the evidence shows this to be an optical illusion. So do poetic structures indeed cause psychological effects? Or is this just another illusion? Most scholars in literary studies also assume these effects and sometimes describe them, but usually in a rather anecdotal way, or as a norm, something we 'should' experience when reading a particular piece of poetry. Again, that is not enough. Maybe we simply live under a delusion. That is precisely where psychopoetics sets in: we want to know for certain that we are not kidding ourselves.

But how? To do so, we must marry age-old traditional poetics to more recent methods of investigation, developed in the social sciences. Such methods often imply interdisciplinary approaches: computational, neurophysiological, or questionnaire-psychological. Various arrangements may be made to this end, which we will introduce in the course of the following chapters. But the bottom line is this: we deliberately confront our assertions with independent data—and gauge the discrepancy between both. By independent data we mean observations that are not directly influenced by the observers themselves. Important for psychopoetics is the question how to arrive at a sensible answer to research questions, so in the following chapters we will consider both the methods and the evidence. We begin in the following chapter with an illustration of what can be done with very simple methods, yet already revealing interesting insights into how sung poetry works.

Core issues

- Psychopoetics is the evidence-based study of the psychological experience of literature, more specifically, of poetry in its various aspects and manifestations.

- While it is difficult to define poetry in a precise and accurate way, a prototypical poem is structured by the white surrounding the lines.

- Poetry is distinctly different from other kinds of literature by its systemic organization, involving verse lines, stanzas, meter, rhyme, etc.

- A fundamental feature of poetry is its use of figurative language.

- Poetry is different from narrative in that it almost always demonstrates a song-like character.

- Poetic structures often come out of traditional, oral folk culture.

- Narrative poems (ballads in particular) tell stories.

- Poetry can be 'high' and 'low' while the boundary between the two is blurred.

Further reading

Dissanayake, E. (2000), *Art and Intimacy: How the Arts Began.* Seattle: University of Washington Press.

Huron, D. (2006), *Sweet Anticipation: Music and the Psychology of Expectation.* Boston: MIT Press.

Simpson, P. (2014), *Stylistics. A Resource Book for Students*, 2nd edn, London and New York: Routledge.

2

Poetry Is Madness

Keywords

fado

questionnaire

descriptive statistics

inference statistics

significance

sample

population

outlier

standard deviation

arithmetic mean

qualitative vs quantitative data

emotional valence

reliability

The previous chapter has laid the foundations of the structures of poetic texts. But how do these patterns work on you when you are reading or listening to them? In this chapter, we will make a beginning with the study of *experiencing* poetic organization.

And we position poetry where it belongs: in the real world, in the social sphere, embedded in a live performance, vibrant with music, and making use of modern technology. Music and voice are at the origin of poetry, which is important for the way it gets across. In ancient times, poetry was often sung for an audience (e.g., the *rhapsode* in Greek culture): the audience listened to the *Iliad* while the singer accompanied himself on the lyre. Initially, literature was public, not private, and often oral, meant to be memorized and recited—as it is still often the case nowadays in poetry festivals or in slam poetry. It is only in the early eighteenth century that people started reading to themselves.

'Loucura'

So now we invite you to look at a London show by the Portuguese singer Mariza: Link 2.1 on the Companion Website.

The song is titled 'Loucura' ('Madness' in Portuguese).[1] It is a *fado*, a classic urban folk song, traditionally enacted by *fadistas*, singers of *fados*. First watch the video and listen to the music and the song (even if you may not understand the words) before reading on. We are not playing tricks on you: listening in before reading the rest of this chapter will make much more sense of what follows—and will be more fun, too. Close your book and meet Mariza's 'Loucura.' When ready, open your book again and read on. Off you go!

We realize that was certainly a lot to take in at once. So we now ask you to look at the clip once again, but this time join in an experiment we ran with some of our students, thirty-five of them (in reports and articles, this would be usually denoted by $N = 35$), mainly postgraduate students—predominantly female, at my[2] university in Kyiv, Ukraine. Like you, most of them did not understand a word of the lyrics. Yet we asked them to fill in *questionnaires*—specifically designed forms that help us obtain reactions from groups of people. This is the major experimental tool we use in psychopoetics so far. Of course, there are other measures researchers can and do apply, but, in view of the examples we are referring to in this book, we will for now limit ourselves to focusing on questionnaires.

So in this experiment students rated their feelings while watching, but also the feelings they thought the singer herself experienced, by giving a number from 1 through 10 for each of the following emotions, with 1 meaning 'very little' and 10 'extremely so.' The emotions involved are:

- surprise;

- joy;

- contempt;

- sadness;

- fear;

- shame;

- anger;

- trust;

- tenderness;

- elation.

Are you ready? Then listen again to Mariza, and give your response to the ten emotions—(1) your feelings while watching, and (2) the feelings you think the singer experienced. You may do so during, but also after the performance. Then pause.

Keep your ratings in front of you. We are going to compare them with the ratings *our* students gave—they will be different, of course, but maybe not all. Let us see. Before we go on, a warning: do not be afraid of the graphs you will see. We say so because there are many people in the Humanities who think that the study of poetry, or music, or art in general, does not (should not) make use of statistics (*descriptive* so far, summarizing results) or graphs. Honestly, we think that this is not a helpful idea. First, why would we not be able to depict listeners' reactions in a graph? Social scientists have been doing this for over a hundred years already. Second, the graphs you will see are about people's reactions to the song, not about the song itself. And, by the way, if you are afraid you may have to draw them yourself, you do not have to build them by hand: computer software will generate them for you. Finally, we will show you from the outset how graphs can be illuminating, if only because they summarize a lot of information. In this book we will be using two computer programs for the statistical analysis, including constructing graphs (SPSS and Microsoft Excel) while several others are available, so it remains up to you to decide which one to use.

So please now inspect Figure 1: it represents the average response of our students to each of the ten emotions. The set of bars on the left-hand

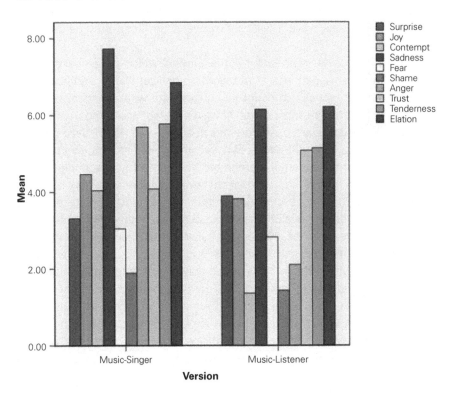

FIGURE 1 *Initial reaction to the performance.*

side are the emotions ascribed to the singer (labeled 'Music-Singer'), while the right-hand side has the emotions the students felt themselves (labeled 'Music-Listener').

One notices immediately that there are marked differences between the various emotions. For instance, 'shame' scores very low for both the singer and the listeners (lower than 2 on the scale of 10), 'fear' scores fairly low as well (around 3), while 'sadness,' 'tenderness,' and 'elation' all score rather high (above 5). So the experiment and the graph already allow us to identify the major emotional fields that the song is located in—according to a group of students.

More interesting, though, are the differences in the emotions ascribed to the singer and those our students said they experienced themselves. You have to compare each bar on the left with the corresponding bar on the right. So our students ascribed 'surprise' to the singer with a value of just above 3 (on the vertical axis), but their own 'surprise' was a bit higher, namely, almost 4. This difference is rather slight: only half a point out of 10. But now compare the bars for 'contempt,' 'sadness,' and 'anger.' For each of these emotions the difference is much larger: 2.4, 1.7, and 3.7, respectively. (We have calculated the averages for you.) That means that for these three emotions our students made a *significant* difference between what they perceived to be the singer's emotions and their own feelings. In each case, their own emotions were *significantly* lower than those they perceived in the singer.

This difference is important for the way in which people experience poetry. But for now, just look at the words 'significant' and 'significantly' in the previous sentences. No doubt you understand what is meant by those words. What you may not realize, however, is that the words, which are deliberately italicized, are used here in a special sense. They mean not only that there was a large difference between the emotions, but also that this difference was not accidental. Remember that only thirty-five students gave us their reaction. Would other students have reacted the same? This is exactly what statistics (*inference* statistics at this stage) does for you: estimate the probability that other students would come up with similar answers. In this case, yes, we can be 99 percent assured that they will—in the case of 'sadness.' In the case of 'contempt' and 'anger' we may be confident that other students in those fields at this university would react in the same way with a confidence higher than 99.9 percent. (You may wonder how one knows this. Well, that is the secret of statistics, in which we will initiate you later in this book.) Another way to explain the notion of 'significance' is 'generalizability': if results are statistically *significant*, it means we may confidently generalize them to the whole group to which the participants belong, to the *population*.

So now we know the major emotions that play a role in witnessing Mariza's performance: 'sadness,' 'tenderness,' and 'elation.' And we also know—with a very high degree of trust—that there were significant differences in reactions between the perceived emotions of the singer and the spectators' own feelings, notably for 'contempt,' 'sadness,' and 'anger.' In each of these cases, the emotions the spectators felt were lower than those they thought the singer went through. There were also two emotions that were stronger in the spectators' experience than those ascribed to the performer: 'surprise' and 'trust.' The differences in these cases were not, however, statistically *significant*, which means that we may not confidently generalize them to other groups of students. Also note that these conclusions are based on an experiment in which participants watched a *video recording* of a performance. Would their reactions have been different if they had witnessed it live? This we do not know. Throughout this book, we are presenting the results of such experiments, not to tell eternal truths, but to demonstrate particular aspects of how people react to songs and to poetry. We invite our readers to look critically at these experiments and try to amend their design as well as the conclusions that may be drawn from them.

So how about your own reactions? Were they similar? Or different? Maybe even dramatically different in some cases? Presumably you do not find this surprising. After all, you are different from our students. And we know that no two individuals are identical, because we all judge the world around us in different ways. Variation should not surprise you.

Then what is the use of such comparisons, you may well wonder? You are thereby asking why this book was written. And why one would want to do such a thing as study poetry—or rather the *experience* of poetry? If the answer boils down to saying that people differ in their reactions, then one may justly be disappointed. But that is not the full answer we would give. Because something considerably more interesting may be at hand when noticing the differences you have registered in your own reactions. To this end, inspect your ratings and see if in some cases they are VERY different from those in Figure 1. If you spot such a large discrepancy, you observed something for which there is a special term: it is called an *outlier*. An outlier's reactions are very far removed from the average response.

There may be many reasons why your observation is an outlier relative to this experiment. The most obvious one is, of course, that you belong to a different group of people than the ones who took part in our experiment. In everyday language, a *population* could be a group of people belonging to a specific region or nation. And people in different populations may differ. They may speak different languages (or dialects of that language), and their country may have gone through different historical developments. Or you may belong to a society that is (politically and socially) organized in a different way. Or it may possess different traditions and mentalities. So it is very well possible that your own reactions to Mariza's performance stem from your belonging to a particular *population*.

Does this mean, then, that people of a particular population all share the same ideas, so that they will all react identically? In no way. Because individual variation exists also *within* populations. In this book we will study variation both *between* and *within* populations. Variation *within* a population may also be different: from minimal to extreme. You can express this by the average deviation from what most people would give as their reaction, i.e., from the average. This is the so-called *standard deviation*: another way of defining this is to call it the 'average deviation from the average.' If this formulation sets you thinking, you are on the right track. Indeed, that is what is meant by the *SD* (the abbreviation for the standard deviation used in books and articles). Look again at the emotion of 'contempt' attributed to the singer in Figure 1. You notice that the average response in our group approached the value of 4. But beware: this is the *average* of all responses. Maybe nobody in the group actually gave the number 4. It is the *arithmetic mean* of all responses in the group. Now notice that it makes a lot of difference if the number 4 is the average of people giving either the number 3 or 5, or whether 4 is the average of groups of people allocating the numbers 2 and 6. In the former case, there is large convergence among listeners, while in the latter there is less uniformity. This is expressed by a small SD in the former, and a larger one in the latter case. Hence a small SD means little variation in responses, and vice versa: a large SD indicates a large variation between people's reactions.

So now we already have a deeper understanding of differences: not only do we notice the various sources of differences (*between* and *within* populations); we now can express also the *degree* of observed differences. The same is true for variation *between* populations. If you ask people in Western societies whether male and female individuals should have the same rights, you will find almost no differences of opinion. At the same time if you ask them whether nuclear power is a good source of energy, you may find considerable variation between various populations (and also *within* each population).

Remember now that only thirty-five students took part in the experiment. That, certainly, is not the whole population of students. It is, in technical terms, a *sample*. This is the hallmark of all scientific work: since we cannot examine everything, we inspect samples. This is the same also in the natural sciences: one cannot study all the stars, all groups of animals, or all fossils. If you go through a blood test, the doctor cannot take all the blood from you to check whether you are ill or not—she will take a *sample* of blood only. In research, we are condemned to look at limited samples. But we hope to generalize from those samples to populations in general, and in order to do so, one must use statistics. Do not be afraid! And do not run away. We will do so in a practical, hands-on way that will allow you to grasp most of the statistics you will see in scientific papers.

Now a basic question presents itself: what is a sample a sample of? Well, you know the answer by now: of a population, of course. A population of what? In the case of our thirty-five students, they certainly are a sample of students in a department at the university where the experiment was held. But was this sample also representative of other departments? Also of other universities in Kyiv? In Ukraine? In other countries in Eastern Europe? In Europe in general? In the whole world? Here we hit upon a notably difficult problem, that of the relation between sample and population. We will not go into that tricky relation any further, but only point out a rule of thumb: generalize *prudently* from a sample to a population. On the other hand, do not be afraid to go beyond your observations when you believe this to be justified.

To illustrate how tricky the relation between sample and population may be, we remind you that our sample consisted of predominantly (in fact, almost exclusively) female students, which is quite typical of Humanities departments in many countries. May we generalize beyond the female gender in this case? Probably not. Why not? Because it may be that male and female listeners react differently. For instance, our women students witnessed a woman performing. It is not too far-fetched to expect that men would see the woman singer differently. Differences may occur, of course, in the possible erotic attraction a performer may exert on audiences with different sexual orientations. If you happen to be male and you noticed considerable differences in your reactions from the ones our students reported, gender may be the source of the difference.

Having considered your reactions so far, let us now return to the performance itself. We guess that most people will agree that it is intense, at the same time emotional and reserved, as the performer revels in the idea of madness (of being a *fado* singer)—a madness that is full of pain and suffering, but also of enthrallment and blessing. The robust and powerful rhythm of the music is in tune with the facial expression and body movements of Mariza who, with her strong voice, utters what seems to be a conflicting combination of sadness and joy. (Remember that in our experiment 'sadness' was the emotion evaluated the highest for both singer and listeners.) The whole piece is a dialogue of guitars that sound steady and almost monotonous, while Mariza's voice is sharply clipped, adding much to the adverse feelings of sadness and joy at the same time.

Mariza is wearing a full-length black dress with a red pattern, and her shoulders are covered with a black shawl of delicate tulle. The black necklace fits the garment, and the musicians in the back accompanying her are also dressed in black—presumably so that no color scheme distracts the attention of the audience from the singer. Is this part of poetry? Yes, it is! The singer has thought seriously about her appearance before stepping in front of the audience. Is this necessary? No. Sometimes a performance can be overwhelming without any special outfit. Dress and make-up may further enhance a performance and make it even more memorable. In the case of Mariza it is she—and her delivery—that is at the center of the stage. Her hair is dyed golden and meticulously plaited in thin braids—almost like a classical warrior, and we see her ears with numerous stud earrings, and her bright red lipstick that is of the same color as the dress ornaments. The singer's deep dark eyes obviously stand out against the pale face, expressing the depth of emotions articulated with her soaring, intense, echo-inducing voice with its exceptional clarity and vocal resonance.

The song is introduced with a prelude by two traditional Portuguese 'guitarras.' Then the accompaniment diminishes, and the sound goes almost to a hushed tone. Mariza slowly walks to the front of the stage. And then there is a moment, only a fraction of a moment, before she joins in the piece with her head bent down, but then sharply looks up and starts 'talking' to us, the listeners, pressing her ringed hands to her chest and stretching the arms out. Her back is straight, and the whole posture is firm. The facial expression of the singer alters from a semi-smile to a nearly painful grimace, all this enhanced with her brisk shudder-like body movements as she is walking on the stage. There comes a moment of certain sacredness, when the public is full of expectation of what is going to happen. It almost feels like a moment of *epiphany* (to which we will come back in Chapter 5): everyone senses that now, at this very moment, something is going to be revealed. And this revelation is instantly delivered, when Mariza bursts out full blaze with her first sentence: *Sou do fado*.

This ungrammatical sentence literally means 'I am *from* fado.' The construction demands a place name as a complement, as in 'I am from Lisbon' or 'I am from Poland.' Which is not the case here: *fado* is a poetic genre, not a place. One can say in Portuguese, '*Sou de Lisboa/São Paulo*' (I am from Lisbon/ São Paolo). So basically the performance begins by saying where she comes from. Not from some place, but from a 'non-place.' That non-place is called *fado*. Which is precisely what the poem will be elaborating on in the following verses. This kind of (linguistic or other) deviation from the norm constitutes the bulk of a lot of poetry, and we will analyze it in depth in Chapter 4.

So this opening immediately reveals the heart of poetry: the singer does not belong 'here'; she comes from a different place, from the land of song— as if *fado* were a country, or a town. That is where she lives. She spends her days in poetry. For us, as spectators, it is not clear whether that is good or bad, whether she likes the place or not, whether her experiences there are pleasant or painful. The whole emotional setup is hanging in full air. It could be both, or it could develop in one direction, but equally well in the opposite one.

Now with the text

People may get shivers at such an opening. Yet you may not have understood the meaning of Mariza's first sentence. So it is time to now have a detailed look at the text of the song. Below you will find the original in Portuguese against its translation into English.

Loucura	**Madness**
Sou do fado!	I'm from Fado!
Como sei!	How I know!
Vivo um poema cantado,	I live a poem sung,
de um fado que eu inventei.	of a fado that I made up.
A falar,	Speaking,
não posso dar-me,	I can't expose myself,
mas ponho a alma a cantar,	but I make my soul sing,
e as almas sabem escutar-me.	and the souls know how to listen to me.
Chorai, chorai,	Cry, cry,
poetas do meu país,	poets of my country,
troncos da mesma raíz,	trunks of the same root,
de vida que nos juntou.	of the life that put us together.
E se vocês,	And if you
não estivessem a meu lado,	weren't by my side,
então, não havia fado,	then fado wouldn't exist,
nem fadistas como eu sou!	nor fadistas as I am!
Esta voz,	This voice,
tão dolorida,	so hurtful,
é culpa de todos vós,	it's all your fault,
poetas da minha vida.	poets of my life.
É loucura!	It's madness!
Ouço dizer,	I hear them say,
mas bendita esta loucura,	but blessed this madness
de cantar e de sofrer.	of singing and suffering.
Chorai, chorai,	Cry, cry,
poetas do meu país,	poets of my country,
troncos da mesma raíz,	trunks of the same root,
de vida que nos juntou.	of the life that put us together,
E se vocês,	And if you
não estivessem a meu lado,	weren't by my side,
então, não havia fado,	then fado wouldn't exist,
nem fadistas como eu sou!	nor fadistas as I am!

At the end of the song, Mariza turns her back to the audience as if leaving, to let the spectators contemplate what they have heard and experienced—then turns back again for the final climactic chords, reinforced with sophisticated cadences of her voice.

Now look at the text. As we showed in the previous chapter, (written or printed) poetry is immediately recognizable by the white surrounding the text, and often also within the text, separating the stanzas. In the text printed above, this is clear enough: we, the authors, have done that for you. In the performance of Mariza, there is no such text visible. So if the surrounding 'white' is so characteristic of poetry, where is it in the singing? Partly it is in the separation of the refrain—which separates itself by virtue of the verbatim repetitions. But the 'white' plays at a deeper level. The 'white' surrounding a poem during this London performance may be seen in the separate stage on which Mariza is standing, isolating her 'poem' from the spectators. There is an unmistakable distancing between the singer/musicians and the people in the audience. It is again, like in printed poetry, a *spatial* separation that marks poetry from its environment. Why? To make us, the spectators, concentrate more than usually on the text, its content, its form, and its meaning—the same way as in the poem by Goethe.

In the previous chapter we dealt with narrative poems that told a story. What is the story here? There is none. No events are recounted, and there is no real movement from beginning to the end. In the first two stanzas the author introduces the vocation of a poet. Stanzas 3 and 4 then spell out that vocation: Mariza is singing, so as to bring the people of her country together (stanza 3), but thereby needs you, the listeners (next to the poets), at her side. Because without them there would be neither the song (*fado*) nor singers (*fadistas*). Stanza 5 then widens the scope toward the society by which she is hurt—she has heard that they declare her mad (stanza 6), which she, however, sees as a blessing, even if it brings suffering. And then the refrain is repeated once more.

This repetition of the refrain might make you think that the song resembles a *ballad*, but there is a profound distinction: there is no action here, no *plot*. Look again at the poems in the previous chapter: in both of them things *happened*. Here no events take place. And no dialogues either, as in the previous chapter: the whole poem here is a monologue. No one else speaks. Another major difference is that usually there is no 'I' in the ballads, no first person (except in direct speech). While here, the *lyrical I* is central: it is the very first word with which the poem begins: *sou* (I am). Finally, ballads recount individual events, things that happened to particular individuals—even when they may stand (allegorically) for persons in general, while the song by Mariza is about *generic* things. It is about the situation of the poet, in general. Central to the portrayal of her plight are her (performed) emotions.

This generic truth to which the poem aspires, however, is bound to the poet seeing herself as mad. There is organic *imagery*: 'trunks' (*troncos*) and 'roots' (*raiz*), metaphors for kinship, indicating her links to her country (*pais*), but her ties are especially to the poets, poets of [her] country (*poetas do meu pais*), who presumably suffer from the same madness (loucura) as she. The general tenor of the song is her position as an outsider, trapped in madness.

The madness here is no ordinary foolishness. One is reminded of the most famous figure illustrating foolishness in English literature: *King Lear* who is still sane at the beginning of the play, but through lack of proper judgment sets himself on the road toward madness. He still does not realize the danger, though he is explicitly warned by the Fool.

> Fools had ne'er less grace in a year;
> For wise men are grown foppish,
> And know not how their wits to wear,
> Their manners are so apish.

(Act I, scene IV, lines 163–6)

Only a few lines later, again it is the Fool who makes things clear when addressing the king:

> Yes, indeed: thou would'st make a good Fool.

(I, V, 36)

And then it begins to dawn on Lear, when he prays:

> O! Let me not be mad, not mad, sweet heaven;
> Keep me in temper; I would not be mad.

(I, V, 43–4)

This is exactly what happens in Mariza's song: things are turned upside down: although she lives in a song and is declared mad (*É loucura! Ouço dizer*), in fact, she is the one who sees things more clearly. It is the one who is mad (the poet) who discerns the generic truth, and it is she who sees through everyday perceptions and illuminates the deeper meaning of reality. The price she has to pay for this is exclusion. And madness here is the metaphor for this exclusion-through-illumination.

All this plays at the level of the poem's *content*, but at the same time a lot of things are going on at the level of the *form*. You may not notice this while listening, but when you see the text printed, all of a sudden a grid of intertwined meanings opens up. Just look at the verse lines. They are end-stopped most of the time, but you hardly notice, as the *syntax* drives you on and on, and there is a marked tension between the printed and the spoken line. Look at the rhyme scheme, which starts off quite regularly, with *A B A B,* but then develops into a much more complicated one. Here it is, stanza per stanza:

A B A B
C D C D
E' E E E'
F G G G.

At this moment, we invite you to yet again listen to the song, just as our students did after the first round, now having the text and its translation at hand. And once more: judge the emotions of the singer and of yourself by rating them on the same scales from 1 through 10 as you did initially. When you are ready, go to the next paragraph and look at our students' reactions, presented in Figure 2. On the left-hand side of the graph are again the emotions ascribed to the singer (labeled 'Text-Singer'), and, on the right-hand side, the emotions the students felt themselves when listening to the music, now knowing what the song is about (labeled 'Text-Listener').

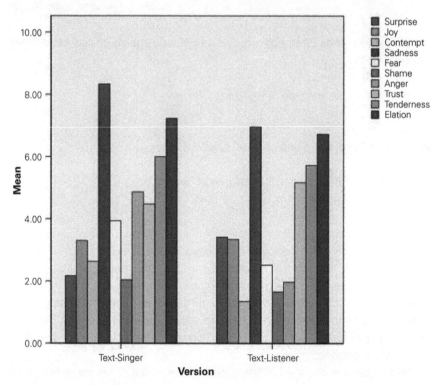

FIGURE 2 *Reactions after learning the lyrics.*

Let us study this graph in some detail. (We will compare Figures 1 and 2 afterward, but for now let us concentrate on the ratings of the performance *with* the text/translation.) Again, 'shame' scores very low: apparently this is an emotion that has little relevance in this poem. The same three emotions as before are high again: 'sadness,' 'tenderness,' and 'elation'—even higher than at the first listening. And 'surprise' and 'trust' are higher for the listener (i.e., for oneself) than for the singer, but now the difference for 'surprise' is *significant* (with a 99 percent confidence level). 'Contempt' and 'anger' (not 'sadness') again differ significantly: these emotions are markedly lower to the spectators themselves than they think they were for the singer.

We see that the basic pattern remains more or less the same. In other words, *understanding* the text of the song did not change much in the spectators' emotional reactions. Of course, the text is only one of many clues that may produce an emotional reaction. There are also numerous visual clues, including lighting, clothing, Mariza's body posture, her facial expressions, etc., next to the auditory aspects: the *guitarras*, the melody and rhythm, the voice and its modulations and so forth. Yet the lack of difference between the two reactions is already a surprising finding.

Now it is time to juxtapose the results of the two stages of the experiment: reacting to Mariza's performance *without* and *with* the texts. We first look at the emotions the participants attributed to the singer as presented in Figure 3:

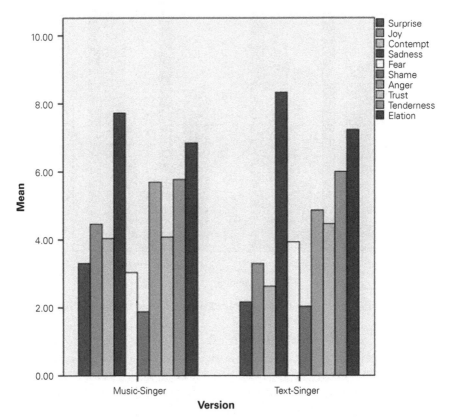

FIGURE 3 *Emotions attributed to the singer in the two conditions (without/with the text).*

As can be seen from Figure 3, the reactions do not differ very much. This should not surprise us, since they represent what emotions the audience noticed in the singer. Knowing the meaning of what she was singing did not seem to make much of a difference in this case. The only difference that was statistically significant was for the emotion of 'surprise,' which was lower after being acquainted with the content of the song. This is, of course, not surprising in itself.

When we compare the emotions of the listeners themselves in the two conditions (without/with the text), one could expect different reactions. But there are hardly any, and none that are (statistically) significant as you can see in Figure 4:

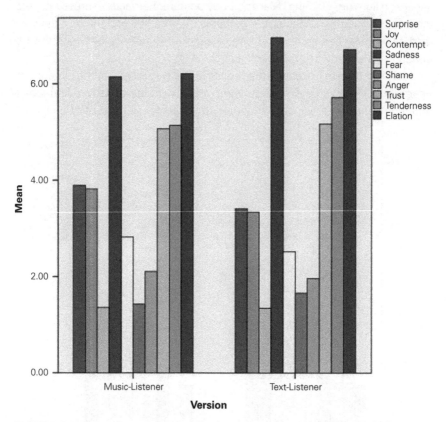

FIGURE 4 *Listeners' own emotions in the two conditions (without/with the text).*

This is certainly an unforeseen result. None of our students understood a word of the poem at the first listening; therefore, one would expect that knowing the meaning of the song would change their emotions. And it did not. So it seems as if the performance as such had an impact that overrode the influence of the words of the song.

(By the way, did you notice that the scales of the graphs are different? Look at the vertical axis: here the graph runs from zero to slightly below 7 while in Figure 3 it went up to 10. This is something you should always pay attention to in illustrations: what are the distances between the bars? If you do not look at the vertical axis, this may be very misleading, and what looks like a considerable difference on a graph could in fact be that of a fraction of the total scale.)

The first stage of the experiment (rating the performance without knowing the words) was followed by a group discussion, led by one of us. The notion of *fado* itself was discussed, and only one student had any background knowledge of the musical genre. Discussing the singer's emotions, participants mentioned: love, memories, catharsis, disappointment, pain, exaltation, anger, and contempt. They also focused on the 'unique manner' and the 'strong voice' of the singer, who—they said—was 'performing with her face.' Some respondents additionally mentioned 'revolution' and commented that the song was gypsy-like and could be about the singer's country and its tragic past, or even about 'the problems of the nation.'

Describing their own emotions, students acknowledged that they were somewhat confused by experiencing two feelings at the same time: on the one hand, they noticed that the mouth corners of the singer were mostly down, indicating some negative emotion, while, on the other hand, noticing that Mariza sounded quite proud. The confusion was increased by being 'jealous that she can express herself so well.'

The discussion was quite in line with the feedback to the song from other listeners you can read below the video. In their comments, viewers acknowledged, among other things, the following reactions (we present them in their original, not edited form):

- 'I'm getting goosebumps',

- 'I shiver when I hear her sing',

- 'my soul leaves the body',

- 'Fado is something inexplicable:)'

- [*sic*] Something to feel this feeling that only Fado makes me feel, love'

and

- 'It brings us sweet and nostalgic memories, asleep in the depths of our conscience and they speak to us, like ancient whispers of the air and the sea, rain and the desire!'.

Most notably, listeners made comments very similar to the ones by our students:

- 'I love your music, I don't understand it, but I feel it.;)
- [*sic*], 'i dont understand the words but i feel fado',
- 'We barely understood a word of Portuguese but we felt Fado',
- 'I don't know the words, but there are tears in my eyes'.

So now we have two sets of data: numerical responses to emotional scales and verbal descriptions of psychological experiences. The former are called *quantitative*, the latter *qualitative*. These two kinds of evidence complement each other—something that we will further elaborate on in Chapter 8 when we will speak about the methods employed by psychopoetics.

These commentaries corroborate the results of our experiment, where we found little difference between the reactions to the performance without and with the translation of the lyrics presented. But wait: there is another possible explanation for these results. It is the actual *performance* by the singer, her presentation, and the whole arrangement of the show. Someone with the professional expertise in acting—like Mariza certainly is—may have achieved more or less the same results if she were singing nonsense words. Please remember: experimental results need interpretation!

Positive vs. negative

Now look again at the emotions we probed: surprise, joy, contempt, sadness, fear, shame, anger, trust, tenderness, and elation. These are quite recognizable emotions, one would say. An uncontroversial theory says that emotions always carry *valence*, i.e., they are experienced as either positive (pleasant) or negative (unpleasant). If you look at the list again, you may notice that five of the emotions have positive valence (surprise, joy, trust, tenderness, and elation), while the other five have negative valence (contempt, sadness, fear, shame, and anger). An interesting question therefore is: what is the *general* reaction of participants to the negative vs. positive emotions? That would show their general orientation toward the performance. Is one allowed to do this? Here again, some basic knowledge of statistics comes in: there is a particular test that can be used to answer this question. The requirement for 'adding' the responses to the two groups of emotions (positive vs. negative) is that they must generally evoke similar reactions. This is called *reliability*, the degree to which the onlookers reliably respond in the same way to the two groups of emotions. The technical term for this measure is *Cronbach's alpha*, a measure that (according to statistical conventions) should be higher than .65 (and statistical software will calculate it from your data). If that is the case, one may conflate the values of individual emotions into an over-arching group of emotions, which is what we did. And look at the result in Figure 5:

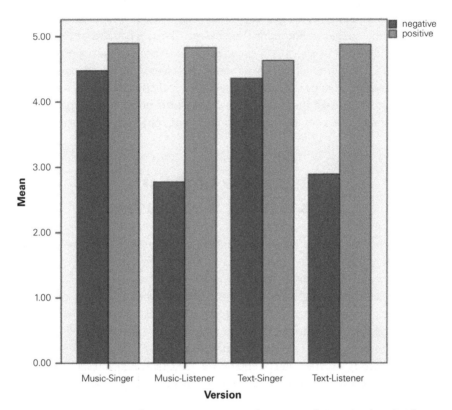

FIGURE 5 *Negative and positive emotions in the two conditions (without/with the text).*

As can be seen from the graph, positive emotions are about the same in all conditions. Second, their averages are rather low: they do not exceed the value of five (on a 10-point scale). The third, and most striking, thing to notice, however, is that listeners (when exposed to the music both without and with the text) attributed more negative feelings to the singer than to themselves. And the differences are highly significant, with a generalizability of 99.9 percent. This is interesting and something one would not expect at face value. Seeing this beautiful woman singing a song would not engender negative reactions. (Of course, they are not negative *to* her, but an estimate of the emotions she is expressing.) Maybe it happened to you too, but you did not realize it. This is one of the (many) reasons why it is necessary (and useful) to do research: because our everyday experiences are often not very trustworthy—or may be obscure even to ourselves. After having studied the poem in detail, we may better understand why the onlookers indeed attributed more negative emotions to the singer: she is truly (in part) revolting, against her own anxieties, against her position as an outsider, against, well, against the world around her. And we now know that this does not lead spectators to have those negative emotions themselves. This is a paradox of the arts, of music, and also of poetry: that we can distinguish between emotions evoked by poetry and the emotions we experience ourselves. One would expect there to be some congruency between both, so that sad poems make a reader sad, and jolly poems make them exhilarated. That turns out *not* to be the case. In many instances, we actually *enjoy* sadness in art, poetry in particular.

The paradox of the arts: Can sad music feel pleasant?

The clearest demonstration of this paradox comes from music. The research by Kawakami et al. (2013) demonstrates this in the clearest possible way. They exposed forty-four listeners (roughly half male/female and roughly half musicians/non-musicians) to three pieces of classical music, each time in a major and in a minor key, lasting thirty seconds each. After listening to the pieces, participants responded to sixty-two emotion-related descriptive words and phrases, to capture both *perceived* and *felt* emotions, each time on a 4-point scale. The results showed a clear (and statistically significant) dissociation between perceived and felt emotions. As the authors summarize:

> [W]e may actually feel positive emotions when we listen to sad music.... [F]elt and perceived emotion may not actually coincide in this respect: sad music would be perceived as sad, but the experience of listening to sad music would evoke positive emotions.
>
> In short, when the participants listened to the sad music, they indeed felt tragic emotion, but the degree to which they actually felt this emotion was lower than that for which they perceived it. Additionally, the listeners experienced romantic and blithe emotions more than they perceived these particular emotions when they listened to the sad music. (...) With respect to the happy music, perceived emotions were rated higher than felt emotions for blithe emotions including feeling merry, feeling animated, and feeling like dancing.
>
> (ibid.: 311)

The differences between both emotional experiences, moreover, were not affected by prior musical experience of the respondents (i.e., there were no significant differences between musicians and non-musicians). The experiment shows, in other ways, that listening to sad music evokes ambivalent emotions, both unpleasant (more gloomy, meditative, and miserable), but at the same time pleasant emotions (blithe, merry, animated, being in love, and feeling like dancing).

The authors themselves suggest that similar emotional processes may be at work in the experience of art in general. Kawakami et al. (ibid.) explain this by the absence of object-related emotions in those art experiences, which they term 'vicarious' emotions. We may mourn the fate of Hamlet or Antigone, we may be moved to tears even, but there is no 'object' Hamlet or Antigone in our daily surroundings. The authors represent this field in Figure 6:

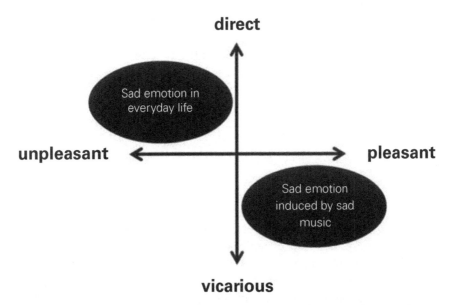

FIGURE 6 *Pleasant-unpleasant, direct-vicarious model; from Kawakami et al. (2014: 6).*

The horizontal axis in the figure demonstrates the emotional evaluation of *felt* emotions (from unpleasant on the left to pleasant on the right) while the vertical axis shows the way in which individuals relate to the trigger of the emotion (direct or vicarious). Thus, emotions experienced in everyday life would be located in the top left-hand quadrant in the figure. Alternatively, emotions triggered by music, or art in general, would be located in the bottom right-hand quadrant. The reason is that music has no direct relationship to listeners who then experience *vicarious* emotions, and this enables them to *feel* pleasant emotion even when they *perceive* the music as sad.

This is not necessarily the only explanation for the phenomenon. In general, however, we must conclude that we are facing a paradox here, namely, that human beings can revel in sad emotions and actually rejoice in the experience of painful feelings.

Madness in poetry: What stands behind Ophelia's folly?

You have certainly noticed that the key emotions in the performance we discussed relate to the idea of madness—in Mariza's case the madness of being a *fado* singer. But this idea is not unique. The sociologist Anton Zijderveld in his *Reality in a Looking-Glass: Rationality through an Analysis of Traditional Folly* (1982) has looked at the history of the fool to conclude that he is, in fact, a precursor to us, moderns, and that a certain degree of tolerable madness is inseparable from humankind.

The *theme* of madness in poetry dates back to ancient texts, and the works of several writers are directly associated with it: Artaud, Charlotte Brontë, Cervantes, Dostoevsky, Erasmus, Gogol, Hölderlin, Ionesco, Poe, Shakespeare, Mary Shelley, and, of course, the mystics (Meister Eckhart, Ruusbroec or San Juan de la Cruz).

And speaking of madness, one is reminded of one of the most tragic figures in literature, Ophelia, in Shakespeare's *Hamlet*, who goes mad, partly because of her father's death, but also (there is a discussion about this in literary criticism) because of her rejection by Hamlet. Ophelia is different from Mariza, as she suffers for nothing and does not gain insight through her madness. The change that has come over Ophelia through her madness makes her speech incoherent, and she has to revert to song. In the case of Mariza, she knows how to handle her madness in such a way that it becomes a force, even employing us to stand beside her to strengthen the value of what she is doing, singing *fado*. In Ophelia's case, the derangement is completely inside her, and she is at the mercy of the forces outside her, rendering her insane.

While *Hamlet* is a play, at some crucial moment the text reverts to poetry and song, particularly in act IV, scene v: Ophelia comes on stage and starts singing intermittently. In fact, just like with Mariza, this is a *performance* Ophelia resorts to in order to reveal her state of mind—a fearsome mixture of anxiety and anguish, of mourning and misery.

Here is her famous 'Valentine song':

Pray let's have no words of this, but when they ask
You what it means, say you this.
    Tomorrow is Saint Valentine's day,
    All in the morning betime,
    And I a maid at your window,
    To be your Valentine.
    Then up he rose, and donn'd his clo'es,
    And dupp'd the chamber door,
    Let in the maid that out a maid
    Never departed more.

(IV, v, 46–55)

And she continues:

    By Gis and by Saint Charity,
    Alack and fie for shame,
    Young men will do't if they come to't –
    By Cock, they are to blame.
    Quoth she, 'Before you tumbled me,
    You promis'd me to wed.'

He answers,

    'so would I a done, by yonder sun,
    And thou hadst not come to my bed.' (58–66)

The language of the song, unlike that of 'Loucura,' is *archaic* ('dupp'd' stands for 'opened,' 'Gis' for 'Jesus,' 'if they come to 't' for 'if they have an opportunity,' etc.). Like Mariza's, it is a bewildered expression of Ophelia's pent up feelings of being betrayed by her lover. (Remember the Goethe poem we analyzed in the previous chapter.) Ophelia starts hers in a rather romantic tone, telling how she woke up early in the morning ('betime') for the man to see her because, as the tradition goes, the first girl he sees on St. Valentine's Day is going to be his love. Obedient and loyal to men in general, she is now 'a maid at [his] window,/To be [his] Valentine,' but then the slant of the song changes to a gloomier and even accusing one as the man took advantage of her: he '[l]et in the maid that out a maid/Never departed more'—a straightforward implication of the sexual relationship they had, of her loss of virginity. Devastated and ashamed, the girl goes on saying that her valentine had promised to marry her if she went to bed with him, but he did not.

So the song is not *about* madness *per se*, but rather the manifestation of Ophelia's mental breakdown. The girl's madness stems from her deep mourning for the death of her beloved father, killed by the man she loved, and at the same time for the unrequited love ('Before you tumbled me,/You promis'd me to wed') and from Hamlet's unexpected departure for England. The complexity of the situation is simply too much—and she breaks down under the weight of the contrary emotions.

In case of Mariza, it is her isolation from fellow human beings, by virtue of being from the country of the *fados*, that makes her mad. Madness is outside daily life, and that is where poetry happens. Indeed, poetry is often striving to alienate you from your everyday surroundings. So encountering a poem in a language that you may not (find easy to) understand plunges you into the depth of what poetry can do. It also means that you may have to come back to the text again and again, as we, the authors of this book, had to do as well: really great literature generally demands effort, serious and prolonged effort—which is something conflicting with present-day habits in (Western) societies, which place much greater emphasis on speed and the rapid change of fashion. Poetry may take you, so to say, into a madhouse, with its own, specific 'being in the world.'

In the chapters that follow, we will look at what in poetry makes you, as readers or listeners, experience the power of the words and rhythm—just as the spectators of Mariza's song did. After all, as we have seen, madness may also destroy someone, as it did with Ophelia. When that happens, we are overwhelmed with fear and pity, two emotions that are central to the experience of poetry. But that is for later.

Meanwhile, in preparation for the next chapter, we request you to do some research on your personal collection of music. The question to be answered is the following one: 'Which of the songs in your collection does not contain any repetition?' By 'repetition' we do not mean words like 'the' or 'you' or 'love' because obviously some words are inevitably repeated, since there is a limited number of words in a language. What we mean is whole phrases or sentences. So please identify in your collection those songs in which there are *no* sentences repeated and keep this information at hand when starting reading Chapter 3 of this volume.

Core issues

- Music and voice are at the origin of poetry. From its outset, literature was not private, but a public oral performance, often meant to be memorized and subsequently recited.

- In research on the experience of poetry basic knowledge of statistics is helpful. Graphs are highly illuminating in summarizing results.

- In evidence-based research, a sample (a group of participants) is usually selected from a population, and statistics is employed to establish whether we can generalize from those samples to populations in general.

- We can distinguish between emotions evoked by poetry and the emotions we as readers/listeners experience ourselves.

- Emotions always carry valence, i.e., they are perceived as either positive (pleasant) or negative (unpleasant). In poetic experience we, paradoxically, often enjoy sadness.

- The theme of madness in poetry dates back to ancient texts. The two emotions that are central to the experience of poetry are fear and pity.

Further reading

Feder, L. (1980), *Madness in Literature*. Princeton: Princeton University Press.

Khalvati, M. (2010), *Saudade: An Anthology of Fado Poetry*. Lisbon: Gulbenkian Foundation.

Sass, L. (1992), *Madness and Modernism: Insanity in the Light of Modern Art, Literature and Thought*. New York: Basic Books.

Small, H. (1998), *Love's Madness: Medicine, the Novel, and Female Madness*. Oxford: Oxford University Press.

Stokes, R. (2018), *The Penguin Book of English Song: Seven Centuries of Poetry from Chaucer to Auden*. London: Penguin Classics.

Weineck, S.-M. (2002), *The Abyss Above: Philosophy and Poetic Madness in Plato, Hölderlin and Nietzsche*. New York: SUNY Press.

3

Poetry Is Prettiness

Keywords

repetition

literariness

foregrounding

parallelism

poetic function

baby talk / motherese

defeated expectancy

falsification

manipulation

factor analysis

experimental group

control group

Likert scales

p-value

Repetition

Let us start with the results of the investigation you carried out in preparation of this chapter. How many of the songs in your personal collection of pop music did *not* contain any repetition of particular phrases, clauses, or sentences?

We do not know the number you came up with in your inspection, but we do know that the number will be low, very low—perhaps there were even none at all. As a matter of fact, this is what we would predict: that among your collection of songs there are hardly any in which no sentences are repeated. Is this not strange? Well no, you may argue, because these are popular songs, meant to provide some entertainment for the general audience, so their content should not be too difficult. They should be easy to be grasped without effort, and so repetitions serve this purpose of making their message easily comprehensible, simply by virtue of being repeated a number of times. But wait! Do inspect the song 'Loucura' in the previous chapter. Do you see any repetitions in the lyrics? Sure there are: stanza 3 (which already opens with internal repetition of '*Chorai, chorai*' or 'Cry, cry') is repeated again as stanza 7, and stanza 4 is identical to stanza 8.

Or the Scottish folk song 'Jock O'Hazeldean' we discussed in Chapter 1. Is it without repetitions? Certainly not: in the very first stanza lines 1 and 2 open with 'Why weep ye by the tide,' and lines 4 and 5, with 'An ye shall be his bride.' All stanzas of the verse close with 'For Jock O'Hazeldean' with the exception of the last one, which closes with 'Wi' Jock O'Hazeldean'—echoing the final lines of the preceding stanzas anyway. The examples of repetitions are, surely, numerous.

The songs we have just mentioned are traditional, with their origins in past history. But they are still meant for large audiences, and indiscriminately at that. They form part of what we called 'low' culture in Chapter 1. So let us look at a song that definitely does *not* belong to popular music. We had an example of this in the poem by Goethe in Chapter 1, 'Heidenröslein,' put to music by a musical genius, Franz Schubert. And what do we find in the text? An amount of repetition that even surmounts the repetitions in popular songs: per just 101 words of the poem, *Röslein* (briar) is repeated as many as seventeen times, and the phrase *Röslein auf der Heiden* (briar on the meadow), six times.

This observation falsifies our hypotheses that repetitions are there because of popularity, easiness of comprehension or entertainment. So what *is* the explanation? In this chapter we will advance another hypothesis, namely that repetition in poetry (and elsewhere) is not just repetition: it is meaningful, while it gives pleasure. The 'pleasure principle' lies at the heart of much poetic experience. When reading a poem or hearing a song, we are delighted when something 'returns,' something that was there a few seconds ago. We will elaborate the hypothesis, but in line with the principles of this book, we will also demonstrate the evidence that speaks in its favor.

So when, for instance, readers encounter the famous ballad-like poem 'The Rime of the Ancient Mariner' (1798) by Coleridge, and have come to Part IV and read the first line 'I fear thee, ancient Mariner!' and then encounter the next line 'I fear thy skinny hand!', they, so our hypotheses goes, experience some kind of delight. And more even in the next stanza:

> I fear thee and thy glittering eye
> And thy skinny hand, so brown.—

Then there follow 121 lines that are very different, so the reader may have thought the game of the first three lines is over, but then may be surprised when in line 345 they read:

> 'I fear thee, ancient Mariner!'

The game of repetition is re-opened. And is played the whole poem through. Sure no one would think that these repetitions are a coincidence. And if they are not, they must be intentional. They bring some kind of an 'Aha' (*Eureka!*) experience in the reader, and poets play this trick to instill awareness in the recipient, but also because the playful elements provide pleasure. That is the theory, at least—it should be submitted to an independent test.

At the same time the reader's experience is one of shared intense heroism with the Mariner. In trying to understand this deeper energy of the poem, it helps to realize that the poem is also an allegoric story, namely of Coleridge's own liberation from his drug addiction. But there are so many stories, movies, and poems about drug addiction. Why would *this* text by Coleridge prevail? The British quality newspaper *The Guardian* nominated it the poem of the week in 2009, whose spell does not seem to weaken over the years. From a psychopoetic point of view, a good part of the explanation has to be sought in the structural characteristics: in the ballad-like thrust of the episodes, in the simple, but obstinate, metrical beat, in the regular rhyme scheme—and in the subtle repetitions that are woven throughout the poem. Time to look at it again (if you have read it in school)!

Roman Jakobson

A theoretical framework for the observed repetitions was proposed by a Russian with an exceptional biography. He formed part of a movement later called Russian Formalism, groups of scholars and artists in Moscow and Saint Petersburg. Their main objective was to develop a systematic study of what literature is—in contrast to the objectives of traditional forms of literary criticism. What is typical for literature, they argued, is *literariness* (*literaturnost'* in Russian). One of the central characteristics of literariness was, according to several scholars in Russian Formalism, the kind of repetitions that we saw in the previous section. From early onwards, roughly 1916, this insight was developed by Roman Jakobson, but then later became known in the West in the 1960s. That was because Jakobson left the country (in 1920), disillusioned by the Bolshevik revolution. He went to Prague, where he was influential in the circle of the so-called Prague Structuralists. In this circle a central term was invented, the one we will have recourse to often in this book. It is the term 'foregrounding,' the English translation of the Czech term *aktualisace*, coined by the Prague Structuralist Jan Mukařovský ([1932] 1964). Let us first explain what is meant by the term, before we go on with the discussion of Roman Jakobson's contribution to it.

In poetics, stylistics and literary studies, the term 'foregrounding' is used to refer to a device, a strategy if you want, by which authors make some part of their texts stand out (put it into the 'foreground'). This can be done in basically two ways: either by *deviations* (which is the subject of the next chapter) or by *parallelism*, which we will focus on in the present one. The two different devices are linked to different theoreticians, as we will see. The concept of parallelism is associated with the name of Roman Jakobson.

In the early 1940s, Jakobson fled West again, and—after several peregrinations—became professor at Harvard University, where he remained until his death (in 1982). Because of his influential position in the United States, his ideas became well known, but (the polyglot) Jakobson was also instrumental in spreading the ideas of other Russian Formalists in the West. Let us concentrate here on one of the central ideas that furthered the study of poetry. It has to do with repetition, or better, with *parallelism*—the term which we will explain later in this chapter.

The most famous expression of Jakobson's ideas in this respect is to be found in a 'Closing Statement' that he delivered at the end of a conference, which was printed with the subtitle 'Linguistics and Poetics' in 1960. In it, Jakobson distinguishes different functions that language may fulfil, like the emotive or referential function. One of these functions that is of special importance to us here, he calls the *poetic function*, one in which full attention is given to language itself, it being, in this sense, *self-referential*. What this means was cast by Jakobson in a rather cryptic sentence, one that has bedeviled students of this work for decades: 'The poetic function projects the principle of equivalence from the axis of selection into the axis of combination' (Jakobson 1960: 358).

Let us clarify what is meant by it. There is talk of two axes, one of *selection* and one of *combination*. Things become much more transparent if we put this in spatial terms. The combination is the horizontal principle. It is: time. In language sounds follow each other horizontally, in the sense that one comes after the other in time. We cannot utter two sounds at exactly the same time. We must 'combine' them, and here is no escaping this principle of combination. But at each point in this horizontal course choices are to be made (by the speaker/writer). Take, for instance, some lines from 'The Raven,' a famous poem by Edgar Allan Poe:

While I nodded, nearly <u>napping</u>, suddenly there came a <u>tapping</u>,
As of some one gently <u>rapping</u>, <u>rapping</u> at my chamber door.

The words 'napping,' 'tapping,' and 'rapping' all three rhyme. They are very similar in sound (in fact, they differ only in their initial consonant), but they are grammatically different: 'tapping' is a noun here while 'napping' and 'rapping' are verbs. So we confront near-equivalence in sound, but difference in grammar. At the same time, there are other instances of repetition: in the phrase 'nodded, nearly napping.' The poet could easily have chosen 'almost' instead of 'nearly,' but then the *alliteration* (that is what it is called when words have identical initial consonants) would have been gone. The choices to be made at each point can be visualized as arranged vertically: at each point in time, one may choose from a 'column' containing different possibilities. The fact that they may all be chosen means that they are equivalent. The same goes for 'nodded': Poe could have used 'dozing,' 'snoozing,' or 'falling asleep.' So the line might as well have run as follows:

> While I nodded, almost dozing

or

> While I nodded, about to fall asleep.

But that is not what the poet has chosen. So intention is behind it. It is clear that the intention was to select words with highly similar sounds. So, instead of choosing words with approximately the same meaning but with a different phonological makeup, the poet chooses to repeat an almost identical sound structure. That is what Jakobson means by this 'projection.'

Another illustration may come from Shakespeare's *Othello*. Right after he has killed Desdemona, his faithful wife, whom he suspected of infidelity, Othello exclaims:[1]

> 'I kiss'd thee ere I kill'd thee!'

The sentence is full of symmetries. Thus the grammatical structure is the same in the two halves: Subject ('I')—Verb ('kiss'd'/'kill'd')—Object ('thee'). On top of it, the tense of the verb is the same (past), and the two initial sounds of the verb are identical, too. For each of these, different choices on the vertical axis of equivalence could have been made. One could cast these possibilities in a table like the following one:

Selection and combination in Othello's line.

I	embraced	you	before	I	killed	you
I	hugged	her	before		killing	her
I	kissed	my wife	before		strangling	her
I	hugged	Desdemona	before	I	took	her life
I	gave you a kiss		before	I	murdered	you
I	kiss'd	thee	ere	I	kill'd	thee

Each of the horizontal combinations would have expressed more or less the same meaning that Othello has in mind. But Shakespeare opted for the bottom one. Why? One reason—and to most analysts a very important one— is the symmetry in it. None of the other variants shows such a high degree of symmetrical shape. And symmetry appeals to our brains, to the human brain. Sasaki et al. (2005) used functional magnetic resonance imaging (fMRI), comparing brain activity in response to symmetrical versus random dots, and found that (visual) symmetry is specifically enhanced in the human brain. We love symmetry because we experience it as harmonious, beautiful, peaceful, delicate, and graceful—whether it is in buildings, painting, rituals, carpets, cutlery, and even in human bodies and faces. And, of course, in music. (Remember your own research on the number of repetitions in your collection.) Symmetry is also present in language, and poetry is the exquisite place where one finds such condensed forms of harmony.

Parallelism

But are the 'symmetries' in poetry we discussed on the previous pages, repetitions in the usual sense of the word? If we compare them with your personal collection of popular songs or with traditional songs, and even with the Goethe poem and its musical version by Schubert, often we are not dealing with real repetition, but with *partial* repetitions. There is a special term for this in literary studies: *parallelism*. The term refers to a repetition with variation. And this actually is the type that is much more frequent—and much more important—in poetry than straightforward repetition. This is also the term that is used when studying the poetic function that Jakobson had in mind. We have already dealt with several forms of parallelism in Chapter 1: rhyme, for instance, is a form of partial repetition—the vowel is repeated, and the consonants vary, as in the Poe example above. So is alliteration, the mirror image of rhyme, so to say: now the initial consonant (cluster) is repeated, but the ensuing vowels differ. The poem by Poe offers examples of this, too. Meter is a form of parallelism, too, and so are verse lines and stanzas.

Basically, a lot of typical poetic structures are forms of parallelism. But one may occasionally find it in prose as well. Here, for instance, are the opening lines of Nabokov's novel *Lolita*: 'Lolita, light of my life, fire of my loins. My sin, my soul.' The lines abound with alliteration and *assonance* (also repetition, but now of vowel sounds). And these cases are no accident, for it goes on like this for several lines, quite clearly intentionally.

Parallelism is also a device that frequently turns up in daily language, proverbs, idioms, or sayings. Consider, for instance:

When the going gets tough, the tough get going;
    Easy come, easy go;
    All's well that ends well;
    First things first;
    Man proposes but God disposes;
    Out of sight, out of mind;
    Use it or lose it.

Even in individual words parallelism in everyday language is not at all uncommon, as becomes clear from examples like 'bye-bye,' 'chit-chat,' 'fifty-fifty,' 'flip-flops,' 'hocus-pocus,' 'blah-blah,' 'wishy-washy,' 'yoyo,' and—of course—'papa' and 'mama.' The last examples bring us to the origins of parallelism in our lives.

From about some thirty weeks after birth, babies begin babbling, as their first step on their way to language mastery. And this babbling is full of parallelism, with words like 'nana,' 'dada,' or 'dodo.'

In 'The Poetics of Babytalk,' Miall and Dissanayake (2003) have uncovered the similarities between the efforts at speaking by babies, on the one hand, and typical forms of parallelism in poetic language. In it, they analyze the speech of a mother to her eight-week infant. And sure, the kind of language used by mothers to talk to their pre-linguistic babies displays a plethora of poetic, mainly parallelistic, devices. It is even the case that babies prefer recorded babytalk to ordinary adult speech, as demonstrated by Fernald and Kuhl (1987). This is an important new direction taken in the study of poetics because one may wonder how come that people, poets and song writers, have some predilection for forms like parallelism. It turns out that this is a penchant which we delight in since very early childhood.

The point is not that parallelism and other poetic structures turn up in babytalk, but that they occur at the very beginning of language development in human life. The consequence is aptly formulated by Miall and Dissanayake (ibid.: 356): 'The existence of sensitivities to such features in the first weeks of life suggests that humans are born with natural (innate, universal) predispositions for aesthetic engagement, from which, we suggest, cultures and individuals have gone on to create their myriad elaborated forms of artistic expression.'

Their analysis of babytalk covers only a brief fragment (of just over a minute) of *motherese*, as it is called. May one base general conclusion on such a minuscule piece of language? Not if it were the only one, but the observations made are echoed by several other studies of mother–infant communication; for instance, by Beebe, Stern, and Jaffé (1979); Malloch (1999); Papoušek and Papoušek (1997); and Trevarthen (1979).

More important still is the fact that the widespread use of such forms of parallelism seems to be universal: at least it is also documented in non-Western societies, such as the Kung people in Namibia (reported in Konner 1977), some Australian aborigines (see Hamilton 1981) and the studies by Tronick, Morelli, and Winn (1987) and Hewlett (1991) on pygmies; for an overview, see Finnegan (1992).

Parallelism is so central to poetry that there have been (serious) efforts to *define* poetry just by the occurrence of parallelism or hyper-regularity (for example, meter, rhyme, or alliteration). The clearest of such proposals is by Anna Christina Ribeiro (2007) who claims that '[a] closer look at the poems from literary traditions around the world will reveal that the history of poetry is one of texts whose universal and enduring characteristic is their exhibiting certain types of repetition schemes' (ibid.: 191). She adds that '[a]s a rule (...), we do not find in prose (or film) the attention to those devices [of repetition]' (ibid.: 195).

On the whole, parallelism implies that some component of the form or meaning of a text is similar to some other component at some abstract level of description. This makes a poem easier to remember, creates expectation and excitement, adds emotive effect, and holds a text together. *Lexical parallelism* involves repetition of words or their meaning; *syntactic parallelism* presupposes repetition of an order of sentence elements, while *phonological parallelism* involves reiteration of sounds.

Next to 'abstract' types of repetition, such as the meter, foot, line, stanza, and poetic form (sonnet, haiku, ballad, etc.), Ribeiro distinguishes between:

- word terminal repetition (e.g., rhyme);

- word initial repetition (e.g., alliteration); and

- the recurrence of specific words or phrases.

All these repetitions may be *dense* or *sparse*, and poets may *follow* the tradition, *transform* it, or *reject* it. And such patterns of poetic form, we believe, are highly effective in shaping the reader's expectation and thus enhancing the emotional effect of the text, which we will illustrate in the following section of this chapter. But let us first, by way of an illustration, look at how such repetitive patterns play out in a non-Western genre, that of Japanese *haiku*. Ribeiro makes an attempt to define poetry by answering the following question: 'What can *Stabat Mater*, Beat poetry, Shakespeare's sonnets, Goethe's *Faust*, and Japanese haiku possibly have in common?' She claims that in poetry '[l]ines, in turn, recur a certain number of times and thereby contribute to producing a stanza type (a ballad quatrain) and/or a poetic form (the haiku)' by way of the so-called abstract level of repetition (similar to sonnet or villanelle).

Thus in the Japanese poetry of haiku the structure involves three groups of five syllables, seven syllables, and five syllables respectively. This is one of the shortest poetic forms in world literature, consisting of seventeen syllables only. Let us look at an example from Matsuo Basho (1644–94), whom we already met in Chapter 1. Here is a haiku by him:[2]

瓜作る　　　君があれなと　　　夕涼み
Uri tsukuru /　Kimi ga arena to /　Yusuzumi

A first thing to remark here is that Japanese uses a different type of *script*, not an alphabet, in which *sounds* are rendered through graphic symbols, called letters, but instead a so-called *ideographic* writing system. It was developed by the Chinese, who call it *hanzi*, and in Japanese it is called *kanji*. In such a script you do not write sounds, but *concepts*. So instead of writing c-o-o-l-n-e-s-s (reproducing how the word sounds), you write just one symbol, 涼, which means, well—coolness. Speakers of Japanese know this, and they also know (of course) how the word for 'coolness' is pronounced, namely, *suzu*. If you look again at the poem by Basho, you will notice that this is the penultimate sign. You can see that there is one more sign after it, namely み, which is transliterated as 'mi.' But this is not a *kanji* sign, but a phonetic symbol, rendering the syllable 'mi.' So in Japanese you do write sounds, but mainly for endings of verbs, grammatical functions, or particles. It is a *syllabary*, a kind of alphabet, but for syllables, called *hiragana*, consisting of forty-six signs. (Are you having an inkling that is complicated? It is—but not to Japanese children! It all depends what you grow up with.)

Let us now return to Basho's poem. A translation could run:

Oh that you were here
Who used to grow gourds –
The cool of evening breezes.

But that fails to capture some of the original's beauty, in which the *kanji* signs stand out on their own. So let us look at the signs in detail:

瓜 (uri)—this is an umbrella term for various fruits such as gourds, melons, etc.
作る (tsuku-ru)—to make, in this context, to grow.

So the first group of five syllables refers back to the growth of melons, a refreshing fruit. The second group of seven syllables is about the present:

君 (kimi)—may have different meanings, but here refers to 'you.' Linked to the previous part, the traditional 5-7-5 structure may here be seen as an

8-4-5 pattern. Or even, when we take the following words into account, a 12-5 structure.

These following words are written wholly in *hiragana*:

> are (あれ) to be
> na (な) wishing
> to (と) that.

The whole phrase should be understood more or less as: I wish you would be here. The final group you already partly understand: it is about coolness (*suzumi*). But what about the first sign, 夕 (yu)? It means (to keep matters simple): evening. So the third group of the poem refers to a cool evening, to spend a refreshing evening with the friend, who is currently absent.

If we now look again at the English translation above, we may notice how far it is from the original. Not only has the order of the groups been reversed, but it also obscures the inherent parallelism in the original: the three parts (5-7-5 syllables) are organized as:

Past (you grew melons)—a present longing (wish you were here)—present (spending a cool evening).

Moreover, the first and final parts echo each other: the melons in the first part provide refreshment, which is echoed in the final part. So our translation would run something like this (retaining the pattern of 5-7-5 syllables in English):

Melons you once grew/wish you were present here now/a cool evening.

We have dwelt somewhat long on this extremely short poem, in order to illustrate the richness and variety in poetic forms across the globe, and the concurrent different experiences they evoke.

Politics, sermon, song: From Caesar to Brodsky

The famous Latin phrase *Veni, vidi, vici* (I came, I saw, I conquered) was allegedly pronounced by Julius Caesar after at the Battle of Zela in 47 BCE he swiftly beat Pharnaces II of Pontus. Do you notice anything special in its form? What is there in this phrase that made it survive 2,000 years?

You have obviously noticed that the phrase consists of three words that belong to the same part of speech (a verb) in the same grammatical form (past tense). More than that—the words contain the same number of letters (four per each) and the same number of syllables (two per unit). The initial consonant sound in each lexeme (/v/) is repeated thrice, a threefold alliteration. Finally, the three words are syntactically linked through omission of conjunctions, or *asyndeton* (which is contrasted to *polysyndeton*, a deliberate repetition of several coordinating conjunctions in succession). All these parallel devices, we believe, make the phrase emotionally attractive, emphatically strong, and thus memorable.

Hence parallelism as a powerful rhetoric device is often employed by politicians who skillfully use it to exert emotional effect on an audience, and there are scores of examples to it. One of them is Sir Winston Churchill, not only the British prime minister, but also the winner of the Nobel Prize in Literature (1953), who produced more words than Dickens and Shakespeare put together. In his speech to the House of Commons in 1940, warning the Parliament of a possible Nazi invasion, Churchill pronounced the following: 'We shall fight on the beaches, we shall fight on the landing grounds, we shall fight in the fields and in the streets.' Quite obviously, the sentence is marked by repetition, *anaphora* in the first place—a stylistic device when the initial component of a structure is reiterated.

Similarly, the 35th president of the United States, John F. Kennedy, in his inaugural address in 1961 says the following to the citizens of his country: 'My fellow Americans, ask not what your country can do for you, ask what you can do for your country.' This type of repetition implies the reverse order of otherwise parallel units ('your country' and 'you'). This is called a *chiasmus*: the elements are repeated, but in reverse order, yielding the pattern A B B A in the example just given. It is especially effective in highlighting opposing positions, like in the Kennedy example, but it is also highly effective in drawing attention to the contrast, and thereby strengthening it in the listener's memory, as, for instance, in Shakespeare's *Julius Caesar* (IV, iii, 18): 'Remember March, the ides of March remember.'

Not only politics but also religion has made extensive use of parallelism—with virtually the same purpose: affecting the audience. Prayers, initially and primarily oral, are meant to be remembered and pronounced numerous times, so that the resulting emotional impact soothes the problems of the one who does so, with the hope of being helped by the celestial force. The peace prayer of Saint Francis of Assisi below is a good example—you can listen to it recited by the staff of St. Francis hospital (giving it the coping power we will discuss in Chapter 6 later): Link 3.1 on the Companion Website. Here are the words:

1 Lord, make me an instrument of your peace:
2 where there is hatred, let me sow love;
3 where there is injury, pardon;
4 where there is doubt, faith;

5 where there is despair, hope;

6 where there is darkness, light;

7 where there is sadness, joy.

8 Divine Master, grant that I may not so much seek

9 to be consoled as to console;

10 to be understood as to understand;

11 to be loved as to love;

12 for it is in giving that we receive,

13 it is in pardoning that we are pardoned,

14 and it is in dying that we are born to eternal life.

The prayer, you have certainly noticed, is full of elements that repeat themselves. Look first at lines 2 through 7. Here the same element, 'where there is,' is anaphorically reiterated. Additionally, the syntactic parallelism is explicit when every line here has the same structure. The parallelism is enhanced by the semantic contrast as the fourth word ('hatred,' 'injury,' 'doubt,' 'despair,' 'darkness,' and 'sadness') in every line is negatively colored and counterbalanced with the element bearing positive connotation ('love,' 'pardon,' 'faith,' 'hope,' 'light,' and 'joy'). In all probability, this optimistic final note in each line is aimed at elevating the faith of the person who pronounces the prayer in its omnipotence.

In the second stanza, lines 9 to 11 demonstrate grammatical parallelism where passive and active forms of the same verb are balanced. In line 12, 'giving' and 'receive' are juxtaposed. Finally, the concluding line of the prayer sounds like a hymn to immortality: 'dying' is just a preamble to 'eternal life'—with the parallelism playing the key role. It is no wonder that this prayer has been put to music as its parallelism goes hand in hand with its musicality.

To show how deep the effects of parallelism run, consider the poem 'A Song' (1989) by the 1987 Nobel laureate Joseph Brodsky. Its topic is highly similar to the haiku by Basho that we discussed a minute ago: longing for an absent beloved person, which forms a common theme in poetry the world over. Listen to the way the author himself reads the poem, to the accompaniment of a piano: Link 3.2 on the Companion Website.

I wish you were here, dear,
I wish you were here.
I wish you sat on the sofa
and I sat near.

The handkerchief could be yours,
the tear could be mine, chin-bound.

Though it could be, of course,
the other way round.

I wish you were here, dear,
I wish you were here.
I wish we were in my car,
and you'd shift the gear.

We'd find ourselves elsewhere,
on an unknown shore.
Or else we'd repair
to where we've been before.

I wish you were here, dear,
I wish you were here.
I wish I knew no astronomy
when stars appear,

when the moon skims the water
that sighs and shifts in its slumber.
I wish it were still a quarter
to dial your number.

I wish you were here, dear,
in this hemisphere,
as I sit on the porch
sipping a beer.

It's evening, the sun is setting;
boys shout and gulls are crying.
What's the point of forgetting
if it's followed by dying?

Quietly and repeatedly, the prayer-like 'I wish you were here' anaphorically opens stanzas 1, 3, 5, and 7, and the final word of the phrase ('here') rhymes not only with the final word in the line ('dear'), but also with the final words in the fourth line of the stanzas ('near,' 'gear,' 'appear,' and 'beer'). Stanza 7 seems to be following the pattern of stanzas 1, 3, and 5, and the reader expects the same second line as they had before ('I wish you were here'), but all of a sudden the expectation is defeated with 'in this hemisphere' coming in (a stylistic device known as *defeated expectancy*)—at the same time deviating from the established syntactic pattern and following the phonetic one as 'hemisphere' rhymes with both 'here' and 'dear.'

Song again: From The Beatles to a soccer match

So *parallelism* as a form of musicality seems to be both a universal and a defining characteristic of poetry. Metricality, for instance, is virtually absent from other genres, but highly prevalent in poetic forms. Although prosodic grouping underlies linguistic processing (also in bird song), the exquisite elaboration of metrical systems seems unique to poetry. Such forms of musicality also heighten the psychological feeling of proximity, mainly through the simultaneous enhancement of several brain centers, notably those of motor skills, emotionality, and creativity. Certain patterns/phrases are powerful on their own, as the rhythm is created by the metricality, musicality, combination of sounds, etc.

Here again we see how similar poetry and music are. According to Ribeiro (2007), '[w]e may recall that (...) the early words for poetry in various languages indicate "making" or "artifice" (for example, *poiesis*, in Greek) or "song" (*shi*, or word-song, in Chinese; *mele*, air or melody, in Greek, besides, of course, *lyra*, one of the instruments that often accompanied performance and that gave us "lyric")' (199). This is 'to be explained by the needs of oral cultures (...) defined by a psychological propensity to pattern language in certain ways— ways that are memorable, both in the cognitive sense that they are more easily remembered, and in the evaluative sense that they are pleasing' (ibid.).

So we face a certain 'magic' of the words, when we know a poem, but without fully grasping its meaning—as it basically happens with music, and that we can repeat it endlessly and enjoy it, without ever arriving at a final understanding of its meaning. Dylan Thomas once described the phenomenon (in a public talk) as such: 'Poetry is what in a poem makes you laugh, cry, prickle, be silent, makes your toe nails twinkle, makes you want to do this or that or nothing, makes you know that you are alone in the unknown world, that your bliss and suffering is forever shared and forever all your own.'

With this idea in mind, let us now look at a very different kind of song—the one Paul McCartney from The Beatles composed in June 1968, while driving from London to Weybridge in Surrey. Originally titled 'Hey Jules,' the song was written for Julian, the son of John and Cynthia Lennon, who had just divorced, so it was meant to cheer the boy up and urge him to move on in the world with an open heart—the idea of poetry helping to cope with troubles, that we will elaborate on in Chapter 6. If you know the song, you will remember that it is full of parallelism. The text consists of six stanzas, four of which anaphorically open with 'Hey Jude, don't + verb.' The text, imitating an informal talk, explicitly focuses on the direct address ('hey Jude' is repeated seven times in all) and imperatives: 'don't make it bad,' 'take a sad song,' 'remember,' etc. The syntactic parallelism is enhanced by rhyme ('it's a <u>fool</u>

who plays it <u>cool'</u>) and alliteration ('**s**ad **s**ong'), while the general optimistic flavor is boosted through persistent repetition of 'make it better' (six times).

The song immediately made it into the top charts and in the United States alone was #1 for as many as nine weeks, to be later performed by Elvis Presley, Smokey Robinson, Diana Ross, and Ella Fitzgerald, to name just a few. But what is interesting for the purpose of this book is the fact that the song also turned into a soccer chant, uniting crowds of fans, who would ceaselessly repeat the 'Na na na nananana, nannana' refrain. Even more surprisingly—a song written by a band from Liverpool now celebrates the achievements of their deadly rivals, Manchester City, demonstrating the power of poetry: Link 3.3 on the Companion Website.

Now the question arises whether this happens also when readers confront poetry. In what follows we will look at this issue in more detail.

Is there good evidence for the effects of parallelism?

Ever since Roman Jakobson formulated his insights into the poetic function, scholars have evaluated his theory at length, first in linguistics (see, for instance, Leech 1969), but then also through reading experiments confronting theoretical assumptions with actual reading behavior. Several such studies were indeed able to demonstrate the psychological validity of insights generated by the Russian Formalists, notably by van Peer (2020), Miall and Kuiken (1994a), and the thematic issue on foregrounding of *Language and Literature* (2007). In all these studies, predictions derived from the theory were corroborated. With the help of such reading experiments, it was possible to uphold the theoretical stance of the theory of foregrounding. To give one example: Russian Formalism (to which Jakobson initially belonged) speaks of *retardation* of perception as a result of the devices of estrangement, used by artists, leading to aesthetic experiences. Miall and Kuiken (1994b) could show this indeed to be the case, in that text passages that contained heavy foregrounding devices were (subconsciously) read significantly slower than non-foregrounded passages. Since participants in the study were totally unaware of the fact that their reading speed was being monitored (by a computer), these results may be taken as clear proof that literary features like foregrounding indeed slow down perception.

In what follows, we will subject Jakobson's theory of the poetic function to a *falsification* procedure, after the philosopher of science Karl Popper (e.g., in his work *Objective Knowledge*): we will try to prove not that the theory is right, but that it is wrong! If the theory is not *falsified* in the test, then we accept it, at least for the time being. The method consists in *manipulating* a poetic text, for instance, by removing the structural characteristic under consideration and then distributing the two versions, the original and the manipulated texts, *randomly* among a group of (highly similar) readers. We hypothesized that parallelism is so essential in poetry that removing it would destroy the prettiness and thus decrease readers' appreciation of the text.

The poem under consideration is by the Modernist poet E. E. Cummings:[3]

anyone lived in a pretty how town
(with up so floating many bells down)
spring summer autumn winter
he sang his didn't he danced his did

Women and men (both little and small)
cared for anyone not at all
they sowed their isn't they reaped their same
sun moon stars rain

children guessed (but only a few
and down they forgot as up they grew
autumn winter spring summer)
that noone loved him more by more

when by now and tree by leaf
she laughed his joy she cried his grief
bird by snow and stir by still
anyone's any was all to her

someones married their everyones
laughed their cryings and did their dance
(sleep wake hope and then)they
said their nevers they slept their dream

stars rain sun moon
(and only the snow can begin to explain
how children are apt to forget to remember
with up so floating many bells down)

one day anyone died i guess
(and noone stooped to kiss his face)
busy folk buried them side by side
little by little and was by was

all by all and deep by deep
and more by more they dream their sleep

noone and anyone earth by april
wish by spirit and if by yes.

Women and men (both dong and ding)
summer autumn winter spring
reaped their sowing and went their came
sun moon stars rain.

You have certainly noticed many ungrammaticalities in the text, but also parallelism that is manifested on various levels. *Phonologically*, there is rhyme, but also alliteration ('dong and ding'). *Lexically*, 'sun moon stars rain' is reiterated in stanzas 2 and 9, and in different order in stanza 6: 'stars rain sun moon.' We also see enumeration of seasons in stanza 1 ('spring summer autumn winter'), but again in different order in stanzas 3 ('autumn winter spring summer') and 9 ('summer autumn winter spring'), thus creating a feeling of endless continuity of the events described.

On the *semantic* level, the poem rests on the opposition of 'women and men' (stanzas 3 and 9), 'little and small' (stanza 3), and 'noone and anyone' (stanza 8). Repetition of mostly monosyllabic words goes together with *syntactic* parallelism, as throughout the whole poem we encounter the same pattern again and again: 'more by more' 'side by side,' 'little by little,' 'was by was,' 'all by all,' and 'deep by deep.' And more could be added if one were to undertake an exhaustive analysis of the text. But the few examples make it clear enough that next to a heavy regime of deviations (which we will explore in detail in the following chapter), the poem abounds in all sorts of parallelism.

Removing a good number of them from the text was our objective, so that—in comparison with the version by E. E. Cummings himself—we could observe what changes in readers' psychological experience of the text were caused by the parallelisms. After the experiment had been carried out, we invited participants to comment on the manipulated version they read, and they said it was 'original,' 'entertaining to read,' though 'a bit confusing' and one that 'need[ed] time.' The fragment of the manipulated version of E. E. Cummings's poem is presented below:

Anyone lived in such a pretty how town
(with up floating down many bells)
spring summer autumn and winter
he sang his did not and he danced his did

Women and men (both small and little)
Cared for anyone not at all
They sowed their isn't and they did reap their own
Sun moon stars and perhaps some rain

Children guessed (but only some
And down they forgot as they grew up
Wind cold flowers and heat)
That noone loved him more forever

When by now and leaf upon tree
She laughed his joy and his grief she cried
Bird by snow stir by quiet
Anyone's something was all to her

Someones married their beloved
Laughed their cryings and performed their dance
(sleep wake hope and then) they
said their nevers they slept their dream

sky storm sunshine night
(and the snow can begin to explain
how children are apt to forget to remember
with down so many chimes floating up).

This manipulated version of the poem was read by 70 participants (65 female; mean age 23), while the original version was read by a *control* group of 71 participants (67 female; mean age 21). The latter are respondents who are not affected by our manipulation, but read the original version. The comparison of their reactions to those of the *experimental group* allows us to witness the repercussions of this manipulation.

But how do we observe readers' responses? There are various ways to do it. In this experiment we requested them to give their reactions by indicating the extent to which they experienced an emotion indicated by an adjective. An easy way to do this is by using the so-called *Likert scales.* You may have seen these yourself in opinion research. Thus, for instance, in our experiment we asked participants to indicate the strength of their emotion on a 7-point scale, with an instruction along the following lines:

Questionnaire sample: control group version

Dear reader,

Below you will find the opening line of a poem. Please read it attentively and then circle the number that corresponds best to your opinion. This is not a matter of right or wrong, but solely how *you* feel about it. That is the only thing we are interested in. There are NO right or wrong answers, as your genuine reactions are what is important to us.

Please consider the order of the answers: number **1** means that you do NOT feel that the statement applies, number **7** indicates your absolute agreement. Thus, for instance, if the question is asked whether you find a particular line 'beautiful,' circle **1** if you think it is not beautiful at all, and **7** if you think it is absolutely beautiful. With all positions in between, of course.

Now read the opening line from the poem:

Anyone Lived in a Pretty How Town

I feel that this line:

is musical	1 2 3 4 5 6 7
has a deep meaning	1 2 3 4 5 6 7
makes me more sensitive	1 2 3 4 5 6 7

But which emotions? We used a battery of thirty adjectives: six dimensions, represented by five adjectives each (aesthetic appreciation, aesthetic structure, cognition, emotion, social context, and attitudes). (The scales were taken from van Peer, Hakemulder, and Zyngier [2007], and you will find the full version in Ancillary Resources at the end of this book.) The reactions were provided at three locations in the poem: after line 1; after the 6th stanza (middle) and after the whole poem. So each reader gave us 90 reactions, which is a lot to look at manually. Yet, just like we demonstrated in the previous chapter, statistics comes to help, and there is a variety of tests that can be applied, depending on the research design. This time we carried out an ANOVA for the six groups of scales. This is a statistical test allowing one to detect the influence of the manipulation (i.e., the elimination of the parallelism) on readers' reactions to the emotion scales.

In Chapter 2, we have already introduced the ideas of *significance* and *generalizability* to you. You already know that statistics helps us conclude whether our findings are accidental, or significant, and thus generalizable beyond the group of participants. Some more technical knowledge is needed at this stage.

One of the results the ANOVA test yields is the so-called *p-value*—a technical term where the letter p stands for 'probability.' It is an estimate of the probability that the observations are flawed, caused by some unknown errors or chance. The value is expressed as a number between 0 and 1. Alternatively, you can think of it in terms of percentage, so then p varies between 1 and 100. You can see this if you move the decimal point two places to the right. It is easy to understand that we want this probability to be as *low* as possible, but conventionally the threshold is .05 or 5 percent. So $p < .05$ means that the probability of chance is lower than 5 percent, and it is *unlikely* that pure chance caused the outcome. Another way of saying this is that when we repeat the experiment 100 times, we will find the same result ninety-five times or more, thus it is allowable to say that your findings are generalizable. At this point, you may wonder: how do we know? The answer is not easy to give, as it is the result of 400 years of research into probability. So if you *really* want to know how people arrive at such an estimate, you should do a course in statistics. There is also a book introducing you to statistics in a hands-on way, written specially for research in the Humanities (van Peer, Hakemulder, and Zyngier 2012).

So in our experiment a statistically significant difference was found for two of these six dimensions: aesthetic structure (AS) and emotive (EM) as demonstrated in Figure 7.

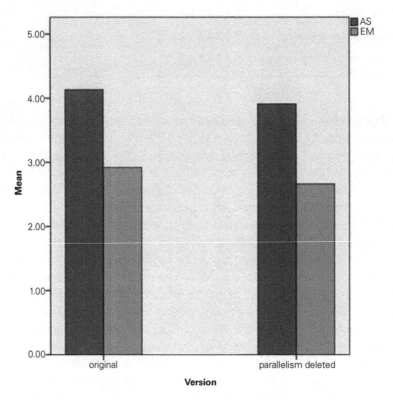

FIGURE 7 *Variables 'aesthetic structure' and 'emotive' in the two versions.*

As can be seen in Figure 7, the differences were in the predicted direction, which means that readers had a lower evaluation for the version from which parallelism was removed. Thus for aesthetic structure (p = .011), the original on average scored 4.07, and the version without parallelism, 3.92. For the emotive dimension (p = .028), the original scored 2.91, and the text form which we removed parallelism, 2.65. You may remember that these categories were composed of five adjective scales that gauged readers' subjective reactions. For the 'emotive' category, these were the scales:

- I find this line moving

- I am touched by it

- It makes me shiver

- Such wording gets under my skin

- Reading this gives me gooseflesh.

We conflated readers' reactions to these five scales into one dimension (after having applied Cronbach's alpha). Thus the *general* emotional response to the manipulated version, the one from which the parallelism had been removed, was significantly lower. For the other dimension, 'aesthetic structure' the individual scales were:

- The sentence does not have a practical application

- The line is complex

- The sentence is elaborate

- The wording is unique

- This is written in a very special style.

In other words, the poem without its original parallelism was perceived as less complex, less elaborate, less unique, less special and—somewhat more difficult to interpret perhaps—of a more practical nature. The difference between the two versions was significant in statistical terms, meaning that we may attach real value to it.

But now look at the graph again. The differences are there, but they are small, are they not? This is what is called the *effect size*. It is the size of the difference. So we must conclude that removing parallelism caused a significant, albeit small, difference. But perhaps this small difference should not surprise us. After all, we are dealing with a brief reading experience, of a rather complex poem—no doubt participants were struggling to make sense of the poem in the first place. And then there are the three other dimensions, for which we could not observe significant differences in the reactions to the two versions.

We therefore applied another statistical technique, *factor analysis*. This is the method to reduce a large amount of observations to a smaller number of underlying variables, called *factors*. Remember that each participant gave us ninety reactions: six dimensions of five adjectives at three moments in the poem. And these ninety responses were provided by a total of 141 participants, thus yielding 12,690 observations! We cannot go into the technicalities of how a factor analysis works, but suffice it to say that it leads to a reduction of the large number of observations to a small number of underlying (but invisible to our everyday eyes) factors. In our case, we found two such factors that revealed significant differences in the response to the two versions of the poem. One factor we identified as 'emotion,' the other one as 'meaning,' and Figure 8 visualizes the differences.

What transpires from the graph is that the removal of parallelism from the original version resulted in lower emotional involvement of readers (p = .047) and a lowering of a meaningful reading (p = .008). Thus it would seem that parallelism contributes both to higher emotional and meaningful readings.

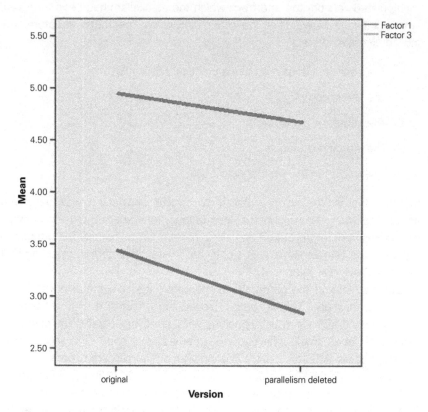

FIGURE 8 *Readers reaction to original and manipulated versions: Factor 1 ('emotion') and Factor 3 ('meaning').*

We are now in a position to answer the question in the title of this section: Is there good evidence for the effects of parallelism? The evidence is not overwhelming, we have to admit. But it is also unmistakable, as some of the differences observed are statistically (sometimes highly) significant, although the effect size is generally small. We have to put these results into perspective. The evidence is independent: it was provided by participants who were unaware of what we were testing, and the data were not influenced by us, the researchers. The relatively modest results must be put in perspective, too. We are dealing with a brief reading experiment that took only a very limited amount of time. In any case, the experiment revealed that there *are* effects of parallelism that can be observed objectively. We are only at the beginning of such evidence gathering, and will have to probe further and deeper into the nature of the workings of parallelism.

Another 'flower'

'Heidenröslein' is, as we saw in Chapter 1, a poem about the brutality a woman undergoes at the hand of a lover—if lover you may call him. The poem has a pendant in the realm of violent love, one that was written at about the same time, when Goethe and Friederike were dallying around. It is called 'The Violet.' You may familiarize yourself with its sound in an English version here, against the background of a portrait of the poet: Link 3.4 on the Companion Website. So here it is, with our English translation next to it. (Ours is slightly different from the text you will find in the video and may sound pretty stilted, but we attempted to give you a more exact translation of the German.)

1 *Ein Veilchen auf der Wiese stand,*	A violet in the meadow stood,
gebückt in sich und unbekannt;	bent over in itself, unknown;
es war ein herzigs Veilchen.	it was a whole-hearted violet.
Da kam ein' junge Schäferin	There came along a shepherdess
5 *mit leichtem Schritt und munterm Sinn*	with gentle step and lively sense,
daher, daher,	from there, from there,
die Wiese her und sang.	the meadow on and sang.
Ach! denkt das Veilchen, wär' ich nur	Ah! thinks the violet, if I was but
die schönste Blume der Natur,	the finest flower on the plain,
10 *ach, nur ein kleines Weilchen,*	oh, but just a little while,
bis mich das Liebchen abgepflückt	until my love desired me
und an dem Busen matt gedrückt,	and on her bosom squeezed me down,
ach, nur, ach nur	oh only, oh only
ein Viertelstündchen lang!	a quarter of an hour long!
15 *Ach, aber ach! Das Mädchen kam*	Ah, but ah! The maiden came,
und nicht in acht das Veilchen nahm,	without a glance or care for it,
ertrat das arme Veilchen.	she trampled down the violet.
Es sank und starb, und freut' sich noch:	It sank and died, but rejoices still:
und sterb' ich denn, so sterb' ich doch	and if I die, then I die
20 *durch sie, durch sie,*	for her, for her,
zu ihren Füßen doch!	beneath her darling feet!

Again, as with 'Heidenröslein,' you may take it for a children's song, pleasant to listen to, but nothing more. It has an appealing character, until you fathom the grim nature of the story: the poor and helpless but dedicated and faithful little flower, the cheap and useless cruelty against its unconditional love, and the lover's indifference to its suffering. Even in its own annihilation the violet still declares its love.

By now you may have left behind the view of a children's song. Again the violet here is not simply a flower, but a metaphor, standing for a person. Presumably for a woman. After all, several first names given to girls are just that, names of flowers: Daisy, Erica, Iris, Jasmine, Lily, Petunia, and, indeed, Violet. Thus flowers tend to be associated with girls. So who is the 'violet' in love with? Clearly with the shepherdess, who came leaping along merrily in lines 4–7. That means that the violet is male, then? That sounds strange, running against all cultural expectations. But poetry is a strange country. (Remember the country of *fado* Mariza lives in?) In it, things tend to be different. Here we have such a strange violation: against all cultural conventions, the violet is to be seen as male—in flagrant contradiction to everyday use.

Or could it be that the violet *is* female, after all, and that it is in love with the shepherdess, so that the poem is about lesbian love? Yes, theoretically that is possible, and nothing forbids such an interpretation of the poem. It would not take away the central idea of the poem at all. But for historical reasons this interpretation must seem unlikely. It was written in 1773 or 1774, the year in which George Washington was elected as the delegate to the then Congress. Is it likely, you think, that people at the time of Washington would be writing poems about lesbian love? Highly unlikely—even with such a libertine like Goethe, who is—again—the author of the poem. He certainly meant the violet to be male, and in this sense this poem is a mirror image of 'Heidenröslein.' In anthologies, the two poems are often printed side by side, or one after the other (another—quite unexpected—kind of parallelism). Before going into this matter, let us first look at the parallelism in the poem. What about meter and rhyme? For that we have to turn to the original, of course.

The meter is easy to recognize: it is the same as in the Scottish ballad we saw before:

x / x / x / x /
x / x / x / x / etc.

So it is an *iambic tetrameter*, with some rhythmic variations, for instance, with the first word of the second stanza: according to the metrical pattern, it should be unstressed, but has quite a strong stress here, emphasizing the deep longing that the violet has for beauty. The same deviation from the pattern (and for the same reason) occurs at the beginning of the third stanza. But apart from these instances, there is little tension between meter and rhythm in this poem.

At the same time the rhyme scheme is quite complicated here. You may check for yourself:

- *A A B C D E F*

- *G G B H H I F*

- *J J B K K L K.*

What is most obvious in the scheme is that the first two verses of each stanza always rhyme and that the third verse always has *Veilchen* or a (somewhat funny) rhyme with it: *ein Weilchen* (a little while). Then there are the rhymes in lines 11–12 in the second stanza (*abgepflückt /gedrückt*) and a similar pattern, but now three times, in the final stanza, lines 18, 19, and 21 (*noch, doch, doch*).

As to figurative language, it has already dawned on us that the violet here, too, as with 'Heidenröslein,' is a metaphor for a human being. But, against the grain of associating flowers with females, here the violet stands for a male person. (One may recognize the genius of a poet like Goethe here, in that he dares to go against such powerful social conventions and turn things upside down.) Just like in 'Heidenröslein,' the loving flower is also destroyed, but now literally, in the final stanza, not by any intention on the part of the shepherdess, but thoughtlessly. She could not care less about the little flower beneath her feet and just tramples on it. The violet dies, but even in the act of dying it still professes its love for the girl, and is happy to have died under her feet. In fact, it says *durch sie* (by her), so that the shepherdess is, in fact, its murderess. So while the rose (the young *woman*) is *socially* killed by the man, the violet (the young *man*) is *literally* killed by the woman. Another difference: the young woman in 'Heidenröslein' defends herself, while the young man in 'Das Veilchen' even rejoices in his own death at his lover's feet.

As with 'Heidenröslein,' also here we notice the alternation between *narration* and *direct speech*. What we have in the first stanza is that someone is describing the violet in the field. We do not know who the person doing this is. It is, again, an *invisible narrator*. But then in the second stanza, all of a sudden we are in the violet's head, witnessing what *it* is thinking, wishing, hoping for. In stanza 3, without warning, we are in the storytelling mode again: the shepherdess comes along and steps on the flower, which then dies. In line 5 of this stanza we are back in the violet's head: its elation at dying under the feet of its beloved shepherdess.

'The Violet' in music

As with 'Heidenröslein,' the text emanates such energy that it attracted the attention of composers. Mozart, for one, gave the poem (in 1785) an eternal appeal. So listen to it (do have the text at hand, so you can follow), sung here by the British tenor Mark Padmore:[4] Link 3.5 on the Companion Website.

There is a brief introduction on the piano, and then the singing starts off blithely until 0:29 when in line 4 the pace is speeded up, reflecting the skipping movements of the shepherdess. Here we have a parallelism between the content of the text, on the one hand, and musical rhythm and melody, on the other. At 0:42 a brief piano intermezzo, repeating the theme of the song, leads to the dramatic change of the second stanza at 0:49. We now shift to a minor key, indicating the ruminations of the violet over its own appearance, while the singing also slows down markedly. But then at 1:06 its melancholy changes to its projecting itself into a happy dream, and the tempo accelerates again, echoing the pace of lines 4–7 before, an internal musical parallelism. But notice the slowing down at 1:15: the violet is dreaming away of being held by the shepherdess, if only for a quarter of an hour. Again we see textual/musical parallelism: the singing 'echoes' the shortness of the event by stalling the rhythm. At 1:26 we enter the dramatic denouement (from line 15): the shepherdess has not the slightest interest in the violet (the male lover) and tramples it in 1:37—the singer underlines the catastrophic event by raising his voice dramatically. When you would expect this to be the end of the story, you are mistaken. There is a brief pause of almost two seconds, and then the singing continues in an almost elegiac soft tone describing the death of the flower. But then, at 1:49 we hear the violet's imagination at its death, and then (at 1:56) are again thrown into yet another acceleration (the third one) that it died for its beloved. The song ends at 2:06. Or—so we expect, but there is something unexpected following, very slowly pronounced and then a verbatim repetition of line 3 of the poem.

You will have noticed: 'Das Veilchen' is not, like 'Heidenröslein,' a strophic *Lied*: there is no refrain. The music of the song follows a trajectory that mirrors the story. It starts in G major, as 'Heidenröslein,' in the same uncomplicated and carefree mood. With the sudden appearance of the shepherdess, the key changes briefly to D major, here clearly merry and euphoric, making one expect some jubilant events to follow. But then with the second stanza we are abruptly thrown into a meditative (and melancholic) reflection by the violet—on what it sees as itself lacking physical beauty. This is reflected in the music: we are now in G minor, a musical key usually associated with worry, discontent, uncertainty, and fretfulness—as indeed the violet is ruminating here on its state of imperfection (or how it perceives itself). The initial joyous melody is now echoed in this minor key, while the little flower is hopeful of becoming beautiful, if only for an instant. And this hope is projected in lines 11–14, where it dreams of being culled and hugged against the girl's bosom, now in B flat major, a key said to be cheerful, joyful, and—indeed—hopeful. But these dreams are shattered in the third stanza, when the violet is being trampled upon by the beloved shepherdess, briefly throwing us back into the G minor key. Finally, however, even while dying (from verse 19 onward), the violet is thrilled and grateful, and we are back in the initial key of G major. When the little violet dies, the music stalls, but then exhilarates into a heart-rending but victorious cry *durch sie, durch sie* (by her, by her): it warms itself in the realization that it has died under the foot of the creature it so longingly loved.

If you followed the singing with the poem's text in hand, you were in for a surprise at the very end. Goethe's poem ends (in line 21) with the violet's joyous cry while it dies. But that is not how the *song* ends, going on, as it does, for another two sentences:

22 *Das arme Veilchen!*   The poor violet!

    Es war ein herzigs Veilchen.   It was a whole-hearted violet.

First of all, there is a complaint about 'the poor violet' (*das arme Veilchen*), and then the third verse of the poem is repeated: *Es war ein herzigs Veilchen* (it was a wholehearted violet). These words are not in the poem by Goethe. It is Mozart who added them. So here one genius is complementing the work of another! Notice the contrastive parallelism here: although the violet is said to be poor (*arme*), we are at the same time reminded that it was sweet (*herzigs*).

This afterpiece shows the same ingredient as we have seen at the end of 'Heidenröslein.' We then said that the final part of classical songs often functions as some sort of solace—that after the horror we witnessed it brings us some peacefulness of mind, some peace with the brutal world. This is even more obvious in the end of 'Das Veilchen,' in the two lines that Mozart added: it was, after all, a lovely violet—and we should remember it. This kind of solace is something of considerable importance, when we will deal with poetry as a source of consolation (in Chapter 6).

This is also some kind of parallelism between most songs in the *Lied* tradition. But important here is yet another form of parallelism: between the two poems by Goethe, as they are each other's mirror image. We said before that they often occur side by side in anthologies, and that is no accident. Both texts deal with the destruction of a lover, female in 'Heidenröslein,' and male in 'Das Veilchen.' The textual treatment of the theme is remarkably different, but we can see the contrastive parallelism in the two poems at an abstract level. Although this is not the usual way in which parallelism is defined in stylistics, it is clear that such forms of parallelism play a role in psychopoetics: reading one poem brings to mind the other one, and their respective interpretations influence each other.

Core issues

- Repetition lies at the heart of most poetry, effecting literariness, the ultimate quality by which literature distinguishes itself prototypically from other uses of language.

- Repetition in poetry is meaningful and gives pleasure. The 'pleasure principle' lies at the heart of poetic experience.

- Foregrounding is a device or a strategy by which authors make some part of their texts stand out from their surroundings. This can be done either by deviation or by parallelism.

- The concept of parallelism is associated with the name of Roman Jakobson. His 'poetic function' shows how poets make the same selection of linguistic elements repeatedly where they have the freedom to vary.

- Parallelism as a form of musicality is both a universal and a defining characteristic of poetry. It is found already in the 'talk' of very young babies.

- Parallelism, or hyper-regularity, implies that some component of the form or meaning of a text is similar to some other component at some abstract level of description: lexical, syntactic, phonological, etc.

- Patterns are powerful on their own, so parallelism is highly effective in shaping the reader's expectation and thus enhancing the emotional effect of poetry.

- A falsification procedure in evidence-based research (after the philosopher of science Karl Popper) is an attempt to prove not that a theory is right, but that it is wrong. If the theory is *not* falsified, it is accepted as, for the time being, true.

Further reading

Fox, J. (2014), *Explorations in Semantic Parallelism*, Canberra: ANU Press.

Frog, E. (ed) (2014), *Parallelism in Verbal Art and Performance. Pre-Print Papers of the Seminar-Workshop, 26th–27th May 2014*. Helsinki: University of Helsinki.

Pinsky, R. (1998), *The Sounds of Poetry. A Brief Guide*. New York: Farrar, Straus and Giroux.

Shklovsky, V. ([1917] 1965), 'Art as Technique,' in L. T. Lemon and M. J. Reis (eds), *Russian Formalist Criticism: Four Essays*, 3–24, Lincoln: University of Nebraska Press.

Tartakovsky, R. (2009), 'E. E. Cummings's Parentheses: Punctuation as poetic device,' *Style*, 43(2): 215–47.

van Peer, W. (1990), 'The Measurement of Metre: Its Cognitive and Affective Functions,' *Poetics*, 19: 259–75.

van Peer, W. and F. Hakemulder (2006), 'Foregrounding,' in K. Brown (ed), *The Pergamon Encyclopaedia of Language and Linguistics*, vol. 4, 546–51, Oxford: Elsevier, 2006.

van Peer, W., S. Zyngier and F. Hakemulder (2007), 'Foregrounding: Past, Present, Future,' in D. Hoover and S. Lattig (eds), *Stylistics: Prospect and Retrospect*, 1–21, Amsterdam, Atlanta: RODOPI.

4

Poetry Is Surprise

Keywords

foregrounding

deviation

poetic licence

hypothesis

alternative hypothesis

null hypothesis

error probability

The world upside down

All texts surely have their producers, so when reading this book, you have probably had some idea about its authors. So this is us in Figure 9 on the next page.

'What?' you might have said. But something is wrong with this picture. It is upside down, and, to make sense of it, I should stop and think about how to make head or tails of it. And you probably did. But did it make you feel good? Or just different? Or maybe strange at first sight, but after some time funny and thus nice?

Have you ever had the feeling of attraction to things that look overtly strange at first sight—even insane? This is a trick sometimes applied in various kinds of art—for instance, in architecture when they build upside-down buildings, like the one in Figure 10 on the next page, to attract people—tourists in this case.

There is even a painter, Georg Baselitz (born 1938), who made it his trademark to hang up his pictures upside down. If you check him out on the internet, you may be surprised that even his portraits are meant to be looked at like that.

In Chapter 2 of this book, we have already talked about poetry as some kind of 'upside down,' of explicit strangeness, of madness. Indeed, poets are sometimes looked upon as fools, and their views could be even mocked and laughed at. Or even worse—they could be threatened or ostracized to the

FIGURE 9 *The authors of this book upside down.*

FIGURE 10 *Upside-down building by Polish artist Daniel Czapiewski.*

point of becoming outcasts. And only later will ridicule be replaced by praise or admiration.

Now let us look at a particular kind of 'madness' that is cultivated in poetry. The rest of this chapter will bring together the different threads we have been weaving so far: the typical structures of poetry and the madness that poetry often involves. They all come together in one great theory, which we will first elucidate. But then we will have to ask ourselves one crucial question: is there any good evidence in favor of this theory—in other words, is it true?

But let us continue for a while with the madness of things turned upside down.

Confused by confusion

In 1886, the famous Russian author Leo Tolstoy published a story *Kholstomer* usually translated as *Strider*. It is a story in which the narrator is a horse, in fact, a gelding, but not like in fairy tales: besides the fact that he can think and talk, he is involved in profound reflections on his own world, contrasting it with the world of humans. To get a taste of it, we request you to look at the following link: Link 4.1 on the Companion Website. In it, the horse is played by an actor; he is in the middle of this reflection. The performance is in Russian, but if you do not speak the language and do not understand what the actor is saying, that is only an advantage for our purposes. We ask you to observe the actor and think of the emotion he is showing right from the first minutes of the video. What the horse is saying is the following (now in translation into English):

> 'Mine, mine, mine … '. Those words had an enormous effect on me. They indicate that men are guided in life not by deeds, but by words. They like not so much to do or abstain from doing anything, as to be able to apply conventional words to different objects. They have agreed that only one person may use the word 'mine', and he who in this game of theirs may use that conventional word about the greatest number of things is considered the happiest. Why this is so I do not know, but it is so.

The horse is totally confused: he cannot understand what humans mean by possession—an idea totally alien to him. So he wonders what on earth the meaning could be of everyday words like 'my' or 'mine'. As readers/listeners we are confused no less, initially at least. How could anyone *not* understand such simple words, that even small children are acquainted with from an early age onwards? Here we confront something many people find puzzling in literature, and especially in poetry. One could even say that this kind of initial confusion often puts people off poetry: it is confusing to many readers. You may have experienced this yourself. Maybe initially you found the poems by Goethe or E. E. Cummings confusing, too—or the songs by Mariza or Dick Gaughan. But now we are confused by confusion. Tolstoy is not a little bit of a genius. He turns the evident upside down, words that we never thought would be complicated, like 'my' or 'mine.'

About fifty years later, another genius recognized the root of the problem by pointing to the limits of our knowledge, as delineated—and thus constrained—by the language we speak. It was the philosopher Ludwig Wittgenstein who, in his *Tractatus Logico-Philosophicus* (1922), wrote that '[t]he limits of my language mean the limits of my world' (no. 5.6). If we do not have words for a thing, then we cannot know it. As the story by Tolstoy vividly illustrates, to the horse there are no words like 'my' or 'mine,' so he cannot understand human concepts of ownership. One encounters such limits of knowledge also when confronted with words, especially emotional words, in other languages. Thus the song 'Loucura' by Mariza can be said to express the feeling of *saudade*, an untranslatable word in Portuguese, referring to a mixture of sadness, loss, distance, nostalgia, and love. Japanese emotion *arugama*, or Finnish *sisu*, are other examples of emotions that are typical within a culture, and difficult to explain to outsiders. Some languages are rich in such 'untranslatables': German especially shows such richness in that its 'unique' words have been imported in other languages, like English. We already are acquainted with *Lied*, but think also of: *Angst, Bildung(sroman), Dasein, Dichtung, Einstellung, Empfindung, Erlebnis, Geisteswissenschaften, Gestalt, Heimat, Schwärmerei, Sehnsucht, unheimlich, Verfremdung,* or *Zeitgeist*.

It is poets, of all people, who try to break through the limits of language, by creating wholly new perspectives on the world, like Tolstoy's story. But precisely because they overstep the boundaries of daily language practice, their poems may create confusion—the consequence of which is that many people find poetry 'difficult.'

On the other hand, this sort of confusion may offer a chance to reflect. Some would even say that it is an indispensable feature of good literature: you get puzzled to later enjoy what made you baffled initially. This is what Silvia (2009), has to say about it:

> Confusion is a metacognitive signal: it informs people that they do not comprehend what is happening and that some shift in action is thus needed, such as a new learning strategy, more effort, or withdrawal and

avoidance. For people in art education, confusion is a major emotion: it is the typical emotion of novices who are faced with works that they cannot understand. Fostering expertise in the arts probably involves both reducing and harnessing the experience of confusion.

(49)

And 'enhancing people's ability to understand something makes it less confusing and more interesting' (ibid.). So as you go through the monologue of the horse (either in its textual form or in the performance), you are struggling—even if you do not realize it—with this 'upside down' feeling, trying to embed it into normality. And this subconscious effort leads to a deeper insight into reality (which may also give aesthetic pleasure). We are confused that the Kholstomer, the horse, is confused. But it makes us reflect on the very issue of ownership: how can one 'own' something?

The idea that poetry throws you back on some basic ideas is not new, and already the Greek/Roman writer Plutarch (46–120 CE) in the chapter 'How the Young Man Should Study Poetry' of his *Moralia* holds that:

> when poetic art is divorced from the truth, then chiefly it employs variety and diversity. For it is the sudden changes that give to its stories the elements of the emotional, the surprising, and the unexpected, and these are attended by very great astonishment and enjoyment; but sameness is unemotional and prosaic.

(1927: 135)

'So in the reading of poetry,' he continues, 'one person culls the flowers of the story, another rivets his attention upon the beauty of the diction and the arrangement of the words' (ibid.: 159).

Foregrounding

At this point you could object that the story of Kholstomer the horse is not poetry. So why did we bother you with it? There is a deeper reason behind our choice: the story by Tolstoy is used in one of the most famous essays written about art in the previous century. We are referring to 'Art as Technique' by Viktor Shklovsky. The original Russian title is 'Iskusstvo kak priyom,' where the latter term is sometimes used in Western literary studies to denote techniques or devices related to foregrounding. Just like Roman Jakobson, whom we have mentioned in the previous chapter, Shklovsky was one of the Russian Formalists, active at the dawn of the 1917 Revolution. In this essay, he confronts the fundamental question why there is such a thing like art (including literature and music). Indeed, as far as we know, there are no—absolutely no—human societies that do not possess forms of art, including (some kind of) poetry. At first sight, art would seem to be superfluous, something we can dispense with. Apparently not—otherwise some groups would have abolished it. Shklovsky challenges the question head-on, in as bold a way as hardly anyone else has.

His starting point is the daily habits by which we live, habits which we need to survive. Trivial this may be, but you do not have to reinvent how to lace your shoes every day, nor how to take a shower or where to find food if there is none in the fridge. These daily routines save an enormous amount of time and energy, so they are conducive to survival. But they have a downside: they make us forget about their value. That is precisely the nature of a habit: you carry it out without thinking—or feeling. This is OK as long as we are dealing with shoe laces or an empty fridge. But what about love? What if love becomes routine-like? Then feelings slip away. Our habits make us forget about our experiences; they make us into some kind of human robots, who no longer recognize their surroundings. Our actions become unconscious, without emotional involvement. Shklovsky has a penetrating image for this: this 'automatization' of our personal lives 'eats away at things, at clothes, at furniture, at our wives, and at our fear of war' ([1929] 1990: 5). No, this is not a poetic exaggeration: even the most gruesome thing on earth, war, will not inspire fear in us once it becomes ingrained in our daily habits. So our need for survival, which happily makes use of necessary routine, kills our emotions.

It is at this point that Shklovsky's argument bites: this is precisely the function of art, he argues: to reinstall our emotional awareness of things around us, stripped of their habitual track. And the way by which art accomplishes this renewal of sensibility is by making us see things in an unusual way. Daily life never demands us to think about the meaning of words like 'my' or 'mine.' In doing so, Tolstoy draws our attention to language that we routinely use without realizing its implication, namely that it is *someone* who owns, in the case of Kholstomer, who even owns other living beings, like the horse himself.

Shklovsky invents a new word for this trick that artists employ: *ostranenie*, which is not a usual Russian word and can be translated as 'making strange'—*strannyi* means 'strange' in Russian. Other words that are used in English as translations are: 'defamiliarization,' 'de-automatization,' but especially '*foregrounding*,' a spatial metaphor—implying that the author puts something in the foreground of perception, against a less important background. This term is, in fact, a translation not of Shklovsky's *ostranenie*, but of *aktualisace* we mentioned in Chapter 3, and it is *foregrounding* that we will use in the rest of this book as a synonym for *ostranenie* (and *aktualisace*), as most psychopoetic studies use this term.

You may now say that 'making strange' is a strange thing in itself. You are right—when a horse is engaged in language philosophy, it is indeed strange. Why would you want something to be strange? To be different? To be mad (as in Chapter 2)? In the history of mankind, what is 'strange' is perceived by people as outlandish, even 'dangerous'—as something to be avoided. So why would anyone actively seek it—as artists and poets apparently do? Shklovsky's article provides an illuminating clarification.

In doing so, art, poetry in particular, supersedes the boundaries of expected normality and thus requires a repositioning on the part of readers. Readers therefore have to leave entrenched categories behind and engage in a form of disencapsulation. This is a difficult task, especially for the inexperienced—in fact, for most people, having grown up and living in a highly controlled environment, without much challenge to a large number of entrenched ideas, categories and arrangements. Dealing with poetry, you have to learn to build a personal involvement with the exceptional, with the unusual, with digressions from the habitual.

As you already know, foregrounding may take two forms: *deviation* and *parallelism*. The previous chapter dealt with the latter, and the present one will explore the other form, i.e., deviation, also traditionally referred to as a '*poetic licence*,' the idea that authors are *allowed* to depart from established norms and conventions. This is how Shklovsky himself saw it:

> a general rule: a work of art is perceived against a background. (...) Whenever we experience anything as a *deviation* from the ordinary, from the normal, (...) we feel within us an emotion of a special nature, which is not distinguished in its kind from the emotions aroused in us by sensuous forms, with the single difference being that its 'referent' may be said to be a perception of a discrepancy. (...) This is a field of inexhaustible richness because these differential perceptions are qualitatively distinguished from each other by their point of departure, by their forcefulness and by their line of divergence.
>
> ([1929] 1990: 20–1)

Shklovsky wrote his seminal essay in the turbulent times at the eve of Russian Revolution of 1917, which brought a lot of social, political and economic confusion—and violence—to the lives of people, even to whole nations. Right after the revolution, this confusion found its vent in literature. This was a period when the *avant-garde* art, which even nowadays can be puzzling, flourished—in painting, in music, in ballet, and certainly in poetry. One such author is a representative of *Futurism*, Vladimir Mayakovsky.

Turbulence enhanced:
Avant-garde and Mayakovsky

A young tall bold contemporary of Shklovsky, bearing a reputation of creating scandals both in his poetry and in private life (the story of his *l'amour à trois* with Osip and Lily Brik is just one example of it), he nevertheless could be deeply lyrical, even sentimental. A *poète maudit* as he was, looking for a way to add extra power to his texts, to make the words alive, in his 'War and Language' essay, Mayakovsky ([1914] 1955: 325) insists that

> [w]e have to sharpen our words. We have to ask for language that would, frugally and accurately, represent every movement. We want words to explode like a bomb, or ache as a wound, or rattle happily as a victorious hurray.

So let us look at the opening of his poem 'Listen' (1914) in Russian with the English translation by its side. To get a taste of Mayakovsky's own form of recitation, you may wish to compare your own reading to how the poet himself recites it at: Link 4.2 on the Companion Website.

Послушайте!	Listen!
Ведь, если звезды зажигают –	But if stars are lit –
значит—это кому-нибудь нужно?	[it] means—someone needs it?
Значит—кто-то хочет, чтобы они были?	[It] means—someone wants them to be?
Значит—кто-то называет эти плевочки жемчужиной?	[It] means—someone calls these spits a pearl?

The poem starts with sharp and direct 'Listen!'—a resolute address to the reader, the one that immediately shortens the distance between the poet and audience. But right away, starting with line 2, the tone abruptly changes to almost narrative. In the previous chapter we discussed how parallelism is at play in poetry, and you have definitely noticed that lines 3, 4, and 5 open with the same short disyllabic verb *znachit* ([it] means). Such deliberate anaphoric repetition of an initial component enhances the rhythm of the poem. Line 6 explicitly breaks the pattern you have probably got used to and, by way of *enjambment* you have already met in Chapter 1, continues line 5 into just one word: 'a pearl.' More than that—a negatively colored metaphor STARS ARE SPITS, in just a glimpse, switches to a romantic one STARS ARE PEARLS.

The case may be described in terms of *internal deviation*: the text sets up a regular structure, a pattern (in this case of a repeated identical phrase in an initial position), and then unexpectedly deviates from the pattern established before. Internal deviations are rather common in poetry, and they have been studied, both in the stylistic analyses of individual poems and from a theoretical point of view (see, for example, Levin 1965; Leech 1985: 39–57; van Peer 2020; Short 1996: 59–61). Thus we are dealing with some well-known device that poets regularly employ to convey a specific idea, message or impression. From the study of such internal deviations it is known that they generally carry extra interpretative weight: if an author first sets up a pattern and then deviates from it, this usually carries a special meaning: the poet wants to alert the reader to something in the pattern that is significant yet overlooked or unexpected. As Leech observes, '[p]articularly through the concept of tertiary or internal deviation, the method [of stylistic analysis] enables us to see a linguistic basis for such critical concepts as "climax", "suspense", "unity"' (ibid.: 56).

Now let us see how the poem ends:

Послушайте!	Listen!
Ведь, если звезды зажигают –	But if stars are lit –
значит—это кому-нибудь нужно?	[it] means—someone needs it?
Значит—это необходимо,	[It] means—it is necessary,
чтобы каждый вечер	so that every night
над крышами	above the roofs
загоралась хоть одна звезда?!	lights up at least one star?!

You have certainly noticed that this is almost the same stanza you have read at the beginning. The reader is returned to the initial pattern in a *frame*-like structure, another clear instance of parallelism, but the closing lines are emphatically different: the poet seems to seek the reader's approval of his words and, by way of an interrogative, but at the same time exclamatory sentence, pleads for agreement. Violent and romantic at the same time.

Pushkin's Mistake with the Spanish ambassador. Formalism is functionalism

So far we have acted as if poetry as a kind of text was unproblematic, but there are complicated cases, because it is in the nature of literature that authors try out the boundaries of readers' expectations. An interesting case in this respect is Alexander Pushkin's *Eugene Onegin*. It is, in actual fact, a novel, but a novel written in verse. It is the love story of Tatiana and Yevgeny,[1] but written in such lighthearted poetic lines that most readers fall in love with the poet's purity and prettiness of diction, together with his simple, but at the same time exquisite style of writing. No wonder, *Eugene Onegin* has attracted much attention of literary critics, and Vladimir Nabokov was one of them.

Let us have a look at an entertaining piece of academia that was exploited in the May 25, 2017, issue of *The New York Review of Books* (Morson 2017). In it, Gary Saul Morson, a Slavist and literary critic, refers to the Russian economist and Harvard professor Alexander Gerschenkron, who pointed out Nabokov's exhibitionist 'pedantry'—which actually criticizes Pushkin for poor scholarship. Gerschenkron observes:

> He [Nabokov] describes the calendar of the novel year by year, month by month, and day by day, accusing Pushkin (…) of having committed mistakes. Tatiana's Saint's Day occurred on January 12, 1821, which in that year fell on a Wednesday, but the careless Pushkin unaccountably made it a Saturday (II, 477). Again, Pushkin causes Tatiana, in 1824, to converse with the Spanish ambassador, but Nabokov (with the help of a Russian scholar) found out that in 1824 Spain had no ambassador at the Court of St. Petersburg.

(III, 183)

What do you make of this? Interesting? The case illustrates that even highly creative people (like Nabokov doubtlessly was) can be mightily mistaken. Obviously Nabokov's remarks are completely off the mark. We can clearly see this when we ask ourselves: would Pushkin's poems have been more moving if the calendar and the other details would have been correct? Is it less moving because of the inaccuracies? Poetry is not history, as Aristotle already argued in the fourth century BCE.

The comments by Nabokov are just the sort of pointless erudition, pedantry indeed, that the Russian Formalists took as representative of all scholarship that misses the very nature of literature. It focuses on irrelevant biographical or social trivia, of which they made fun in an ironic article 'Did Pushkin smoke?' Instead they proposed to unravel the mysteries of poetry through systematic research. In their spirit, we will now turn to the question whether this approach is compatible with the aim we set ourselves, namely, to develop an evidence-based psychopoetics.

Truth? A sample of experimental design

It is now some hundred years ago that Shklovsky formulated his theory. Since then numerous articles have been devoted to his work, and Berlina (2016) provides an excellent overview. A central question for psychopoetics is, however, whether the theory is a *valid* one, whether its assertions are upheld by reality. Such knowledge requires an *empirical* perspective, one based on independent data, controllable observations and evidence. You already had a look at how *empirical research methods* work in Chapters 2 and 3. So if we want to gain insight into what *real* readers *really* experience in poetry, we have to observe—in our case to observe real readers by way of a carefully organized experiment. Not just one or two, but several. And these observations should not be biased in the sense that the concomitant data should be analyzed in some *objective* way. 'Objective' here means open to control by other researchers. Not studying real experiences of poetry is like medicine involving mere opinions about diseases, without looking at real patients, going into the causes and consequences of an illness. And what experiences one has in poetry is what psychopoetics tries to lay bare. Or do we want to find out whether Pushkin smoked?

So can we say that the views proposed in the previous section make valid assertions? This presents us with a methodological question: HOW does one find out? How can we somehow 'prove' that this is really how literature functions? This is the question that will occupy us in the rest of this chapter.

In order to investigate the correctness of the claims in question, we will have to marry two fields that have hitherto remained largely separate: on the one hand, age-old *poetics* (since the Greeks, in fact), and, on the other, more recent methods of inquiry developed mostly in the *social sciences*. How does that go?

The whole idea is to *test* the theory, of course. But theories are often rather abstract, so an essential step in this process is to reformulate this abstract nature into something concrete. We basically use our imagination: if we accept that the theory is correct, what, then, could we expect? Compare this to astronomy where, if the theories are correct, we should be able to accurately say when a solar or lunar eclipse will occur. Needless to say, astronomers are exceedingly successful in doing so. If psychopoetics aspires to a likewise status, it has to convert theoretical statements (like the ones by Shklovsky) into concrete assertions. These will then be held against independently collected data bearing on the assertions made. For instance, a claim will be that—given the nature of art as described by the *ostranenie* concept—spectators (of art works, movies, opera, theatre plays, or literature) will be surprised. *Ostranenie* is making our everyday perceptions strange, and strangeness will (initially, at least) surprise us. So here we have a starting point: we may expect that readers of *ostranenie* passages will be surprised. Maybe our observations may not be very accurate when compared with the astronomers' precision, but one has to start somewhere, preferably in a clear and simple situation.

So far for making the theory concrete, but what about *data*? Surprise is a momentary emotion, caused by an unexpected event. How to collect independent data on people's surprise emotions? It is difficult to 'measure' such an emotion. So we have to find a roundabout way to gain access to it. An easy way is, of course, to simply ask people. Turning to literature as a form of art, the theory of foregrounding may now be reformulated as follows:

If you request readers to indicate their surprise emotion while reading, they will preferably indicate passages that are characterized by *ostranenie*.

We could do this by asking readers to underline such passages. So far, so good. But how do we determine which passages we should count as foregrounded? Shklovsky gives several examples of foregrounding in his writings, but how to generalize from these? The method developed in this respect starts from the fundamental distinction made in linguistics between (at least) three levels or organization: phonology, grammar, and semantics. Human languages operate simultaneously on these three levels. They are *sounds*, produced by our vocal system. The study of these sounds is phonology (and phonetics). Sounds are essential for language. But not just any sounds. Each individual language requires the sounds to be grouped and arranged in a highly specific way. This *order* is what we call 'grammar.' If this condition (of ordering the sounds correctly) is met, the sounds acquire *meaning*, studied in the area of linguistics called semantics. Each of these sub-areas (phonology, grammar and semantics) has produced a relatively rich body of insights. We can use these to descriptively take stock of the various cases of foregrounding in the text.

Which text? It would be best not to execute the test with just one particular fragment, so as to avoid that observations are limited to it, which may have unique characteristics. So more texts are needed. How many? That is difficult to say, but more important is the difference between texts, so they should not be from the same kind of authors. For instance, one could imagine that gender may play a role, so that it is important to include both male and female poets in the *corpus* used.

In the research I conducted (van Peer 2020), six poems were selected, rather intuitively. They were by such different writers as E. E. Cummings, Emily Dickinson, Christina Rossetti, Theodore Roethke, Dylan Thomas, and William Wordsworth. For each of these six poems a highly detailed analysis of all foregrounding devices was undertaken, separately for each of the three levels just indicated: phonology, grammar, and semantics. Let us look in somewhat detail, by way of an example, at the most unusual poem of the six, the one by E. E. Cummings, whom we have already met in the previous chapter. Here is the first stanza:

yes is a pleasant country:
if's wintry
(my lovely)
let's open the year.

We will not go into a detailed analysis here (you can find it in ibid.: 70–2), but it is immediately clear that line 3 hardly contains any *ostranenie*, while lines 1 and 2 are more foregrounded. This plays at the phonological level: the *assonance* of the /e/ vowel in 'y**e**s'/'pl**ea**sant' and the /i/ vowel in '**if**'s'/ 'w**i**ntry', but also on the grammatical level: both lines are a-grammatical in English: 'yes' is not a place name (e.g., the name of a country), as grammar requires, and 'if' is not a time indication, as in 'today's wintry' or 'January's wintry.' The strong grammatical deviations therefore have substantial consequences for the semantic level. Since the grammatical construction makes no sense, readers have to construct a meaning themselves. The road by which they can arrive at some kind of interpretation goes more or less like this: there is some invisible speaker addressing a loved one ('my lovely' in line 3). In the first two lines the speaker is basically inviting the beloved to say 'yes' to him/her, not 'if.' The grammatical parallelism between the two initial verses helps to underscore an interpretation along those lines. In other words, the first stanza is a *modernist* variation on a love poem. This leads to line 4, which also contains a deviation, but now a very mild one: the formulation 'let's open' is a bit unusual, but it is not at all unusual to speak about the 'opening of the year.'

These are merely a few of the many instances of foregrounding found in this stanza. Their extensive analysis was then turned into some visualization, in which all instances from this inventory were indicated in the text of the poem itself. The result of this can be seen in Figure 11 on the next page.

Dotted lines represent foregrounding on the phonological level, straight underlining denotes grammatical forms, and frames are used to indicate semantic foregrounding. The visualization allows one to distinguish between locations where one sees a *nexus* of heavy foregrounding devices, as in lines 1, 2, and 9—contrasted with other regions in the text where little or no foregrounding can be detected, as, for instance in lines 3, 7, and 11. On the basis of these differences, rank order numbers were allocated to verse lines, leading to what we are aiming at, namely, concrete expectations. *If* Shklovksy's theory is correct, then readers should be most surprised by the verse lines where we observed an accumulation of foregrounding instances. And we can even rank them in descending order, for instance, like this:

Line number	Foregrounding rank order
1	2
2	3
3	11
4	8
5	5
6	6
7	12
8	7
9	1
10	9
11	10
12	4

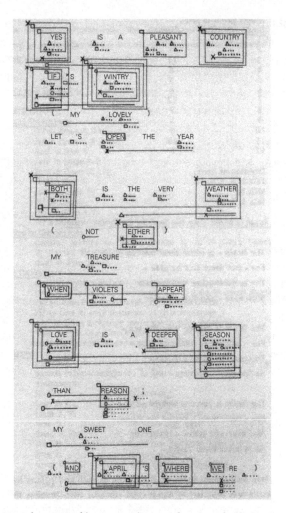

FIGURE 11 *Visualization of* foregrounding *in the poem by E. E. Cummings (van Peer 2020: 73), reproduced with permission.*

We now have a concrete instrument anticipating an outcome if we would try to detect readers' surprise reaction. That, however, is an internal mental event, not open to direct observation. So we will have to have recourse to another method: we simply ask readers to indicate where in the text they were surprised, by underlining (parts of) words where that was the case.

We have come a long way from Shklovsky's formulations, and our theoretical speculation has now become much more concrete. But it is still not concrete enough. That is why in actual research we use a reformulation of theories that is more down to earth still. We will devote the next paragraphs to it: to *hypotheses.*

We now turn the prediction into a 'yes/no' question: is the prediction borne out by the facts? The 'facts' in this case are the passages underlined by readers. That could be individual letters, syllables, words, phrases, clauses, or whole (groups of) sentences. But how to deal with these 'facts'? In order to allow us to practically handle them, we now reformulate the prediction in the form of the following hypothesis (traditionally marked as 'H'):

H: Text passages that had been identified as containing a high degree of foregrounding will be underlined more frequently.

If we submit a hypothesis *that* concrete, one will notice immediately that it is a risky statement. Could we really expect readers to behave in such a 'predictable' way? Reading poetry being a highly subjective kind of reading, in which individual emotional reactions play a major role, should one not rather expect readers to react in an idiosyncratic way? If so, then the distribution of underlinings would be more or less random—depending on each reader's individual reaction, and no obvious pattern would emerge. One can conceive of this view as another hypothesis, one that is contrary to the one we have derived from Shklovsky's theory. In research, these two opposite hypotheses are used to facilitate a decision: whether the theory is correct or not. The two forms of hypotheses allow us such a decision, since we will gather evidence (underlinings) that will speak more in favor of either. They are usually indicated by two technical terms: the *alternative hypothesis* (often abbreviated as H_a) and the *null hypothesis* (H_0). The former suggests that there is indeed a difference between the groups while the latter implies the lack of difference. Since the two hypotheses are logical opposites, only one of them can be true. So the search is now for the evidence, which, as we said before, should be independent. But independent of whom? Of the researchers, of course. There is an obvious danger that they might wish to influence the results in a direction they would prefer as an outcome. That is why we ask other people to do it—preferably people we do not know, because they might also be influenced by us and may wish to comply with what they believe are our aims or preferences.

We had recourse to university students (not our own): they are easy to get hold of, they are intelligent, they do not need long introductions to an experiment and have no reason to give other than their own reactions. But could not they be influenced by their study object—for instance, if they were all students of literature? That could perhaps be the case, so three groups of students (or *samples*, now that you know the term) were asked to participate:

1 students who were familiar with the notion of foregrounding;

2 students of literature who were *not* familiar with the notion of foregrounding; and

3   students outside the Humanities departments (those majoring in physics, engineering, oceanography, etc.).

By comparing the reactions of these three groups of readers, the influence of familiarity with the theory, or with literature in general, could be controlled. In that way one can raise the chances that the observations are not limited to one particular group, but may be generalized. It turned out indeed that the differences between the three groups in their underlinings of what they experienced as surprising were negligible. But can we really generalize any results that we thus obtain?

To answer this question, we have to compare our expectation with the underlinings, which we can quantify: we count the number of underlinings in verses with heavy foregrounding and those in which little foregrounding was observed. The first question is, of course: were there more underlinings in the former than in the latter? If not, the theory is not worth the name. But if so, how large must the difference be before we can accept it. It is here that statistics comes in again.

From the previous chapter, you already know what a p-value is, and for our purposes, may it suffice to understand that it is a (reliable) estimate of the *error probability*. Let us remind you that there is a convention to accept results that have a p-value below 5 percent, i.e., with $p < .05$, so rather close to 0—which makes sense, because ideally we would wish there to be zero flaws. If it is so, then we accept that our claims, derived from the theory, are corroborated by the independent data. And then the theory is accepted—at least for the time being. But if $p > .05$ (i.e., higher than 5 percent), then we judge the theory is not supported by the independent data. In that case, we reject the claims of the theory at this moment in time.

Now what were the data for the underlining task in the poem by E. E. Cummings? If we divide the verse lines of the poem according to the amount of foregrounding (as revealed in our previous text analysis), the 'foregrounded' verse lines obtained a total of 497 underlinings, and the 'background' verse lines, 135. The difference is marked, of course, and in the direction that the theory asserted.

And what is the error probability of this difference? We will not bother you at this point with the question *how* you calculate this—suffice it to say that a test revealed that the observed difference for 497/135 has a p-value of .00003. In other words, the probability that this difference is caused by some error in our observations is 3 in 100,000! It hardly needs any further clarification that with Shklovsky's theory we are in good hands. It is not a mere speculation, but strongly supported by independent evidence, evidence that could easily have turned against the predictions. But it did not.

Falsification attempt failed

This chapter has provided a theoretical framework for the study of poetic experiences. The theory of foregrounding was seen as an explanatory model that could furnish this study with insights into the fundamental function of art in general and of poetry in particular. Furthermore, this theoretical model was put to a test: to a *falsification* procedure that we have already mentioned in Chapter 3.

The argument runs as follows: instead of trying to 'prove' the theory, we aim to falsify, i.e., to reject it, by exposing its assertions to data that could contradict them. This is exactly what we did—in two stages. Prior to the collection of data, extensive stylistic analyses of six poems were made on three linguistic levels: phonology, grammar and semantics. The results of these analyses were subsequently conflated, and concrete predictions, in the form of hypotheses, were made as to the degree of foregrounding in the different verse lines of the poems. Then readers underlined those passages in the poems that they were most surprised by, and they did this at their own discretion. Therefore, the test contained a real risk for the theory: the data could, in principle, have shown that the theory is wrong. Finally, by comparing the amount of underlining per verse line it was shown that the hypotheses were confirmed—with a statistically high confidence level. In similar experiments readers were asked not to underline, but to rank order the verses according to what they judged to be *important* in the poem or *worth of discussion*. Comparison with rank orders predicted on the basis of the textual analyses again provided strong evidence in favor of the theory.

The theory of foregrounding has thus survived a number of falsification procedures and can be accepted—that is, corroborated by independent evidence—at least for the time being. Let us emphasize, by way of a conclusion, that in terms of its substance, the theory provides a framework which may explain the issues of madness and surprise, as well as the effects of structures, discussed in the previous chapters.

Core issues

- According to Viktor Shklovsky, the function of art is to reinstall the emotional awareness of things around us, by making us see them in an unusual way.

- Poetry supersedes the boundaries of expected normality and thus requires a repositioning on the part of readers by building a personal involvement with the unusual, with digressions from the habitual. Readers' initial reaction may be confusion.

- Deviation (poetic license) in poetry means that authors are allowed to depart from established norms and conventions. After overcoming initial confusion, deviation induces pleasure in readers, as it triggers attraction to things that have been made strange.

- In case of internal deviation, the text first sets up a regular pattern and then unexpectedly breaks it.

- In evidence-based research we reformulate theories in the form of testable claims, or hypotheses.

- We collect independent data to hold against the hypothesis proposed. A statistical analysis is carried out to estimate the error probability of our observations. To accept a theory, this p-value should be as low as possible, but in any case lower than 5 percent.

Further reading

Balint, K., F. Hakemulder, M. Kuijpers, M. Doicaru and E. S. Tan (2016), 'Reconceptualizing Foregrounding: Identifying Response Strategies to Deviation in Absorbing Narratives,' *Scientific Study of Literature*, 6 (2): 176–207.

Cassin, B., ed. (2014), *Dictionary of Untranslatables. A Philosophical Lexicon.* Princeton: Princeton University Press.

Miall, D. S. (2007), 'Foregrounding and the Sublime: Shelley in Chamonix,' *Language and Literature*, 16: 155–68.

Shen, Y. (2007), 'Foregrounding in Poetic Discourse: Between Deviation and Cognitive Constraints,' *Language and Literature*, 16: 169–81.

Sopčák, P. (2007), '"Creation from Nothing": A Foregrounding Study of James Joyce's Drafts for *Ulysses*,' *Language and Literature*, 16: 183–96.

Zyngier, S., W. van Peer and F. Hakemulder (2007), 'Complexity and Foregrounding: In the Eye of the Beholder?' *Poetics Today*, 28: 653–82.

5

Poetry Is Revelation

Keywords

(Petrarchan) sonnet

archaism

tercet, quatraine, sextet, octave

volta

epiphany

qualitative vs quantitative methods

intertextuality

situation model

When I went to university and we had our first lecture on English literature, we, young people, just fresh from school, were naturally expecting things about Shakespeare or Wordsworth, something about love, nature, loneliness or heroic deeds. Instead, we got an assignment to read a poem about, well, we did not really *know* what it was about. There was a vivid shock, but also some kind of revelation: is *this* what literature is about? Our professor took us right into the matter by showing us what poetry might do to people. To us, young people of eighteen, this had quite an impact. What was it about?

A reading experience

It is the year 1816. A young man, twenty-one years of age, writes down an experience. Not just any experience, but one that changed his life. Seen from our time and today's expectations, it looks strange. The life-changing experience for him is reading a poem. One can imagine such a thing: someone vulnerable, depressed, or in search of the meaning of things, encounters a text and feels overwhelmed, stops short in his/her tracks—an experience never encountered before. However, things are a bit more complicated in this case, because the young man already *knew* the poem, had known it for quite a while. But now he read it in another translation, one he had not seen before. Let us explain.

For nearly 3,000 years, the works of the Greek poet Homer hung like a shadow over Western civilization. His works, the *Iliad* and *Odyssey*, counted as the pinnacle of literature. Poets would try to emulate his art. But it was written in classical Greek, a language few have mastered. Therefore, his works were mostly read in translation. And because translations are imperfect, new efforts were (and are) made all the time to improve on previous ones, until this very day. So it came about that in 1616, 200 years before our young man wrote down his experience, a new translation of Homer's poems appeared in print. It was made by George Chapman, a classical scholar. Our young man, when discovering this translation, was so exhilarated that he wrote down his experience in another poem. This was the poem I had to read in our first year at university. It is time to reveal the young man's name: John Keats (1795–1821), and the poem's title is 'On First Looking into Chapman's Homer.' Keats is remembered today for this and many other poems, written in his short life. His work exerted a profound influence on later authors, such as Percy Bysshe Shelley, Algernon Swinburne, Alfred Tennyson, John Ruskin, Oscar Wilde, Edgar Allan Poe, Henry James, W. B. Yeats, T. S. Eliot, Wilfred Owen, William Carlos Williams, Vladimir Nabokov, Jorge Luis Borges, Adrienne Rich, and many others.

Keats's reading experience turned out to be memorable. Together with a friend, he had started reading the translation by Chapman. The poem, the *Iliad*, is long (more than 15,000 verse lines!), yet both were so enraptured by the vigor of the text that they sat up all night until daylight. At ten o'clock the next morning the friend found a poem celebrating the reading experience on his breakfast table. Here is the poem:

1   Much have I travell'd in the realms of gold,

2   And many goodly states and kingdoms seen;

3   Round many western islands have I been

4   Which bards in fealty to Apollo hold.

5   Oft of one wide expanse had I been told

6   That deep-brow'd Homer ruled as his demesne;

7   Yet did I never breathe its pure serene

8   Till I heard Chapman speak out loud and bold:

9   Then felt I like some watcher of the skies

10   When a new planet swims into his ken;

11   Or like stout Cortez when with eagle eyes

12   He star'd at the Pacific—and all his men

13   Look'd at each other with a wild surmise –

14   Silent, upon a peak in Darien.

Some explanations

In all probability, you will find this text, as I did, quite puzzling. It is not just words that sound *archaic* to us, like 'bards,' 'fealty,' or 'demesne.' After all, a dictionary may bring clarification to these *archaisms*:

- 'bard' = a traditional poet reciting *epics* in an oral tradition;

- 'fealty' (pronounced [ˈfiːəltɪ]) = a tenant of land by sworn loyalty to a lord;

- 'deep-brow'd' = with a high and broad brow, implying deep intellect;

- 'demesne' (pronounced [dɪˈmeɪn]) = property of land possessed by a lord;

- 'surmise' = guess.

Beyond those words, there are also archaic phrases, like

- 'the realms of gold', for 'kingdoms or cities in possession of material wealth (i.e., gold)';

- 'wide expanse', for 'the horizon';

- 'pure serene', for 'clear calmness';

- 'some watcher of the skies', for 'an astronomer';

- 'swim into his ken', for 'came into his field of observation/ knowledge'.

Then there are proper names you may not know: Apollo (the Greek god of knowledge and beauty, and here, especially, the god of poetry), Cortez (also spelled 'Cortés,' the sixteenth-century Spanish explorer) and Darien (a region in what is now Panama).

The poem starts with a recollection of past travels—and of wealth: the 'realms of gold' may be also taken metaphorically for the realm of poetry. The western islands and the reference to Homer, the classical poet, make clear that the travels took place in the world of Greek Antiquity. Memories of all these travels in poetry come to mind, but the memories were insignificant: he did 'never breathe its pure serene' until now. The word 'Yet' in line 7 indicates this shift. All former recollections are now diminished in significance: 'never' contrasts these past experiences with what is *now* a totally new feeling (in line 8): hearing 'Chapman speak out loud and bold.' Even if we do not know who this Chapman is or was, his sweeping superiority over past experiences is recognized.

More important still is the 'Then' in line 9: a whole new vista now opens up. The Greek isles are left behind, and a cosmic view breaks through: of an astronomer witnessing a new planet in his field of perception. And this change of perspective is followed immediately by another shift. From the astronomer, presumably looking through a telescope, we are now on top of a mountain—a peak in Darien where the explorer Cortez[1] (who conquered Mexico) suddenly sees the Pacific Ocean, 'with eagle eyes.' Mark especially the word 'silent': the ocean is viewed with awe. And all the men standing around him are speechless. Like the astronomer, and like the explorers of the New World, the young man in the poem experiences something totally new: the language of Chapman's translation of Homeric poetry. As noted by Rumi (2003: 71), '[p]oetry can be dangerous, especially beautiful poetry, because it gives the illusion of having had the experience without actually going through it.' This is exactly how Keats's poem makes you feel.

Structure again

As we saw before, you can see the 'white' above/under and left/right of the poem. But apparently in the poem by Keats no stanzas are indicated by white space. This is misleading, and you can find it out, if you look at the rhyme scheme. It is a very regular and well-known one: *A B B A/A B B A/C D C/D C D*. The rhyme scheme clearly indicates a grouping of lines: 4—4—3—3. (Alternatively, the final six lines could be grouped as three pairs, i.e., *C D/C D/C D*.) This is the structure of the *Petrarchan sonnet*, after the Italian poet Petrarch being the 'inventor' of it. Francesco Petrarca (1304–74), as he is called in Italian, is the founder of Renaissance Humanism,[2] together with Dante (1265–1321) and Boccaccio (1313–75). His major work, the *Canzoniere* ('Book of Songs'), is a collection of poems, 317 of which are *sonnets*, the majority of them dedicated to Laura, his lifelong, but distant, love. (Historically, he is not the 'inventor' of the sonnet form, but through his poetry the form acquired its wide dissemination.) The poem by Keats you have just read is such a sonnet. It consists of fourteen lines, divided in parts along the lines of the rhyme scheme we have just seen.

First there are two stanzas of four lines each, called a *quatrain*. Together they form the *octave* (eight lines), describing his worldly and poetic travels, ending with the revelation in line 8. Then comes a sudden change, indicated by 'Then' in line 9, called a *volta*, Italian for a 'turn,' typically occurring in sonnets between the octave and the next six lines, called the *sextet*, which is composed of two stanzas of three lines each, called a *tercet*. (Here, however, in the Keats poem, the grouping is slightly different: there are three groups of two lines, as already indicated in the rhyme scheme above.) The octave generally lays down some general or abstract proposition, a description, a problem, a question, etc. The *volta* then announces the transition into a concrete illustration, an answer to the question or generally some kind of resolution. Here, in the poem by Keats, the change is (in line 9) from the past to the present, from his former extensive travels that only revealed the personal and intimate experiences (in the octave) to the present, the sextet, exposing how he now discovered a whole new world, offering a vast new vista, opened by the translation of Chapman.

So the stanzas here are not marked by a white space surrounding them. But anyone familiar with the sonnet as a literary form will immediately recognize them. Why did Keats not mark them separately? We do not know. Obviously he preferred to have them linked in one sequence of thoughts. There is some argument in favor of this explanation when we look at the meter. It is a rather strict *iambic pentameter*: five iambic feet per verse line (except line 12, with an extra line-internal syllable before the pause). This is *the* classic English meter, for instance, employed standardly by Shakespeare in his sonnets. But the lines are not end-stopped. From line 3 onward, nearly all of them are linked to the next one: 3 to 4, 5 to 6, 7 to 8, 9 to 10, with very strong *enjambments* in lines 11 and 12, when everything seems to suddenly come to a halt at the end of line 13. So there is an ongoing movement throughout the poem—which would have been broken if the stanzas had been separated from each other. Notice that there is a deviation from the meter exactly at the moment of the *volta* (in line 9): the first word ('Then') should be unstressed, according to the metrical pattern, but its syntax forbids it, and so it draws a strong stress. Similar discrepancies are found in the final two lines: syntactically, the first syllables must have stress in these lines. The result is a succession of two stressed syllables: 'm**e**n l**oo**k'd' and 'surm**ise** **Si**lent,' causing a *retardation*: the regular beat of the meter is halted and the rhythm stalls, thereby drawing attention to itself. It is almost as if the poet took us by the hand in the first verse, led us through the poem by the meter he had set up, and then, in the final two lines, makes us stand still where he wants us to be, so that we can contemplate the vastness of the newly found ocean, i.e., the vastness of the new world of poetry that opened itself to him, and that he now wants to share with us.

Mark also the cases of *parallelism*, a chain of parallels between Homer → Chapman → Astronomer → Cortez → Keats → you. For Keats, the 'Then I felt ... ' is not a mere astonishment in reading the translation by Chapman, but an existential experience, which will transform his whole life— *and* that of English literature. A year later, Keats (1817) will write to another friend, Benjamin Bailey: 'I am certain of nothing but the holiness of the Heart's affections and the truth of the imagination. What the imagination seizes as

Beauty must be truth.' This passage would eventually be transmuted into the concluding lines of his 'Ode on a Grecian Urn':

> Beauty is truth, truth beauty,—that is all
> Ye know on earth, and all ye need to know.

Over the past 200 years, those words have been a source of beauty, consolation, and inspiration to millions of people. This, then, is an *epiphany*, from the Greek *epiphaneia*, meaning 'appearance' or 'manifestation,' echoing the beginning of Western philosophy and aesthetics where, in Plato's *Dialogues* (especially in the *Republic*), the intimate relation between the Good, the True, and the Beautiful, is established.

Students reading Keats

We began this chapter by describing my own reading experience with the poem as a beginning student. But how would students today (and in a different cultural context) react to the poem? After all, in psychopoetics we are after reading experiences of people *generally*. So we ran a simple study with forty-one of our students during a class on literature. We first presented them with the poem, without any information about its author, background, or origin. And then we asked them to give us their reaction to the following questions as demonstrated in the table below (you may recognize the Likert scales and some categories from Chapter 3):

Questionnaire sample

I find the text very striking.
1 2 3 4 5 6 7

This is an interesting text to discuss with pupils in class.
1 2 3 4 5 6 7

The text has important things to communicate.
1 2 3 4 5 6 7

I would recommend this poem to good friend.
1 2 3 4 5 6 7

This is a good example of high quality literature.
1 2 3 4 5 6 7

The text made me see things in a new light.
1 2 3 4 5 6 7

And we also asked the students how beautiful they found the poem. But here we gave them five possibilities on a polarized scale—another tool to use in evidence-based research:

(   ) Not beautiful at all.
(   ) Somewhat beautiful.
(   ) Undecided.
(   ) Rather beautiful.
(   ) Very beautiful.

We then had to convert the answers in numerical data, so 1 now meant that the poem was regarded as 'not beautiful at all,' 2 as 'somewhat beautiful,' etc.

To begin with this question, the average response was 4 (on a scale of 5), meaning that generally readers found the poem 'rather beautiful.' But more importantly, the answers given to the scales in the table above were all rather high as well, as you can see in following graph in Figure 12:

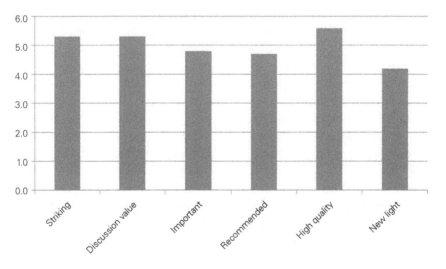

FIGURE 12 *Students' reactions to Keats's 'On First Looking into Chapman's Homer.'*

The vertical bars represent the average answers on a scale of 7. Clearly readers judged the poem above or around the value of 5 for all qualities except the final one ('The text made me see things in a new light'). Especially interesting here is the highest evaluation for the poem's quality ('This is a good example of high quality literature'): 5.6. In other words, readers judged the text as being of very high literary quality.

But here we bump into the limits of our method (of using numerical scales). The numbers do not tell us much, except that the students rated the poem's qualities as high. But then maybe that is to be expected, as they were given the text by their professor—in a literature class at that. This is why we also tried to probe deeper into their reading experiences by employing a *qualitative* method. In a group discussion it emerged from the very beginning that everyone found 'On First Looking into Chapman's Homer' a difficult poem. There were comments on the 'difficulty of the language' and on 'many allusions that were hard to understand' (henceforth the students' comments are quoted *ipsis litteris*). We did not reveal the name of the author or anything out of the background, so one student said: '[i]f I had a dictionary, I would understand the poem better'; someone said: 'My lack of knowledge about what is Darien and who is Chapman does not allow me to appreciate all allusions.' At the same time, however, two people stated that they would like to read more works of the author.

Given the experience of difficulty, it is nevertheless astounding how much insight was gained through reading. One contrast that turned up in various comments was the one between materialism and spirituality. As one participant put it: 'People should think less about the material, but more about the beauty around.' Is that 'in' the poem? In a sense, yes, certainly if one takes the first line of the poem literally. Beauty as an important issue in the poem turned up in about a quarter of all comments. There are also interpretations that stay within a narrative mode, though, such as the one saying that the poem focuses on '[f]eelings of an experienced traveler, probably sailor, his adoreness of nature and his voyages.' But others interpreted the travels more symbolically, for instance: 'Reading and literature in general allows us to travel and get experience.' Or even more pertinently: the poem is about '[t]raveling, exploring new things, new worlds through our imagination and literature.' And then, amazingly, given readers' predicament, some isolated the central experience that Keats describes pretty accurately, as in these two comments made during the discussion: here we deal with '[t]he power of poetry. The effect of Homer on people' and '[a] man experiencing a land, place, thing via the words of someone named Chapman.'

All in all, then, these comments allow us some insight into the kind of psychological experiences that readers were going through. Above all, they are a witness to the cognitive struggle readers were involved in while trying to make sense of the text. At the same time, the comments indicate the readers' interest and motivation to get to know more about the poet and the circumstances of the poem.

There were not really remarks about something like an epiphany, but some might have gone that way with a little bit more comprehension. Please remember that our readers were confronted out of any context with a poem (in a foreign language) for which they had no clue what it was about. In that way, their reading efforts resembled mine as a beginning student. I also had no inkling what the poet was trying to get across after a first reading. So we will come back later in this chapter to the question of whether our students know about the experience of epiphany.

A religious epiphany

No doubt the most famous case of epiphany, and the one that has had the most profound impact on the history of the world, is the one that Paul, one of the founders of Christianity, experienced on his way to Damascus. Paul (or Saul, as he was still called then by his Jewish name), it will be recalled, was a persecutor of the followers of Jesus, and not of a meek type. It says in the *Acts of the Apostles* that he was 'breathing out threatenings and slaughter against the disciples of the Lord' (9, 1). But then something happens to him:

> And as he journeyed, he came near Damascus: and suddenly there shined round about him a light from heaven:
>
> And he fell to the earth, and heard a voice saying to him, Saul, Saul, why persecutes thou me?
>
> And he said, Who art thou, Lord? And the Lord said: I am Jesus whom thou persecutes; it is hard for thee to kick against the pricks.
>
> And he trembling and astonished said, Lord, what wilt thou have me to do? And the Lord said unto him. Arise, and go into the city and it shall be told thee what thou must do.
>
> And the men which journeyed with him stood speechless, hearing a voice, but seeing no man. (9, 3–6)

The rest of the story is known to many: after this experience, Saul is now converted to the very religion he was persecuting. He even changes his name, from Saul to Paul, from the Greek *paulos* (the small one). The account is not poetry, of course, though the language of the Bible (think of the parables) has many poetic overtones. But look at the end of the passage: it is highly similar in a number of ways to the end of the Keats poem. Just like with Chapman's translation experience, there are two senses that are singularly activated: sight and hearing. In Keats, it is the vision of the planet (line 10), the 'eagle eyes' (line 11), 'star'd' (line 12) and 'look'd' (line 13). With Paul, the vision aspects are less outspoken, but there is the 'light from heaven' that blasts Paul to the ground. Similarly, both turn to some kind of dialogic exchange where voice (Chapman's and God's) is significant: Keats first 'hears' Chapman speaking and then talks to his reader, while Paul communicates with God as his men stand speechless, just hearing God's voice without seeing him. Mark that the setting is almost identical to Keats's poem: the men are all 'silent.' Moreover, the spatial aspects are likewise highlighted: it starts with the travels in the octave, but then acquires visionary dimensions in lines 9–10 as astronomical observations are witnessed. Until finally, a bird's-eye view ('with eagle eyes'), high upon a 'peak.' With Paul, it is a 'downfall': he is smitten to the ground and must look up to the voice. And finally there are the bodily sensations: Paul trembles, and the men around Cortez look with 'wild surmise.'

Poetic revelation

One may wonder whether these formulations of the experience are 'passed on.' Has Keats somehow or other been influenced by the biblical story? Then we would say that the biblical text has exerted an *influence* on Keats. This is a whole realm of literary studies where influences of one text on other texts are investigated. Such study goes under the name of *intertextuality*.

With some texts, the influence is widespread, and Keats's sonnet is one of them. Intertextuality and influence studies may become involved in far-flung relations, as with the novel/poem *Pale Fire* by Vladimir Nabokov (1962), an extraordinary work, consisting of exactly 1,000 verse lines, by a fictional poet, John Shade, which are subsequently 'analyzed' line by line by Shade's neighbor and academic colleague, Charles Kinbote. In lines 86–98, we find a description of the inventory of the poet's aunt Maud, which ends with:

A curio: *Red Sox Beat Yanks 5–4.*
On Chapman's Homer, thumbtacked to the door.

You certainly would not expect Keats's poem next to the Red Sox baseball team, but there they are: adjacent in another poem. The commentator of the verses ironically remarks on the lines: 'A reference to the title of Keats's famous sonnet (often quoted in America) which, owing to a printer's absentmindedness, has been drolly transposed, from some other article, into the account of a sports event' (Nabokov 1962: 96).

So here the reference is quite clear, showing the influence of Keats's poem over a time span of 150 years. But such similarities between texts are not necessarily a matter of intercultural influence. What matters most, for both Keats and Paul, was the experience of a turning point in their lives—one that made them re-examine and re-evaluate what had come before. To Keats and his friend, reading Chapman's translation of Homer meant an experience comparable to the one Cortez and his companions had when staring in amazement at the newly discovered ocean. To me, a beginning student, Keats's poem initially presented a riddle. But after having applied all I had learnt until then and having looked at the text in depth, word by word, metaphor by metaphor (a task that took quite some time and energy), it became something of an epiphany for me and my fellow students, too: that poetry is not the sentimental stuff about loneliness, beautiful nature or romantic love, but that it is a force that may deeply affect your life. Having gone through hard work on Keats's text, we now saw poetry as we had not surmised before. And through that revelation we had now become members of an eminent group, one that had *seen*, the way Cortez is imagined to have seen the Pacific, the way Keats saw the beauty of Chapman's translation—and, by implication, the way poetry works in life in general.

Epiphany

Maybe you wonder now what this has to do with you yourself. Or you may feel that this kind of experience is for highbrow aesthetes only, for intellectuals or ivory tower academics, not for ordinary people like you. But just enter the word 'epiphany' in any internet search engine, and you will find literally thousands of references to it, many in the form of poetry. In what follows, we shall delve deeper into the nature of such epiphany and refer to it as 'feelings of significance and ineffability,' which is the term proposed by Fabb (2022).

If you *have* had such experiences, you know that they are often accompanied by physical symptoms, like a shudder, shiver, gooseflesh, chills, or bristling skin, a lump in your throat or tears. Such experiences are especially prominent when listening to music, which is the art where they have been studied most. These physiological signs may arise suddenly, without former warning. They are unusual and unannounced peaks in *arousal*. Why is that the case? Chills are normally an expression of fear, but in art, music, and literature, they are actually *sought*. And they seem to provide a pleasant feeling, rather than the feeling of being threatened.

Epiphanies can come in many different forms and are often generated by a complex combination of experience, memory, knowledge, predisposition, and context (see McDonald 2008). A contemporary example of an epiphany is the situation which is no doubt familiar to you: a friend, a relative, or a teacher explains something to you—a concept or a theory that you did not really fathom before, and all of a sudden in a flash you grasp it. You then *feel* something. Something unusual, something special.

The fact that it is sudden may make you forget that epiphany is the result of significant mental work on the part of the discoverer and is only the satisfying result of a long process. The clarification that the epiphany brings has an emotional counterpart in the feeling of fulfilment. Cognitive achievement and emotional gratification go hand in hand. The feeling of epiphany is so satisfying because one cannot predict when one's labor will bear fruit, and our subconscious can play a significant part in delivering the solution. The experience is fulfilling because it is a reward for a strenuous and sustained effort. A reward for what? First of all, for an openness, a readiness to submit to an experience one cannot predict. Second, a reward for the sustained effort to keep working. The same applies to poetry: without openness and without an honest effort, no revelation is to be expected.

A bit of biography

In 1818, Keats had met Fanny (Frances) Brawne and soon a (non-sexual) intimacy developed between the two, Keats lending her books, they reading together, and he dedicating poems to her, especially 'Bright Star', a poem that led to Jane Campion's delicate and excellent movie by that title; a beautiful clip from the movie, beside other ones you may find on YouTube, is: Link 5.2 on the Companion Website.

But their relationship was clouded by Keats's slim prospects of financial independence, foreclosing marriage. As a consequence, he suffered severe moods of darkness and depression, witnessed in poems from that time, such as 'La Belle Dame sans Merci' or 'The Eve of Saint-Agnes.' Soon after, however, a further major catastrophe shook their lives: he was diagnosed with tuberculosis—a very common and deadly disease at that time. Doctors advised him to move south, to a more benign climate. In September 1820, he left for Rome (his journey being paid for by friends), realizing that he would never see his beloved again. Five months later he was dead. During those months he was (both emotionally and physically) unable to write to Fanny, not even responding to her letters (none of which have survived). Another difference with our present time: it took a month for the news of his death to reach England. Fanny went into mourning for six years and married later, more than twelve years after his death. The small apartment where he lived can still be visited at the Piazza di Spagna in Rome, right at the foot of the Spanish Steps, a quiet and intimate place of pilgrimage for lovers of his poetry. In the Protestant cemetery is his grave. On his tombstone (without his name) it reads what he himself had requested, in full harmony with his life as a poet:

Here lies One
whose Name was writ in Water.

Beauty and truth

Maybe the foregoing discussion gives you the impression that great poetry must be written by adventurous, romantic people, who often die an early and heroic death. Not necessarily. Around 1862, someone else wrote a poem not unlike that of Keats: Emily Dickinson (1830–86), who lived a reclusive life in her home town of Amherst in Massachusetts. She never wandered far from home, but preferred the quiet surroundings of her family. Only seven of her (nearly 1,800) poems were published in her lifetime. Interest in her poetry grew only after she died, culminating in the edition of the collected poems by Johnson in 1955. Since then her fame at the pinnacle of English poetry has been unchallenged. And since the 1998 edition by Ralph Franklin this reputation as one of America's major poets is unequivocal. She is held in great esteem by ordinary readers, in spite of the fact that her texts are brimming with dense meaning, imagery, symbols, and allegory.

In a letter written on August 17, 1870, to Th. W. Higginson, a co-editor of her poetic collections, Dickinson describes the *experience* of poetry in the following way: 'If I read a book and it makes my whole body so cold no fire can ever warm me, I know that is poetry. If I feel physically as if the top of my head were taken off, I know that is poetry. These are the only way [*sic*] I know it. Is there any other way?' (Todd 1894: 315).

Now familiarize yourself with one of her well-known verses: Link 5.3 on the Companion Website. This is one of her stunning poems (numbered 448 or 449 in the editions by Franklin and Johnson respectively). We render it here as it is found in her own handwriting:

I died for Beauty: but
was scarce
Adjusted in the Tomb
When One who died for
Truth, was lain
In an adjoining Room –

He questioned softly why I
failed?
'For Beauty –', I replied –
'And I—for Truth—Themself
are One –
We Brethren, are', He said –

And so, as Kinsmen, met
a Night –

We talked between the Rooms –
Until the Moss had reached
our lips –
And covered up—Our names –

One of the first things when encountering a new text is to have a grasp of the situation *within* the text. We, as readers, are *outside* the poem, and in order to understand it, we must get into the 'world in the text.' In psychology we call this a *situation model*, meaning a mental representation of an event or a situation. Think back of the ballad in Chapter 1: if you did not construct a 'picture' in your head of a young woman weeping at the side of a river and an old man addressing her, you could not have understood what it was all about. And if you had not adapted this current situation model when arriving at stanza 4, you would again have missed what was going on. The same applies to the poem by Emily Dickinson here.

Written in an iambic *tetrameter* (eight syllables, four feet) and *trimeter*, with enjambment in lines 1, 2, and 3, very strong at the end of line 1, the poem describes how two individuals, in fact, neighbors in 'Rooms' next to each other (metaphorically standing for graves), discuss why they died. This immediately makes it clear that we are in a *fictional* world: someone lying in a grave next to yours, and able to converse with each other, though you are both dead. The reader may picture some kind of vault that families had (like the one where Juliet is buried in *Romeo and Juliet*).

The narrator is the first one to be laid in the tomb, and she was hardly used to being there, when another body is entered, who starts a 'conversation,' in the course of which they share the reasons why they are there. Clearly they are dead. But their discussion turns to why they are dead in the first place. The answer is not that they have died *of* something. Instead of an accident, an illness, old age or whatever, they discuss what they have died *for*: Beauty and Truth. The capital letters indicate that these are important things. Remember Keats's 'Ode on a Grecian Urn,' with its 'Beauty is truth, truth beauty' echoing the philosophical discussion about the relationship between Beauty and Truth, a topic that reverberates through the whole history of Western poetry and poetics since the Greek philosopher Plato.

One thing that stands out in the poem is deviant *punctuation*, quite clearly a form of deviational foregrounding: there are no periods (but one question mark). This is no accident, but typical of Emily Dickinson's style as she makes the reader pause after the reasons are made explicit: 'For Beauty –', I replied –/'And I—for Truth—Themself.' The revelation makes the two 'Bretheren' and 'Kinsmen' while 'for' remains highly ambiguous: it can stand both for 'the object of a perception, or desire' and 'in the cause of.' The ending of the poem is surprisingly physical: the two dead people still feel how 'the Moss had reached [their] lips –.'

We are dealing here with a *personification*, a stylistic device through which characters embody certain ideas or qualities. Thus both beauty and truth in the poem are 'represented' by people. Although dead, they 'speak' and even have a conversation. There is no symbolism of light here, as with the previous epiphanies, for an obvious reason: we are underground, in a grave. Remember what we said about the importance of the voice in epiphany: the Lord speaking to Paul, Chapman speaking 'out loud and bold,' which subsequently makes place for stillness—and here the moss reaching the protagonists' lips. Through silence and the obliteration of their names, their dialogue (and hence the poem) reaches out to the world. As with Keats, things will no longer be the same.

A simple epiphany

So is all poetry of this kind? Is poetry to be equated with epiphany? That depends on how you define the concept. Until now we have dealt with some very famous experiences of epiphany—and they are famous because of the undeniable changes they caused in people. But could we not conceive of somewhat 'lesser' epiphanies? If that is the case, then we may perhaps conceive of the 'experiences of significant ineffability' as graded on a scale, from small-scale mini-epiphanies to some grand-scale, monumental changes caused by them. If that be so, then there is a case for arguing that poetry always aims at some kind of epiphany, from the most puny and humble one, when the poet attempts to capture a moment of stillness, in which things all of a sudden acquire a new quality, a new eminence, an experience worth communicating, to others. Indeed, epiphany in poetry need not be complex (as in Keats) or profound (as with Dickinson), but can be worded relatively simply, as in the haiku by Basho. The following poem exemplifies this: it is by William Wordsworth (1770–1850), and it is one of the best known poems in the English language:

I wandered lonely as a cloud
That floats on high o'er vales and hills,
When all at once I saw a crowd,
A host, of golden daffodils;
Beside the lake, beneath the trees,
Fluttering and dancing in the breeze.

Continuous as the stars that shine
And twinkle on the milky way,
They stretched in never-ending line
Along the margin of a bay:
Ten thousand saw I at a glance,
Tossing their heads in sprightly dance.

The waves beside them danced; but they
Out-did the sparkling waves in glee:
A poet could not but be gay,
In such a jocund company:
I gazed—and gazed—but little thought
What wealth the show to me had brought:

For oft, when on my couch I lie
In vacant or in pensive mood,
They flash upon that inward eye
Which is the bliss of solitude;
And then my heart with pleasure fills,
And dances with the daffodils.

By now you can no doubt see through the structural characteristics of the poem, employing a very simple and very regular rhyme scheme (*A B A B C C*) and written in the typical iambic pentameter, with predominantly end-stopped lines in the first stanza, but increasing enjambments from stanza 2 to the end. The situation model is quite simple. There is one speaker only, who recounts an experience which turned into a vision that will last forever: the view of the daffodils has changed the course of his personal history, as they have given him a new resource of delight and understanding. Life goes on, as ever, but the memory of that epiphany will hang around him from now on. The poem clearly demonstrates how poetic epiphany may manifest itself in a lucid piece of wisdom, accompanying one through life.

Revelation

What the life and work of Keats, Dickinson, and Wordsworth show us in baffling detail is the supreme power of poetry. It attests to the extraordinary significance poems can have for human life. The poem with which we started this chapter, about reading a book (and a translation at that), might at first sight seem unlikely to agitate young people to elation. Less even would one expect readers of *a poem about reading a poem* raise the spirits to such levels of intoxication. Yet that is what happened. Generation upon generation has been confronted with this simple but inspiring little text. Why? Marilynne Robinson (2018), the famous American novelist and essayist, sees in the sonnet an expression of being 'ravished' by a book, of finding its suggestive power beyond its subject matter, leading to the humanizing insight that some things are so brilliant they have to be understood as emanating from virtuoso minds, emanating in the pure joy of itself.

It is testimonies like these that allow us to discuss the revelatory character of poetry. As has become abundantly clear in the previous pages, epiphany is an experience that comes unannounced. Although it may be the fruit of a long (and subconscious) incubation process, it manifests itself suddenly, without any forewarning. And it cannot be forced or invited. Moreover, the experience is such that it falls outside the scope of everyday habits: it is what one could call the 'thrilling' character of the revelation experience. It is so overwhelming that our usual categories of description fall short of it. That is why its study cannot make use of experimental designs that we have witnessed in other cases. It is impossible to call forth a poetic epiphany through some external intervention. From Chapter 2 you already know about qualitative and quantitative data, so here we have to rely on what are called *qualitative methods*—for instance, (various kinds of) interviews, diaries, correspondence, personal notes, focus groups, and the like. These are usually contrasted with *quantitative* ones, in which data collected can be turned into numerical form and subjected to quantitative, i.e., statistical analysis. Obviously no such approach can be used in the study of epiphany experiences. Actually, earlier in this chapter we have already informed you of how our students gave their comments on the poem by Keats, and how these were highly informative. It is these methods that psychopoetics has to employ if it wants to gain access to the experiences of epiphany that readers of poetry may have. There is a sense in which we could call critical analyses or interpretations of poems also qualitative. But they rarely deal with experiences of revelation.

So we did a little research of our own. We first asked a group of (forty-five, all female) students whether they themselves had had such revelatory experiences. We asked them the following:

> Have you ever had a SUDDEN moment where you felt you had a totally new and totally DEEP insight in the world, an insight that made you change your thoughts, ideas, and feelings—in short, that it deeply influenced your life?

One would perhaps not expect this, but thirty-eight of the participants said they had had such experiences several times, and seven of them once. No one answered that they had never had such experiences! So it would seem that revelations, as we have been discussing them in this chapter, are not at all rare, at least not for this group of people. One has to be careful, however: with qualitative data, one may not generalize the results.

We also asked participants what they associated these revelatory experiences with and offered them nine alternatives, of which they could choose several. The answers have been summarized in Figure 13 on the next page.

As you can see in the graph, some alternatives did not generate many experiences of this kind, in fact, less than 10 percent (the bars represent percentages). These are: pictures, buildings, and—yes, surprisingly perhaps—religion! The study was run in Kyiv, Ukraine. It may be that answers would be very different in other countries or contexts. Basically three sources of revelation experiences stand out (with roughly 50 percent or more): music, movies, and—the highest of all—literature, but with poetry only some 15 percent. The human face and art occupy a middle position. Most important, perhaps, is the fact that artistic sources seem to be the most important ones for this group of people.

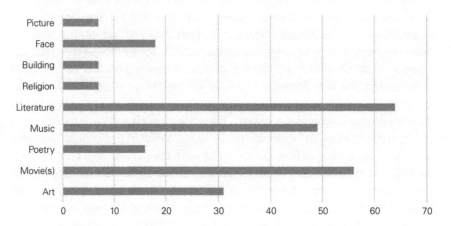

FIGURE 13 *Revelation source.*

We were likewise interested in the kind of situations in which such experiences turned up, so we presented them with nine alternatives. The reactions you find in Figure 14:

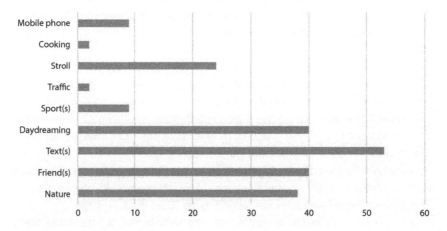

FIGURE 14 *Revelation situation.*

As could be expected, perhaps, some situations are not at all conductive to revelatory experiences and were used by us as a kind of filters to make sure the respondents were indeed honest in their responses: cooking, traffic, sports or using their mobile phone. Having a walk may lead to the experience, but the major situations (indicated by about 40 percent of participants) are: daydreaming, friends, nature, and—again the highest value of over 50 percent—texts (though we do not know what kind of texts).

What of the evidential character of such qualitative methods? Because of the highly subjective and individual character of such experiences, it is hard to generalize about them. But all in all, the surprising thing about our questionnaire is that it revealed much more positive answers than we had ourselves expected intuitively.

As an illustration, we may also look on what Keats wrote in a famous poem, 'Endymion,' published in 1818, which starts with the unforgettable lines:

A thing of beauty is a joy for ever:
Its loveliness increases; it will never
Pass into nothingness; but still will keep
A bower quiet for us, and a sleep
Full of dreams, and health, and quiet breathing.

Here we have in a few words a whole philosophy of poetry. Apparently, reading poetry can offer sudden insights that are emotionally so gripping that they are powerful agents of change in life. Some call it mystical, spiritual, or significant, while others call it ecstasy, being moved or a peak experience, in one word: a Revelation. The key to such experiences is a decisive change in perceiving the world. It is the automatic processing of our environment, as it is shaped in our habits and routines, that impedes the revelation. Breaking through such automatisms is a crucial part of creative thinking—in all areas of life. As we have seen, such revelations can be extremely strong. In the case of Paul, it revolutionized religion in Antiquity; in the case of Keats, it revolutionized his vision of poetry—and opened up a new vista for writers and readers coming after him. Dickinson took it to the grave—and beyond. All this means that poetry is an agent of change, and that such change may be fundamentally innovative, but thereby also disquieting. That will be the stuff of Chapter 6.

Core issues

- The sonnet is one of the most widespread forms of poetry, composed of fourteen lines, arranged both formally and semantically in two quatrains (four lines), together forming the octave, followed by two tercets (three lines), forming the sextet, with a volta (turning point) between the octave and the sextet.

- Poetry has a revelatory character. Often it is an epiphany, a life-changing experience, which falls outside the scope of everyday life.

- Reading poetry can offer sudden insights that are emotionally so gripping that they may be accompanied by strong physical sensations.

- Such experiences are powerful agents of fundamentally innovative change in life.

- In evidence-based research, both qualitative and quantitative methods are used.

- Qualitative methods involve raw data and include interviews, correspondence, personal notes, focus groups, etc.

- When quantitative methods are applied, data collected are turned into numerical form and subjected to quantitative (i.e., statistical) analysis.

- Intertextuality involves the influence of one text on another, so that one text 'echoes' an earlier one.

Further reading

Boitano, P. (2021), *Anagnorisis: Scenes and Themes of Recognition and Revelation in Western Literature*. Leiden: Brill.

Franke, W. (2015), *The Revelation of Imagination: From Homer and the Bible through Virgil and Augustine to Dante*. Evanston: Northwestern University Press.

Patterson, R. (1951), *The Riddle of Emily Dickinson*. Boston and New York: Houghton Mifflin Company.

Regan, S. (2019), *The Sonnet*. Oxford: Oxford University Press.

6

Poetry Is Power

Keywords

canto

coping

consolation

bibliotherapy

empathy

meta-analysis

A youthful experience

When I was seventeen, at school, one morning our teacher walked into the classroom with a record player, which surprised us. To us, a record player was for listening to Elvis Presley, Little Richard, or—in general—rock-and-roll music. So we were puzzled. The teacher put up a record, told us to open our study books (in Dutch) on page such and such (where there was something we did not understand), and to listen. Through the classroom those words reverberated:

Nel mezzo del cammin di nostra vita
Mi ritrovai per una selva oscura.
Ché la diritta via era smarrita.

And then a strange thing happened. Here a bunch of seventeen-year-old boys (no girls at that time) were listening to something they did not understand, and yet there was a dead silence in the classroom—you could hear a pin drop. Strange? Yes, because we were trained to become scientists and engineers, not humanists. And our interests were: football, rock-and-roll, girls, smoking a cigarette, or drinking a beer on the sly. Certainly, not some poetry lines in Italian—which we did not understand. Yet there seemed to be some magic coming from the words, something that made us feel that this was something special, something to pay attention to. It is a story heard often: the words exert an almost bewitching appeal.

Then our teacher explained. This was the beginning of a world-famous poem called the *Divine Comedy* (*Divina Commedia* in Italian), written some 700 years ago by someone called Dante Alighieri, who was banned for political reasons from his beloved town of Florence, writing in the embitterment of his banishment. It turned out to be a revolutionary poem. It formed the basis of the present Italian language and is widely considered as one of the greatest masterpieces of poetry in the world.

There are numerous English translations of the work. The three initial verse lines above are translated by H. W. Longfellow,[1] a professor of Italian at Harvard University and himself a poet, in the nineteenth century, as follows:

Midway upon the journey of our life
I found myself within a forest dark,
For the straightforward pathway had been lost.

It is a *narrative* poem (like those we discussed in Chapter 1), telling the story of Dante himself traveling, under the guidance of the Roman poet Virgil, through the (Catholic) afterlife: first through Hell (*Inferno*), then Purgatory (*Purgatorio*) and Heaven (*Paradiso*), describing what he sees and experiences there, which persons he meets, and how his encounters enlarge the meaning of his life (think of the *revelation* idea we discussed in the previous chapter). Before entering Heaven, Virgil, as a pagan, has to give over the lead to Dante's lifelong love, Beatrice, whom he only met twice (when they were both nine and eighteen), but for whom he kept a perennial love, even though she married another man (and he married another woman). After Beatrice's untimely death, Dante composed a series of poems dedicated to her, which came to be collected in a volume called *La Vita Nuova* (The New Life), another pinnacle of world literature.

Although the *Divina Commedia* is a kind of story (both external and symbolic), it is poetry to the very heart. It is long, altogether 14,233 verse lines! Each of the three books consists of thirty-three *cantos* (from the Latin *cantus*, 'song'), but the first, introductory canto, of which we have just read the first three lines, is an 'extra' canto, bringing the total number to 100. The verses are written in *terza rime* (English 'tercet'), a verse form developed by Dante himself, which consists of interlocking lines of eleven syllables each, with a rhyme scheme *A B A/B C B/C D C*, etc., so that each tercet contains thirty-three metrical syllables, the same as the number of cantos. Imagine writing a poem of nearly 15,000 lines adhering to such a scheme. If ever proof was needed that poetry is structure, as we maintained in Chapter 1, *here* it is!

I myself was so enraptured after this introduction by our teacher that I went to the local library to look for the work. Fortunately, the librarian helped me and found a bilingual edition, with the Italian original on the left and its Dutch translation on the right-hand side. I did not know any Italian at the time, but the magic of Dante's language had such a strong appeal that I started learning parts of it by heart, which I then kept in memory all my life. They are my magic spells, for moments in life when things are going the hard way. Since then I always have Dante's beautiful verses ready at hand in my head.

My life would have been completely different if our teacher had not put on that record with Dante's poetry that morning. Other poets may have influenced other people. Unfortunately, the habit of learning poetry by heart has virtually disappeared, in spite of its consoling effects. One has to find poetry that is *worth* memorizing, of course. With a 700-year-old poem that is still alive, the risks are small. But there are also some poets who are well known for their meditative poetry. In English, Robert Frost is one. Listen, for instance, to him reading himself one of his famous poems, 'The Road Not Taken': Link 6.1 on the Companion Website.

Why should we consider this important? Because all of us have moments or patches in our lives when things go wrong. The degree of this 'wrongness' varies, of course—from a quarrel with a boyfriend or a girlfriend, to wars, or deaths of people we love. Tolstoy wrote, '[h]appy families are all alike; every unhappy family is unhappy in its own way.' You can say the same about individual persons, of course. If catastrophe strikes, you have to *cope* with the trouble (personal or global), this way or another.

The sources of soothing suffering are numerous, of course. To name only a few: nature, family, friends, hobbies, humor, intimacy, sports, or religion. And literature, poetry in particular, may be one of them, as poetry has always occupied an important place in people's lives—in tumultuous moments in particular. Just think of the fact that there was a boom in the popularity of poetry in the UK during the rise of Chartism in the nineteenth century as well as during the miners' strike in the 1980s. According to Katy Shaw, professor of contemporary writings at Northumbria University, '[i]n the miners' strike, we had poetry being written on the side of instruction manuals and printed on typewriters, distributed by hand or sent through the post. Similarly, we have evidence of a lot of Chartist poetry being publicly read out and shared between different groups of workers' (Ferguson 2019).

But where is poetry?

We guess that not all of you have the collected poems by Baudelaire, Longfellow, or Neruda on your bookshelf at home. So how do you find interesting, moving, worthwhile poetry? Maybe you can make a list of instances, situations, or places when you think you may encounter poetry in your daily life. Now compare it with the list we have compiled from our own experience. We believe that poetry is frequently encountered in the following situations:

- in public places (in a hospital or in the street)—look at Figure 23 on p. 174 in Chapter 9, for instance;

- on stage (at festivals and poetry slams, with regularly over 10,000 participants. YouTube video clips of such happenings may go viral on the internet and be watched by, in one case, almost 2 million people: see Link 6.2 on the Companion Website);

- on articles of use (such as the products of the Dutch 'Stichting Plint,' a nonprofit foundation that produces and distributes printed poetry on pillowcases, cushion covers, placemats, mugs, tissues, greeting cards, posters, stationery, and even apps);

- over the radio (for instance, 'Candlelight poems');

- on television (for example, poems performed by TV program's 'house poets');

- on the internet (on social media and on YouTube);

- in newspapers (poems written by 'city poets' or the Poet Laureate);

- on the body (poetry in tattoos);

- on special occasions (marriages, birthdays, celebrations, obituaries, presidential inaugurations, and commencement addresses).

You may perhaps think that some present-day forms, like festivals of slam poetry by Aiya Meilani or Kendrick Lamar, or the songs by Bob Dylan are only about current forms of poetry. But think of Roberto Benigni, one of the most famous Italian movie actors. You may want to watch him in *La Vita é Bella* (Life is Beautiful) or *Down by Law*. (If you wish to familiarize yourself with his sense of humor, there are several short clips to look at on the internet.) But he also recites whole *cantos* from Dante's *Divina Commedia* for thousands of listeners in public squares in Italian towns. Here is one recording, of the very beginning of the poem (see the opening of this chapter), recorded in the square in front of the *Duomo* (cathedral) in Florence, the home town of Dante, from which he was banned, which caused him to start writing the *Divine Comedy* as a political exile: Link 6.3 on the Companion Website. (You can switch on an automatic translation in several languages, by clicking on 'settings,' then 'autotranslate,' and then choosing your language.) Thousands of people stand in the square to listen to the power of this miraculous poem.

Join them! And note, this is not a 'reading': he knows the whole poem (thousands of verse lines) by heart, as you can see.

So poetry can be an event that moves masses of people. But has it always been like that? The historical research by Rubin (2007) claims that poetry has a long-term effect on people as it 'survives in memory even when readers no longer confronted words on a page' (ibid.: 4). In doing so, she, through accountable and lively record, shows what place poetry occupied in the lives of Americans in the past, informing us about how society dealt with poetry in the years between 1880 and 1950. At that time, the value of poetry in the life of Americans can hardly be overestimated, as they invested poems as well as the figure of the poet himself with the values, beliefs, and emotions that they experienced in various social settings.

The author holds that the national history of poetry readings in America included both personal and social examples. Americans treated it as lived experience, and ordinary people read poems aloud not only in family circles (even at the bedside of sick relatives to bring them spiritual and moral comfort), but also in public places, with reading being a social act: at school and during gatherings, the so-called 'group recitations by means of the verse speaking choir' (ibid.: 136), during worship services, camp outings, military campaigns, and various civic affairs. Rubin claims that this brought people not only aesthetic pleasure, but also emotional and spiritual comfort, as poetry has a unique capacity to 'disseminate images in brief, concentrated form,' which proved to be 'an efficacious method of ingraining shared values' of the country (ibid.: 171). A poem contributed to the feeling of cultural continuity and brought people together, creating a sense of togetherness, thus cementing social cohesion.

By supplying a range of personalized examples, Rubin demonstrates how poetry in America helped readers meet social and personal needs. Drawing a connection between the uses of literature in the country with the 'untold chronicle of emotional life in America' (ibid.: 7), she narrates the stories of *actual* readers in helping them find meaning and orientation in life through the words of a poet. These stories include that of the mourner, desperately tragic at a funeral, or the grandparent seeking to be closer to his grandchildren (ibid.: 138). Similarly, reciting poetry assisted in weakening the foreign accent of immigrants looking for acceptance in their new homeland or legitimizing the culture of minority groups when verses could represent dialects of Americans outside the white Anglo-Saxon Protestant mainstream (ibid.: 215). At the same time, Rubin holds, it is controversially remarkable that American publishers shared the common view that poetry had no commercial or market value: they claimed that, unlike prose, it would not sell well (ibid.: 80).

This is a historical perspective, of course, but what about the situation today? Fortunately, there is the large-scale *Poetry in America* national in-depth survey of people's attitudes toward and experiences with poetry, conducted by the National Opinion Research Center (NORC) at the University of Chicago, on behalf of The Poetry Foundation, and it gives a rather all-embracing picture of the present-day situation. The survey among more than 1,000 adult readers with varying levels of interest in poetry reports that '[p]eople remember poems for a variety of reasons but many mention poetry's ability to touch their lives as one reason why a particular poem has stayed with them' (Schwartz et al. 2006: VI).

Today, according to a past US Poet Laureate Tracy K. Smith, who teaches at Princeton University, poetry can be viewed as a counterbalance to the widely popular social media, especially in moments when its power may be uplifting. 'In my teaching of undergraduates,' she claims, 'I see them turning to the art form in their attempts to grapple with questions related to forced migration, shifting gender norms, the environment, mental illness and technology— along with old standbys of love, loss and the changing of the seasons' (Charles 2018).

But, you may ask, what is the current situation in the world in general? Book production has never been so high as nowadays, and about one-third of all new titles produced is 'fiction,' so leans toward—or simply *is*—literature. But within this segment, what is the share of poetry? Most people will think that this is minimal, and that the bulk of published literature consists of stories and novels. Volumes of poetry represent only a minor percentage of the book market. But to conclude from there that poetry is a marginal phenomenon in the lives of most people is jumping to conclusions. And to unjustified conclusions—which can be refuted by evidence.

Statistics from UK book sales monitor Nielsen BookScan shows that poetry sales keep growing in the country by more than 10 percent a year (Ferguson 2019), and its audience is changing. Thus in 2018, two-thirds of poetry buyers were people younger than thirty-four and 41 percent were aged thirteen to twenty-two, with teenage girls and young women identified as the biggest consumers. The reasons, we believe, could be linked to the emotional power of poetry to alleviate predicaments, social in particular. According to Susannah Herbert, director of the Forward Arts Foundation, which runs the Forward prizes for poetry and National Poetry Day, '[a]t these moments of national crisis, the words that spread and the words that were heard were not the words of politicians, they were the words of poets ... Almost everything a politician says is incredibly forgettable. There is a hunger out there for more nuanced and memorable forms of language' (ibid.).

Similarly, van der Starre (2021), in a Dutch replication study based on Schwartz et al. (2006), which we mentioned earlier, confirmed the previous observation that printed poetry has little impact in the population at large. Nevertheless, poetry is present in 97 percent of people's lives—but occasionally only and in non-book form. Generally, women have slightly more frequent encounters with poetry than men, and younger people more than older ones. At the same time, poetry is valued highly: on a scale from 1 through 10 people on average rated it as 6.4, with more than half of the participants valuing it with a score higher than 7.

In a nutshell, adults in the Netherlands experience poetry in an *oral*, *collective*, and *social* form outside the traditional book—think again of Benigni's reading in the square in Florence. Thus poetry is a multimedia genre that most often is experienced on social media (64 percent) and internet websites (57 percent). Also, 35 percent of Dutch adults actively search for poetry online, while 30 percent read poetry books they bought for themselves. Reading a poetry book which someone else gave you as a present happens more often (40 percent), and this shows that even the solitary reading of a poetry book has a social aspect to it.

On nearly all those occasions poetic texts are appropriated for diverse aims and needs. But essential in all these uses is—not surprisingly—an *emotional* component: the texts are used to move others, who wish to be touched affectively by them. It is the thrill of this sensation, of being drawn in by words that is sought, met, confronted, and surrendered to. Poetry derives *meaning and sense*, in this process of spontaneous electrifying fulfilment where people undergo its power. It is, so to say, a mini-*epiphany*, a revelation of things hitherto vaguely sensed but now clarified emotionally, to speak in terms of Chapter 5.

Consolation

One of the areas where the power of poetry becomes quite visible is that of consolation. This chapter has already pointed out the adversities of life. What becomes clear if one looks at the history of world literature, is how much great works from the past deal with suffering, with loss, abandonment, injustice, pain, or mourning. A few titles may be enough of a reminder that literature often exists by the grace of suffering. Think, for instance, of Aphra Behn's *Oroonoko*, of Emily Brontë's *Wuthering Heights*, of Charles Dickens's *Hard Times*, of *The Diary of Anne Frank*, of Victor Hugo's *Les Misérables*, of works by Françoise Sagan and George Sand, of Dostoevsky's *Humiliated and Insulted*, of Simone De Beauvoir's *The Woman Destroyed*, of Leo Tolstoy's *The Death of Ivan Ilyich*, of Harriet Beecher Stowe's *Uncle Tom's Cabin*, of Lu Xun's *A Madman's Diary*, of Gabriel García Marquez's *One Hundred Years of Solitude*, or of Svetlana Alexievich's (2015 Nobel Prize winner) *War Does Not Have a Woman's Face*. All these works excel in their depiction of hardships and misfortune as well as the concomitant distress and pain that humans suffered.

But there are also works in which suffering is mitigated or soothed. One of the most famous, and perhaps also most moving passages of this kind, is in the final chapter of Homer's *Iliad*—yes, the same Homer as the one in Keats's poem that we read in Chapter 5. The *Iliad* is the story of the last weeks of the Trojan war, in which the major Greeks' hero, Achilles, declines to fight. While he is sulking, his dearest friend, Patroclus, ends up being slain by Hector, the son of the Trojan king. This so enrages Achilles that he plunges himself in the melée again, and (with the help of the goddess Athena) kills Hector in a dramatic duel. Achilles's fury is so great that he laces Hector's corpse behind his chariot and on each of the following nine days drags it around Patroclus's funeral bier. But the gods decide that Hector deserves a burial according to the rites of his people. And so Hermes, the divine Messenger, sends old Priam, Hector's father and King of Troy, into the Greek camp, where he meets with Achilles, imploring him to render him the (heavily mutilated) body of his son, to bury it. His plea is not without danger, in view of the fiery temperament of Achilles that we have witnessed in previous parts of the story.

When he enters Achilles's tent, Priam falls to his knees and performs the supplication ritual of *hiketeia*, used in situations of extreme need: the supplicant was to kneel in front of his benefactor, Achilles in this case, grasp his right hand, clasp both his knees and beg—thus acknowledging his complete dependence. The ritual was steeped deeply in Greek religion, and the benefactor was required to respect the sanctity of the request. And then some magic intrudes: Achilles, the heroic slayer, stands dumbfounded by the old man and his courage to confront him in his own tent—how did he break through the sentry?

> All gaze, all wonder: thus Achilles gazed:
> Thus stood the attendants stupid with surprise:
> All mute, yet seem'd to question with their eyes:
> Each look'd on other, none the silence broke...

Until Priam implores Achilles to think of his own (deceased) father, whom he will never see again:

> Till thus at last the kingly suppliant spoke:
> 'Ah think, thou favour'd of the powers divine!
> Think of thy father's age, and pity mine!
> In me that father's reverend image trace,
> Those silver hairs, that venerable face;
> His trembling limbs, his helpless person, see!
> In all my equal, but in misery!'

And Achilles is moved, so then the two are united, bound together in their grief. In Alexander Pope's (1715–20) translation:

> Now each by turns indulged the gush of woe;
> And now the mingled tides together flow:
> This low on earth, that gently bending o'er;
> A father one, and one a son deplore.

Achilles is moved to the bone, by the memory not only of his friend Patroclus, but now also by that of his own father, and relents: he restores Hector's body to his father.

The scene gives us a deep insight in what the Greeks called *eleos*, what we would call pity. This emotion played a central role in their literature indeed. Aristotle, in his *Poetics* (about 335 BCE) sees as one of the major effects of literature a purification (also clarification) of emotions, for which he invents the term *catharsis*, the result of pity and fear, of *eleos* and *phobos*: in seeing a good man/woman suffer for reasons beyond their own will, spectators will experience pity and fear, which will at the same time purify and enlighten them concerning their own emotions.

In Homer's poem, we fear that Achilles might enrage and kill Priam or send him back empty-handed. But then we are shown his pity. In his *Rhetoric*, Aristotle delves deeper into the psychology of pity. It is, he writes, 'a kind of pain excited by the sight of something evil, deadly or painful, which befalls one who does not deserve it; an evil which one might expect to come upon himself or one of his friends, and when it seems near' (Book II, 8, 2, 1385b2). This is the kind of feeling the reader of Homer's poem experiences, and this will cause *catharsis*, a purification. Poetry thus has the power to change our emotional makeup.

The poem shows us yet another mechanism of pity: when Achilles reenters his tent (after having placed Hector's body on a bier which is lifted on to the wagon), he invites old Priam to a meal of bread and roasted meat. Together they eat in silence, each immersed in his own sadness. Here we may think of the widespread habit in many cultures to commemorate the dead with a common meal. Eating together means staying alive together. All these meanings (danger, pride, humiliation, pity, and mourning) are woven together in Homer's text and vivify the emotional experience of the reader.

This, then, is one aspect of the power of poetry: that it conjures up before our mental eye the processes of suffering and healing, leading to readers' enlightenment and emotional relief. The standard overview of such workings of literature is Jürgen Pieters's *Literature and Consolation* (2021), from which some of the following illustrations are taken.

At the same time, there is a second, more direct, form in which poetry may exert its power, namely in directly influencing the reader. In other words, readers profit directly from reading, which is a very old idea. It has been related (by the Greek historian Diodorus Siculus) that there was an inscription above the entrance of the royal chamber, where the books were stored, of the Egyptian pharaoh Ramesses II (1303–1213 BCE), which ran: ψγxhσ Iatpeion (the healing of the soul). If the information is correct, then this was the oldest known library in the world. And it served mental well-being!

Today the notion goes under a specialized name, *bibliotherapy*. There is a broad sense of the word, meaning that reading literature in general, and poetry specifically, enhances readers' creative potential and thereby also their ability to handle personal or social problems. In this sense, reading poetry contributes to the quality of life. In a narrower sense, the term refers to a real therapy, namely to support healing processes—for instance, in the case of depression, psychosis, substance abuse, post-traumatic stress disorder (PTSD), and the like.

This form, too, can boast of a venerable age. One of the first expressions is found in Boethius's *The Consolation of Philosophy*, written around the year 524 by the Roman statesman and philosopher of that name, while he was incarcerated by King Theoderic as a result of court intrigues, awaiting his execution—certainly a situation in which consolation is of vital value. The book begins as follows (in a very loose translation):

> Pleasant poems I used to write, joyful and full of life,
> But now my eyes are damp with tears, and my poems are
> Full of grief as the Muses oblige me to write down,
> Grievous lines from a cheerless, suffering man.
> But these lyrics are my companions, consoling me.

But then he will be visited by an allegorical woman, Lady Philosophy, who will teach him how to be consoled by philosophy.

Is there good evidence that poetry may indeed alleviate suffering? In case of proper medical therapy, there are indeed a number of RCT (randomized control trials) studies. We have seen this design in earlier chapters: one group of participants, the *experimental* one, receives a particular treatment or intervention while another, the *control* group, receives no such intervention. Crucial for RCT studies is that the allocation of participants to either group is done *randomly*, as in that way the chances for bias are minimized. Several such RCT studies on bibliotherapy have been carried out, e.g., for carers of young people with psychosis or for people with social anxiety disorder, depression and post-traumatic stress disorder. McNicol and Brewster (2018) summarize the results as follows: 'Meta-analyses which draw together RCT's together to pool effect size and draw more significant conclusions showed that there were statistically significant positive effects on participants in RCT's of bibliotherapy' (ibid.: 11).

Convincing as these results may be, there is also other compelling evidence for the power of poetry. We just learned that Boethius composed his book about consolation, partly written in poetic form, partly in prose, while in prison. Aptly, so to say, are programs that bring poetry into today's prisons. One such program is called *Shakespeare Behind Bars* (SBB, for short), in which convicted inmates perform Shakespeare plays inside a penitentiary. There is a book by Amy Scott-Douglass (2007), documenting the repercussions of these poetic experiences: *Shakespeare Inside: The Bard Behind Bars*. The book is literally full of testimonies demonstrating the power that the confrontation with the literary works had, in terms of self-knowledge of their own destructive tendencies. The texts drove the convicts into deep layers of self-reflection, not just intellectually, but emotionally and socially, 'live' self-reflection, so to say.

A similar project is described by Laura Bates (2013) in her book *Shakespeare Saved My Life: Ten Years in Solitary with the Bard*, literally the record of ten years of interaction with inmates in solitary confinement whom she confronted with Shakespeare. As one of the major characters testifies, after being acquainted with Macbeth, '[a]s a consequence of that, I had to ask myself what was motivating me in my deeds, and I came face-to-face with the realization that I was fake, that I was motivated by this need to impress those around me, that none of my choices were truly my own' (quoted in Pieters 2021: 113).

You do not have to read the whole book by Laura Bates, because you can get an excellent impression of what the texts by Shakespeare can do in such circumstances from a very moving (and persuasive) TED-UCLA talk, 'Shakespeare in shackles: the transformative power of literature.' You may indeed be surprised what poetry can do: Link 6.4 on the Companion Website.

Poetry and coping

In this book, we again and again refer to the notion of foregrounding, in poetry in particular, and its emotional influence on readers. Apart from emotions induced, *ostranenie* leads to a more reflective frame of mind, as testified in the research by Kuijpers (2014), corroborated in another context by Koopman (2016), who studied the role of reading literature in situations of suffering. The emotions depicted in literary texts are often of a positive kind: 'Clearly, literature of all kinds gives more weight to positive than to negative emotions, and has done so consistently for as long as words have been written' (Lindauer 2009: 84). On the other hand, as we have mentioned earlier in this chapter, from its very beginnings, at the dawn of human civilization, literature has also extensively probed the depths of human suffering with above-average frequencies. In the oldest extant literary work of humanity, the *Epic of Gilgamesh* (which we will discuss at length in Chapter 7), the hero complains bitterly of his friend's death. And it is not difficult to compose a list of major works of poetry that focus on human suffering: tragedies as a genre, whether the Ancient Greek ones or those by Shakespeare, works by Racine or Schiller, Robert Burns's 'Address to the Toothache,' T. S. Eliot's 'The Wasteland,' and Robert Frost's 'The Death of a Hired Man' are just a few examples.

Though positive emotions may generally emanate from literature, the number of works dealing with deep human suffering matches the more pleasant feelings if not in quantity then certainly in acuteness and profundity. This has been most powerfully said by the American poet Robert Frost. In a letter to the critic Louis Untermeyer dated January 1, 1906, Frost wrote: 'A poem begins as a lump in the throat, a sense of wrong, a homesickness, a lovesickness.'

Why this is so, is a paradox: why do people wallow in descriptions of misery, hardships, and distress? And, perhaps even more important: does such reading *help* in coping with suffering? And if yes, *what exactly* is there in the texts that exerts this influence on readers? Presumably, the emotions induced by such confrontations with suffering must be unpleasant. Why? So far, the paradox is unresolved, although some recent empirical work, notably by Menninghaus et al. (2017) and van Peer, Chesnokova, and Springer (2017), has begun to unravel the mystery. And do not forget the research by Kawakami et al. (2013) that we discussed in Chapter 2.

Koopman (2011; 2016) has added to this in her study of suffering in literature, and her findings in many ways corroborate Shklovsky's theory we referred to in Chapter 4. What she found was that readers say they are first and foremost looking for 'meta-emotions': the need for feeling, enjoying the feel of emotions while reading. Like Kuijpers (2014), Koopman (2016) explains this effect through reflection-triggering that foregrounding apparently provides. In having readers confront three different versions of the same story, she found that 'those readers who had read the most original text (containing most foregrounding) had the highest empathic understanding [of suffering] afterwards. This effect was upheld when controlling for personal factors like trait empathy' (ibid.: 239–40). What does this mean, 'trait empathy'? One could presume that it is precisely readers who themselves are already strongly inclined toward feelings of solidarity (with someone suffering) who would experience the strongest feelings of *empathy*. They would therefore be less influenced by the concrete *form* of language. But this was not the case: 'trait empathy' refers to the personality characteristic that distinguishes people's empathic inclinations. This personality trait did *not* make a difference: it was the *language* that did. So what is perhaps most striking in Koopman's findings is the fact that, as with Miall and Kuiken (1994a) and Kuijpers (2014), the formal makeup of the language plays a dominant role.

As the superior empathic effects caused by foregrounding registered in Koopman's (ibid.) research occurred after reading a mere 1,500 words within the context of an experimental study, we could hypothesize that the same can happen with poetry as a shorter form—a claim which definitely requires empirical verification. What is clear, though, is that literature is able to call forth strong feelings of empathy through its formal makeup, and this feeling, we believe, has the power of affecting our emotions.

Earlier in this chapter we spoke of circumstances in life when things go utterly wrong and one needs support to cope with the trouble. How a poet comes to terms with his family's tragic past and how writing poetry helps him grapple with the immense trauma of genocide can be read in Peter Balakian's poetry books *June-Tree* and *Ozone Journal.*

Of course, out of all hardships, war occupies an extreme position. And out of all kinds of literature, it is poetry that has a unique power to alleviate suffering in war conditions. The authors of war poems are numerous: just think of Siegfried Sassoon, Wilfred Owen, Rupert Brooke, and other British poets in the trenches during the First World War. In what follows we will look at one example of such poem from a more recent period, the one your families might remember—the Second World War.

We invite you to look at the video clip (which currently has more than 2 million views), promoting a war game on the internet and listen to the voice-over. The game is called 'World of Warships' (WoWS or World of Ships); some of you may know it. It is a free online game from Wargaming, in which you can take part in epic naval battles, involving legendary warships from the first half of the twentieth century. Listen to the voice-over of the video because we are going to deal with it extensively in a moment. Although the ships and airplanes you see in this video are American and Japanese, the voice-over is in Russian. Listen to one particular word that will turn up again and again. It is *zhdi*, the Russian word for 'wait!' Listen how often it is repeated: Link 6.5 on the Companion Website.

So how many times did you hear it? And do you have any idea what the voice was talking about? Maybe your idea is that it has to do with tactics or skills in using naval weapons. But no, what you hear in the voice-over is—you might not expect it—a poem! It is the famous 'Wait for Me,' written in 1941 by a then–war correspondent Konstantin Simonov. Here is its (loose) English translation:

Wait for me, and I'll come back.
Just wait for me very much.
Wait, when sorrow is brought
By yellow rains,
Wait, in the snowstorm,
Wait, in heat,
Wait, when they don't wait for others,
Having forgotten them yesterday.
Wait, where there are no letters
From far-away places,
Wait, when others, who are waiting together with you,
Get bored (get enough of it).

Wait for me, and I'll come back,
Do not wish well
To those who know too well
That it's time to forget.
Let my son and my mother believe
That I no longer exist.
Let my friends get tired of waiting
And sit by the fire,
Drinking bitter wine
In memory of my soul …
Wait. And together with them
Don't hurry to drink.

Wait for me, and I'll come back,
All the deaths to spite.
Let all those who were not waiting for me
Say: 'He just was lucky'.
They won't understand, those who were not waiting,
How, in the heat of the battle,
With your waiting
You have saved me.
How I survived, only you and I
Will know, —
It's just that you knew how to wait,
Like nobody else.[2]

The poem, which is written from the first-person author's perspective, is addressed to the stunningly beautiful Valentina Serova, a famous Russian actress Simonov would marry in 1943. It still remains one of the most popular war verses in a country that lost around 20 million of its population in the war, a poem many people can still recite from memory. It reputably gave hope to soldiers whose only faith at the terrible time was the thought of a woman waiting for them at home. My grandmother told me stories of how my grandfather and his friends had been copying the text by hand on scraps of paper they could find in trenches and read it at the front—both privately and to each other. He said it had kept them alive.

As Merridale (2005: 271) points out, soldiers knew the text by heart, carried a locket with a picture of their wives or girlfriends in it, with a copy of 'Wait for Me' wrapped around (ibid.: 168) or simply 'kept a copy of [the] ... poem ... folded against their hearts. The veterans explain that they did this for good luck' as the poem

> with its recurrent promise, 'Wait for me, and I'll come back,' offered a protective totem, a sort of individual spell. The soldier who sang the words— for they were quickly set to music—was thinking of his own survival, for, as the poem concludes, 'Only you and I will know/how I survived./It's just that you knew how to wait/as no other person'.
>
> (ibid.: 272)

But how did the poem become that popular and that powerful? What is there in it that gives it its attraction? A good deal of the poem's magnetism hinges on parallelism. Remember that parallelism is common in prayers, which are thus remembered by people who pronounce them, and repeated again and again—to soothe some moral pain in particular. This is exactly what Simonov does in his poem. It indeed sounds like a spell or a charm, when the author addresses his beloved woman with the only monosyllabic plea: *zhdi* (wait), in the poem's opening line Жди меня, и я вернусь. This is the Russian word we encouraged you to listen to at the beginning of this section.

Structurally, the text is divided into three stanzas, and each of them opens exactly with the same line: 'Wait for me, and I'll come back.' More than that, out of thirty-six lines in the poem, ten start with the same word you already know, *zhdi* (which, in various grammatical forms, is used in the text as many as seventeen times). In Chapter 3, discussing parallelism, we have already seen how this device, known as anaphora, works, but the same game is played on final elements—a literary device called *epiphora*. So the monotonous mantra-like rhythm of the poem is enhanced by echoing of *zhdi* in an anaphoric position with the epiphoric one at the end of line 2, as well as with the second syllable of *dozhdi* (rains). The effect is strengthened by multiple usage of nouns, verbs, and participles with the same root, including *ne zhdut* (do not wait), *zhdyot* (is waiting), *zhdat'* (to wait), *ne zhdal* (did not wait), *ne zhdavshim* (those who did not wait), and *ozhidaniyem* (by waiting).

Semantically, the poem is built on a striking emotional contrast: the lyrical hero implores his beloved woman to wait for him (and holds the strong belief that she will) while others (including his friends, his son and even his mother) will accept the idea that he is dead, and that waiting longer makes no sense. Only her waiting, he says, can save his life, as he will thus know that the world beyond the sufferings of war exists, or at least *will* exist when he comes back home 'all the deaths to spite' (the phrase that has become aphoristic after the poem was published), so he has something to live for. This opposition between two worlds—the one in which she is waiting for him, and the other one where they are not—is intensified by extensive usage of negative particles, prefixes, and pronouns: *ne/ne-*, *net*, *nikto* (nobody)—with the hope that with her waiting she will save the soldier.

The evidence for the power of poetry?

Now that we have extensively talked about the power of poetry, we wish to know whether there is such power at all. There is some research that may cast light on the effects of reading stories and novels. The problem with much research is that different studies may throw up different results. The solution to this problem is a *meta-analysis*, a statistical method that allows you to collect the various studies under consideration and then draw a conclusion about what they reveal in general. Such a meta-analysis was undertaken by Mumper and Gerrig (2017). What they wanted to know was whether there is any relationship between lifelong leisure reading of fiction, on the one hand, and, on the other hand, empathy and 'theory-of-mind' (basically understanding others). The conclusion was that there is a small, but significant effect for reading fiction—but not for reading non-fiction. The authors remark that although the effect is small, it is important because of 'the potential interpersonal and societal benefits of greater empathy and theory of mind' (ibid.: 118). So literature does have power in our lives.

The problem here is that this research examined the effects of narratives, not poetry. So is there any real *evidence* to our earlier assumption that poetry, with its highly emotional makeup, will affect people's lives? Lüdtke, Meyer-Sickendieck, and Jacobs (2014) hold that poetry 'is predisposed to induce a variety of different kinds of affective responses and feelings' (ibid.: 363) and put forward '*the mood empathy hypothesis*, according to which poems expressing moods of persons, situations, or objects should engage readers to mentally simulate and affectively resonate with the depicted state of affairs' (ibid.).

The authors start from Jacobs's (2015a; 2015b) neurocognitive poetics model of literary reading (short NCPM) that outlines a dual route for literary text processing: a *fast* route handling text elements that belong to the 'background'—basically what the text is about, and a *slow* route for processing the 'foregrounded' elements—basically what falls outside entrenched ideas, expectations, and everyday language. The fast route is sort of automatic: you recognize words and sentence structures, you pinpoint the kind of situation that is being evoked, so that you form a mental picture of what is described in the text. The slow route, by contrast, goes beyond these automatic processes and makes you pay extra attention to features that strike you, to possible causes or outcomes that are not mentioned, to a pattern or a design that you noted. The model claims that all literary texts elicit two kinds of feelings: *aesthetic* and *nonaesthetic* as well as their underlying neuronal correlates as a function of their *foregrounding* and *backgrounding* features. The fast route facilitates emotional involvement (mood empathy or induced mood) while the slow route promotes aesthetic evaluation (aesthetic liking). Thus Lüdtke, Meyer-Sickendieck, and Jacobs (ibid.: 365) claim that reading poetry causes not only aesthetic emotions associated with the appreciation of poetic features, but also other kinds of emotional involvement like empathy, special moods or sadness. They identify different predictors for the two processes: familiarity and situational embedding as the main factors mediating mood empathy, and aesthetic liking as best predicted from foregrounding features (like style and form). Lüdtke, Meyer-Sickendieck, and Jacobs (ibid.) report evidence that 'mood poetry' induces the described mood (or associated ones) in the reader, and that readers of such texts experience the depicted mood itself—a process similar to empathy, *Einfühlung* or 'feeling in.' These findings thus very well explain the power of Simonov's poem, where the repeated line 'Wait for me, and I'll come back' may induce the positive feeling of belief: the beloved woman *is waiting* for the person reading or reciting the poem, so he is sure to survive.

We started this chapter with a personal remembrance, how the *Divina Commedia* by Dante is a work of eminent complexity and balance, and how it may deeply affect people. And I was not the only one. Consider the fate of Joseph Luzzi, an American professor of Italian literature. On a cold November morning, within one hour his life was changed. From a happily married young man whose wife was eight and a half months pregnant, he lost her in a gruesome car accident. Fate indeed it was, and a terrible one: within minutes he became a widower and a first-time father: doctors were able to save the baby, but not his beloved wife. Imagine what you would do in such a situation, what you would feel.

His book, *In a Dark Wood*, recalls the opening lines that we quoted at the beginning of this chapter: *una selva oscura* (a dark forest). Indeed, the horrible grief he is going through is compared to the feeling of total bereavement, total loneliness, and the colossal affliction is tantamount to what Dante is experiencing, lost in a hostile place he does not recognize, threatened by wild animals, not knowing what is going to happen to him. In Luzzi's own words, 'Katherine's death would bring with it boundless chaos and flux, but there was one constant throughout the entire aftermath. My reading of Dante had always been deep and personal, but when I found myself in the dark wood, his words became a matter of life and death' (Luzzi 2015: 287). And Joseph is lost because the right pathway has been lost: *la diritta via era smarrita* (the straight path was lost). Mind the powerful rhyme in this phrase! It is precisely in the poetry by Dante that Luzzi finds comfort and the strength to work on his grief and forge a new life for himself, 'all ordered by unfaltering eleven-syllable lines in rhyming tercets' (ibid.: 15) while the memory of his deceased wife keeps haunting him, reminding him of the heart-wrenching words spoken by Francesca di Rimini in Canto 5:

Nessun maggior dolore
(There is no greater sorrow)
Che ricordarsi del tempo felice
(Than to be mindful of the happy time)
Nella miseria.
(In misery.)

(lines 104–6)

He then takes to reading the text aloud to himself, and 'the poem's soothing sounds one of the few things that could calm [him]' (ibid.: 37). And he means this literally: part of him was 'sounding Dante's tercets over and over, as if they were a charm to ward off evil spirits' (ibid.: 45). So it is not so much the content of the story that offers him consolation as the form, the structure, the makeup. The review in the *New York Journal of Books* (on the back cover of the book) refers to 'the luminous power of literature to transform sorrow's exile into a kind of blessing.' Do we need to say more about the power of poetry?

Core issues

- Poetic texts are appropriated for diverse aims and needs, and consolation is one of them.

- Poetry is a powerful source of coping, of mitigating or soothing suffering.

- Reading poetry enhances readers' creative potential as well as their ability to handle personal or social problems.

- Foregrounding in literature causes strong empathic effects.

- Meta-analysis in evidence-based research allows you to collect several studies addressing the same question and draw a conclusion about what they reveal in general.

Further reading

Kennedy, D. (2012), *The Waldorf Book of Poetry*. Viroqua: Living Arts Books.
Mazza, N. (2016), *Poetry Therapy: Theory and Practice*. London: Routledge.
McNicol, S. and L. Brewster (2018), *Bibliotherapy*. London: Facet Publishing.
Scott, G. L. (2018), *Aristotle on Dramatic Musical Composition. The Real Role of Literature, Catharsis, Music and Dance in the* Poetics. New York: ExistencePS Press.
Sieghart, W. (2017), *The Poetry Pharmacy: Tried-and-True Prescriptions for the Heart, Mind and Soul*. London: Particular Books.
Stanley, J. (1999), *Reading to Heal: How to Use Bibliotherapy to Improve Your Life*. Boston: Element Books.
Took, J. (2020), *Why Dante Matters. An Intelligent Person's Guide*. London: Bloomsbury Continuum.
Veprinska, A. (2021), *Empathy in Contemporary Poetry after Crisis*. London: Palgrave MacMillan.

7

Poetry Is Persistence

Ars longa, vita brevis

Keywords

aphorism

cuneiform

epic

emotion theory

oral text

theme

metamorphosis

Have you noticed the motto under the title of this chapter? It is a (famous) saying, meaning, literally, 'art is long—life is short.' It is a Latin translation of an original Greek verse, namely, from the *Aphorisms* by the ancient physician Hippocrates (460–370 BCE), one of the greatest figures in the history of medicine, often even referred to as the 'Father of Medicine.' But beware: Latin *ars* is indeed what we nowadays call *art*; however, Hippocrates used the Greek word τέχνη (*tékhnē*), meaning 'technique'—that is where our word comes from. So basically he says that it takes a long time to learn one's craft (medicine, in his case), and one has little time, since life is short. The Latin translation emphasizes not just the craft, but also the creative and aesthetic side of it. It now refers specifically to sculpture, painting, music and to literature. We will all die and be forgotten, but art will outlive us all: life is short, art is long. This goes for poetry no less. You have already noticed that, for in previous chapters we spoke of Homer's *Iliad*, written in the eighth century BCE, and we still treasure it and keep coming back to the text. Art and poetry speak to us over the edge of time. The great works of art are timeless, you could say.

The oldest poem in the world

If we wish to build a psychopoetics as a general understanding of the workings of poetry, it is imperative to investigate the issue outside a Western context. Only in that way can we be certain that the theory has a universal quality. So, in order to illuminate poetry's persistence, we are bound to look at literary techniques used in pre-Western literature.

An example of this is the oldest poem we have, the *Epic of Gilgamesh*, written on clay tablets in *cuneiform* script in ancient Mesopotamia in Sumerian language (not related to any known tongues), but soon taken over by other people, especially Akkadians, who spoke a Semitic language. To say that it is a 'poem' is a bit misleading, for it is in fact a conglomerate of stories that sprung up over a very long time, all related in some way to the protagonist, King Gilgamesh. You may see what the 'text' looks like in Figure 15.

FIGURE 15 *The Deluge tablet of the* Epic of Gilgamesh *in Akkadian* © *British Museum. Reproduced with the permission of the British Museum.*

There are dozens of such tablets (in fact thousands of fragments), from which scholars have collated the epic. It is an *epic* indeed, relating the heroic deeds (but also the emotions) of its main character in poetic form. So what is it about?

Gilgamesh, the protagonist, is named as one of the first kings of Uruk, one of the oldest cities in Mesopotamia, the cradle of civilization. His name is mentioned in a list of Gods from 2600 BCE, so that we are perhaps dealing with a deified historical figure from the early third millennium BCE.

Heroic deeds attributed to him are praised in a cycle of poems. The oldest texts date back to somewhere around 2100 BCE, but they do not present a unified plot. Instead, we have several strands of narratives, centering around different episodes in the life of the hero. The version with the most comprehensive story dates from the time of the first Babylonian empire (from around 1800 BCE). Another millennium later a whole range of clay tablets discovered in the library of King Ashurbanipal (seventh century BCE) has given us the most complete insight in the structure of the poem. All in all, we can say that we are dealing here with the oldest extant literary work of humanity.

The plot consists of two parts, the first of which is basically the story of Gilgamesh and Enkidu, a wild man who becomes civilized and develops into Gilgamesh's friend. Because of a religious infringement, the gods decide to put Enkidu to death. Gilgamesh is devastated by the loss of his friend, and inconsolable. To acquire the secret of eternal life, Gilgamesh then undertakes long and dangerous travels in this effort. This is the second part of the epic, in which the confrontation with the immortal man Utnapishtim teaches him that eternal life is in the hands of the gods, and that humans have to accept their mortality. So Gilgamesh also dies, but his fame lives on after his death. Some parts of the plot may reverberate with you, especially an episode about a worldwide deluge, similar to the biblical story of the flood, in which Noah resembles the figure of Utnapishtim in the Sumerian epic. In fact, the picture of the tablet in Figure 15 contains this very story, and it predates the well-known biblical plot.

A considerable part of the epic focuses on the emotions that Gilgamesh goes through after the death of Enkidu. We become witness to two universal ones: mourning (for a beloved person) and fear (of death). We surely have no difficulty recognizing (and sharing) them. But what do we mean by 'emotions'?

We have used this word so often already in previous chapters, but what are they in fact? We follow the groundbreaking insights of Frijda (1986) here: emotions are fine-tuned evaluation mechanisms with both bodily and mental aspects (and being partly codified culturally). But evaluation of what? Basically of events and their repercussions for a person's plans and concerns. The importance of the concerns in question is a yardstick for the strength of the emotion. If the events pertain to only a passing plan of little bearing on my general well-being, the emotion will be of fleeting significance—it will pass and not occupy me either deeply or long. But such are not the emotions in *Gilgamesh*. The relevance of the events here is of vital significance to him. His life-plans involved an uninterrupted continuation of his friendship with Enkidu, whose untimely death thwarted these plans and cruelly destroyed his present concerns. *Gilgamesh* is thus a meditation on some fundamental issues of human existence.

We know relatively little about how the poem functioned in these ancient societies. Was it meant only for the elite? For the court? Was it read aloud to (illiterate) audiences? Was it based on the oral version that circulated in society through professional singers? All this we do not know. As Charpin, one of the leading Assyriologists, states, '[o]ddly, the problem of readers has almost never been considered, though I find it crucial' (2010: 211).

The importance of this text for our purposes lies in two of its central aspects: its *thematic material* and its *poetic form*. It is truly astonishing that at the dawn of human civilization this text opens up themes (a notion we will discuss instantly) that we recognize as central to our present lives as well: friendship and heroism, glorious deeds and tragic death, the search for immortality and the bitter way of all flesh. None of these concerns has lost any of their immediacy in human life. *Ars longa, vita brevis* indeed.

These topics are presented and evoked in a poetic *form* that is at once elaborate and persistent. The verse is metrical, generally *trochaic*, with four stresses alternated with 1–3 unstressed syllables. Furthermore, rhyme and alliteration may be used to highlight specific aspect. Syntactically, parallelism is abundant, sometimes interwoven with chiasmus, and we will discuss it in the next section of this chapter.

Here is a part of the dialogue between Gilgamesh and Siduri, the female wine maker, which in the standard translation of Campbell Thompson (2017) runs as below. You will notice that in some places there is a hiatus in the text, where the tablet has been damaged and is illegible.

Column II.
There in the Gates (?) of the mountains (?); with me enduring all hardships,
Enkidu, (he was) my comrade—the lions we slaughter'd (together),
(Aye), enduring all hardships—and him his fate hath o'ertaken.
(So) did I mourn him six days, (yea), a se'nnight, until unto burial
I could consign (?) him .... (then) did I fear .....
Death did I dread, that I range o'er the desert]: the hap of my comrade
[Lay on me heavy(?)—O 'tis a long road that I range o'er] the desert!
Enkidu, (yea), [of my comrade the hap lay heavy (?) upon me]—
['Tis a long road] that I range o'er the desert—O, how to be silent],
(Aye, or) how to give voice? [(For) the comrade I ha' (so) lovéd]
Like to the dust [hath become]; O Enkidu, (he was) my comrade,
He whom I loved hath become alike the dust]—[I,] shall I not, also,
Lay me down [like him], throughout all eternity [never returning]?'

Here may be interpolated, for convenience, the Old Babylonian Version of this episode in the Berlin tablet of 2000 B.C. Column II, 1, III, 14:

<u>Column II.</u>
'He who enduréd all hardships with me, whom I lovéd dearly,
Enkidu,—he who enduréd all hardships with me (is now perish'd),
Gone to the common lot of mankind! (And) I have bewail'd him
Day and night long: (and) unto the tomb I have not consign'd him.
(O but) my friend cometh not (?) to my call—six days, (yea), a se'nnight
He like a worm hath lain on his face—(and) I for this reason
Find no life, (but must needs) roam the desert like to a hunter,
(Wherefore), O Wine-maker, now that (at last) I look on thy visage,
Death which I dread I will see not!'

This passage is, in fact, a lament that largely rests on repetition (the name of Enkidu, 'my comrade,' 'enduring all hardships,' etc.). Gilgamesh is in utter grief caused by the death of his friend, as 'the lions [they] slaughter'd (together)/ … enduring all hardships.' He is mourning his companion for six days and seven nights, in hope of his return to life, until he finally realizes the futility of hope and lets Enkidu be buried. Fearful of death, Gilgamesh shares with Siduri his deep concern: his dearest friend was overtaken by the fate that nobody can escape and 'hath become alike the dust.' So is it, Gilgamesh worries, what will happen to him as well? '[S]hall I not, also,/Lay me down [like him], throughout all eternity [never returning]?' And it is these emotions of grief, of fear, of friendship, of longing for immortality that link this text to our modern concerns.

Is it necessary to speak Sumerian?

As you noticed, the text of the *Epic* is highly foregrounded, full of parallelism in particular. But in psychopoetics, we are not content with textual analysis alone. We also seek evidence-based support for the effects of these stylistic observations. In particular, we are interested in the question whether this profusion of parallelism is connected to the meaning, whether, in other words, this extra structure generates extra meaning. From earlier chapters, you are already familiar with the methodology that can help us verify or refute the hypothesis.

An experiment involving forty-five participants (BA and MA, almost exclusively female) was conducted in a conventional academic setting. The research material consisted of an abundantly parallelistic fragment from the

Epic of Gilgamesh, in Sumerian, a language the respondents were certainly not familiar with. And we intentionally did not supply any background information on the poem. So here is the passage with the English translation by its side (from Jones 1998–1999):

Ud ri a ud su du ri a	In those days, in those distant days,
Gig ri a gig bad du ri a	In those nights, in those far-off nights,
Mu ri a mu su du ri a	In those years, in those distant years.

Every line in this stanza ends epiphorically with 'du ri a,' and the same 'ri a' constitutes the second and the third syllables of every verse, so there is parallelism inside the line as well as between the lines. In the English translation, this is rendered through 'in those' elements coupled with the internal semantic repetition of 'days,' 'nights,' and 'years.'

In Chapter 3, we have already introduced you to the method of manipulation in evidence-based research. Here we apply the same procedure: to check whether readers would be able to 'trap' any superimposed meaning of parallelism from the (incomprehensible) text, we removed the parallelism from it. Please note that, unlike in the manipulation we ran with E. E. Cummings's 'Anyone Lived in a Pretty How Town,' the rhythm of *Gilgamesh* was difficult to change, as the words were all monosyllables. Here is the altered version:

Ud di a ad ma du ri a
Gig ru u gig bad da gi u
Mu gu i mi su bu ma i.

The repetitive 'du ri a' is no longer there, and the internally repetitive 'ri a' is gone as well.

The sample of participants was split in two: Group 1 ($N = 22$) read the stanza in the original, and Group 2 ($N = 23$) read the manipulated version. Both groups evaluated the poem's beauty, strikingness, and importance, on a 7-point Likert scale. Additionally, they assessed (on the same scale) whether the text is an interesting one to discuss in class, whether they would recommend this poem to a good friend, whether they considered it to be a good example of high-quality literature and whether it made them see things in a new light. The participants also answered questions about the message of the text. On top of that, we asked them to indicate its possible source, saying whether they thought the text was from a warning, a hymn, an advertisement, an instruction manual, a spell, a traffic sign, a newspaper, a recipe, a novel, or a song.

Results indicate that respondents of both groups did not understand what the poem was about, which was quite predictable in view of the language of the text. Yet in their comments about a half of participants clearly attributed religious meaning to it as they said that

- '[i]t seems to be a religious verse, possibly related to a historical event,'

- 'I have a feeling it is used in some kind of ritual, or religious ceremony,' and

- '[i]t reminds me some kind of a spell or prayer. It sounds divine or supernatural.'

The task of attributing meaning appeared to be harder for the participants of the group that read the manipulated version of the text, where numerous comments characterized the verse as

- '[s]omething without a meaning,

- Just a flow of poet's mind,'

- a text '[a]bout nothing, frankly speaking,'

- '[j]ust a combination of letters,'

- or even the one that 'looks too similar to Tolkien's made up languages.'

Thus we may deduce that the structure of the poem, abundant parallelism in particular, does carry a superimposed sense of its own, so that associations are born and (partly meaningful) conclusions drawn from it.

The quantitative data indicated that implicit religious coloring was attributed to the otherwise unintelligible text. As can be seen in Figure 16, more than

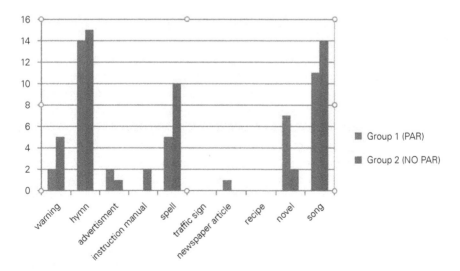

FIGURE 16 *Responses to the question 'What do you think the text is from?'*

half of the participants in both groups indicated that the text could be part of a hymn, of a song (religious in particular) or of a spell.

Please note that in this case removal of parallelism did not affect the general pattern of the reactions: the same three variables ('hymn,' 'spell,' and 'song') score the highest, though participants in Group 2 were more inclined than those in Group 1 to relate the text to a spell (43 percent vs. 23 percent) or to a song (60 percent vs. 50 percent). We may attribute this to the repetitive monosyllabic nature of the text rhythm, which remained unchanged in the manipulated version and possibly influenced appreciation. In fact, one of the participants mentioned that the poem could be '[a]bout people doing the same thing'—a clear indication of monotony felt.

Additionally, results indicate that average appreciation of the poem was lower than the middle on a scale from 1 to 7, and removal of parallelism did not have an influence. The group that read the manipulated version did evaluate the text as less beautiful (3.2 against 3.8), less striking (2.4 against 2.9), of lower quality (2.8 against 3.1), communicating less important things (2.7 against 3.5) and less making people see things in a new light (1.6 against 2.2), but these differences were not statistically significant. In any case, the results point in the same direction, namely, that evaluations are higher for the original, containing ample parallelism. The conclusion from the experiment is that there is some weak evidence that the extra structure introduced by the high degree of parallelism does seem to create some extra meaning, at least in the form of a greater coherence.

African poetry

Texts are ways to overcome 'vita brevis.' They bridge the gaps between generations: we can still read what people in the past said, thought, and felt. Many of such texts that have come down to us in a written form existed in an oral form long before. This was the case for traditional songs of the kind that we analyzed in previous chapters, for instance, 'Jock O'Hazeldean' and *fado* songs. Even the Goethe poem 'Heidenröslein' had ancestors in oral folk tradition. And the pinnacles of Western literature, like Homer's epics, existed in oral forms for hundreds of years before they got written down. So we wish to know whether in such oral manifestation, the typical poetic qualities that we have outlined so far also hold.

The study of oral poetry is necessarily dependent on some recording technique. The person who profoundly changed our whole understanding of oral culture was Milman Parry (1988), an American researcher who defended his dissertation at the Sorbonne in 1928. In it he showed how the Homeric heroic poems in their original oral form were based on formulas, fixed phrases, such as the epithets and metrical structure. As a young professor at Harvard University, he made audio recordings (then a revolutionary technology) of Serbo-Croatian singers of traditional poetry in the Balkans between 1933 and 1935. They showed how oral poets memorized their performance while adapting it to local conditions. This made Parry the founder of research in oral literature, a flourishing discipline, as publications by Ong (1982), Havelock (1988), Finnegan (1992), Rubin (1998), and others convincingly demonstrate. Parry died young—he was only thirty-three when he was killed in an accident. His assistant, Albert Lord (1912–91), continued his work in *The Singer of Tales* (1960). Their work sparked off a completely new way of looking at classic works, drawing attention to their oral nature.

Here we have to briefly clarify the notion of an 'oral text.' We are so used to written or printed texts nowadays that we hardly realize what oral texts are. We have already pointed to prayers, in Chapter 3, or poems learned by heart and then recited again and again in Chapter 6. Well, they are a prime example of what is meant by oral texts. How do they exist? Not in any material form, like written texts. They exist only in the minds of the people who 'know' them. So they are 'invisible'; they are mental phenomena, belonging to a person's memory. And just like written texts may be destroyed (for instance, by fire or water), oral texts may also get lost, because memories are fallible. The most dramatic form of loss of oral texts is when all the people who know a particular text have died. Written texts—that is one of their great advantages—may outlive their authors, but when no people are there to pass on an oral one, it is lost forever.

The volatility of oral texts had already been brought to light by Parry and Lord (1960) who discovered that in oral cultures the events of a story are not literally repeated. Parry found that when Avdo, a singer he knew, recited a long narrative poem for him, of which Parry took closely worded notes. The story was 12,323 verses long. A few years later, when Parry asked Avdo to recite the story again, it was only 8,488 verses long. Another time, he asked Avdo to recite a song by another singer, and Avdo stated that he had sung the same song as his colleague. Only: Avdo's version was three times as long!

Parry's findings were later expanded upon by Jack Goody in his book *The Domestication of the Savage Mind* (1977),[1] making similar observations among the Bagre, a tribe from Ghana in West Africa. Although the singers themselves as well as the local listeners insisted that there was only one correct version of the myth, Goody found significant differences in the length of their performances, which were sometimes as much as five times as long. And elements of the myth considered essential in a 1951 performance were omitted in a 1970 recitation. The Belgian historian and anthropologist Jan

Vansina (2006) came to exactly the same conclusion in his research in Rwanda and Burundi.

In short, the transmission of stories in oral cultures is not stable, but subject to all sorts of influences. There must have been such constant changes because oral culture depends on the laws of human memory, and these laws have become increasingly clear in recent years. In an oral culture, stories must be passed on orally; that goes without saying. Now, in this process of reproduction, significant biases arise, as we have learned from psychological research on memory. Today, no one doubts the vulnerability of much orally transmitted text (though we also know of traditions where texts were orally preserved exactly as they were, for instance, of some Australian traditions, of classical Sanskrit verse and of some oral laws). The distortion that occurs is caused by limitations of the human brain, of memory, but also by specific interests and purposes of the teller and listener. So the persistence of oral texts differs from that of written ones: it is much more 'fluid' and versatile. Nevertheless, they may exist over very long periods of time.

One such interesting poem is the *Epic of Sunjata*. It originated in the kingdom of Mali in the fourteenth century, narrating events from the thirteenth century, when Sunjata Keita founded the great Mande kingdom. That region is called the Mande region, grouping a number of languages (dialects) like Maninka, Bamanan, or Jula, all languages spoken in West-Africa, from Ivory Coast, Guinea, parts of Senegal and Gambia and Mali, and into Burkina Faso and Ghana in the East, thus comprising an enormous geographic region. Sunjata died around 1255. Passed on orally by professional singers from father to son/daughter, the text of *Sunjata* is well known and still highly important for the culture of all Mande people.

The epic tells the story of a child who is disabled and mocked for it: he is lame and cannot speak. But through his willpower he overcomes his disability and finally becomes the first king of a great empire. Generation after generation, a Malian bard, a *jali* (plural *jaliw*), sometimes also called, in French, a *griot* (or *griotte* for the female singer), passed on the poem. These singers are actually both poets and historians, recording and transmitting accounts of important events, always exclusively orally—nothing is ever written down. Until researchers from the West became interested.

Moser (1974) investigated foregrounding in *Sunjata*, using a recording made by Charles Bird in 1969 in the village of Kita, some 200 km west of the capital Bamako in the present Republic of Mali. The singer is Kele Monson Jabaté, a well-known and highly respected performer in the whole region. The recording is subsequently transcribed and a line-by-line translation is furnished. On the basis of this material, Moser distinguishes *phonological* foregrounding from *conceptual*. With the latter he means devices like metaphor, simile, imagery or symbolism. All of these are well known in poetics, but important for our considerations they also turn up in this old African epic. As to phonological foregrounding, poetic devices of parallelism (such as alliteration and assonance) occur in the *Sunjata* epic as well, with one exception: end rhyme is rare if not non-existent.

Oral poetry is basically a performance art. And we know from recordings that each performance will differ somewhat from others, depending on the audience and the inspiration of the singer—improvisation is part of oral poetry. Normally, a performance of *Sunjata* takes between four and six hours, but the one used by Moser (ibid.) only took two. The singer accompanies himself on the *ngoni*, a kind of guitar. The rhythm is a steady 4:4.[2] Seated next to him is the *namu* sayer, usually a young apprentice. The function of the *namu* sayer is to support the singer by saying 'naam' regularly (from Arabic *naam*, meaning 'yes,' 'that's right'), thus 'echoing' the story but also enhancing the rhythm of the song. The singer himself also refers to the *namu* singer a few times, calling him by his name. It should be mentioned also that traditional oral poetry of the kind analyzed by Moser has not undergone any Western influences, not even in modern times. We are dealing with a genuine indigenous tradition of West-Africa.

The bulk of Moser's work is a detailed analysis of the various kinds of parallelism in the text/performance. He begins by pointing out that Jabaté's versification is non-systematic and compares his verse to that of Walt Whitman, especially to 'Song of Myself.' But the overwhelming device to be found in this performance of *Sunjata*, he points out, is alliteration. Apparently the singer has 'unquestionable sensitivity to consonant similarity' (ibid.: 47).

Consider, as an example, the opening of the epic (as registered by Johnson 1986) with the side-by-side English translation:

Nare Magan Konate!	Nare Magan Konate!
Subaa-Mine-Subaa!	Sorcerer-Seizing-Sorcerer!
Sin-lula le soro man di de.	A man of power is hard to find.
Ani ngara naani.	And four meistersingers.
Kala Jula Sangoyi!	Kala Jula Sangoyi!
Subaa-Mine-Subaa!	Sorcerer-Seizing-Sorcerer!
A Hadama le ma.	It is of Adam that I sing.
Hadama le ma,	Of Adam.
Bani Hadama.	Ben Adam.
N'I for a mogo dolu kom	As you succeeded some,
Mogo dolu de f'i ko.	So shall you have successors!
A Hadama le ma. Hadama.	It is of Adam that I sing. Of Adam. (ibid.: 98)

More important, however, for our current purposes, is an indication of the different cases of parallelism: 'Subaa-Mine-Subaa,' 'Hadama le ma,' etc. as they are marked in the extract below:

Nare Magan Konate!
<u>Subaa-Mine-Subaa!</u>
Sin-lula le soro man di de.
<u>Ani</u> ngara na<u>ani</u>.
Kala Jula Sangoyi!
<u>Subaa-Mine-Subaa!</u>
A *Hadama le ma*.
Hadama le ma,
Bani *Hadama*.
N'i fora a **mogo dolu ko**,
Mogo dolu de f'i **ko**.
A *Hadama le ma. Hadama*.

So also in the case of this African, oral epic, foregrounding devices abound. Most work following the proposals by the Russian Formalists referred to poetry from the Western tradition, and Moser is one of the first (and few) to study foregrounding in non-Western poetry. Thus the motto with which we began the chapter holds here, too: *ars longa, vita brevis*. To the listeners, the poem illustrates the vicissitudes and frugality of life, but also the importance of values like willpower and perseverance. It makes them aware of the limits of their own lives (*vita brevis*), but of the persistence of art (*ars longa*).

As to the psychopoetics of the *Sunjata* epic, the same as what we have said about Mariza's performance in Chapter 2 applies, albeit that music plays a less important role here. Remember what we said at the end of that chapter? That Mariza's performance takes you out of your ordinary everyday habits, and plunges you into what it means to be 'mad,' to be isolated from your fellow human beings, by virtue of poetic insight. It is not very different in *Sunjata*: the hero is also an outsider. This time not mad, but severely disabled: he cannot walk, nor stand. He also cannot talk—and is mocked by the people around him because of his deficiencies. Poetry takes on issues that we usually exclude from our daily routines.

Themes that last

How persistent poetry may be can be seen in the study of *themes*. There are other terms in use also, like *motif*, *topos*, or the German word *Stoff* or *Stoffgeschichte*. In what follows, we will use the term *theme*, though it can already have two distinct meanings, which are to be separated. A first, general, meaning refers to the content of a poem, to what it is about, and this is applicable not just to narrative poems. So what is Keats's poem in Chapter 5 'about'? You could say that it is 'about' first reading Chatman's translation of Homer. But is that not a rather trivial statement? After having read the chapter, you will have to conclude that there is another 'about' in Keats's poem. We called it revelation, epiphany, an ineffable experience. This is the second meaning of *theme*: a recurrent content that makes up the true significance of the poem. Why do we still read Keats's poem? Not so much because of the actual translation by Chapman, but because of something that transcends the obvious content of the text. We read the poem because of the very special emotion: the sudden bolt of insight and its concomitant powerful experience.

Poetry is a kind of knowledge, or insight, and themes are a kind of shorthand for a particular bundle of knowledge. But it is knowledge that surmounts what is immediately given in the text. A description of a person lying in bed in a room may be the theme of a story in the first, trivial, sense, but it becomes a *literary* theme when the person wakes up in his bed to find himself to have been transformed overnight into some monstrous insect. That is indeed how the story by Kafka, *The Metamorphosis*, starts. Its title immediately betrays the *intertextual* link: it is rooted in a tradition of 2,000 years, beginning with the poem *Metamorphoses* by the Roman poet Ovid (Pūblius Ovidius Nāsō in Latin, 43 BCE–17/18 CE). It is some 12,000 verses long, and in these some 250 stories are told, in a mythical framework, all about transformations, in which humans are—for some reason or other—converted into another mode of existence, usually an animal or a plant.

Ovid's *Metamorphoses* exerted a long and deep influence on literature during 2,000 years: witness the story by Kafka, published in 1915. Many of these stories gradually became *themes*. To give one example: the poem about the love of 'Pyramus and Thisbe' (in Book IV). They are two lovers, forbidden to wed by their respective parents. Through a crack in the wall, separating their houses, they profess their love for each other and arrange a meeting, under a mulberry tree at the tomb of King Ninus. When Thisbe arrives, a lion appears. She flees, but loses her coat, which the lion tears up. Believing that Thisbe has been killed by a lion, Pyramus commits suicide by stabbing himself with his sword. When she returns to the grave and finds Pyramus dead, she also stabs herself. Their splashed blood stained the mulberry fruit, which is now forever turned the color of blood, in remembrance and in honor of their forbidden but faithful love.

The metamorphosis of the mulberry fruit is subtly announced in the beginning of the poem, when one of the Theban women asks whether she should tell the story:

Donec idem passa est, an, quae poma alba ferebat,
Ut nunc nigra ferat con tactu sanguinis arbor.
(Or how the tree that formerly had white fruit,
now bears black ones, because they were sprinkled with blood.)

And then this image is taken up at the end of the poem, in a *soliloquy* (internal monologue addressed to the character herself) by Thisbe:

Ut quos certus amor, quos hora novissima iunxit
Componi tumulo non invideatis eodem.
(While our love has united us in this hour
grant us to be buried together in the same grave.)

(Note that we will not occupy ourselves with rhyme or meter in this case. For one, meter is of a different nature altogether in Latin and Greek, but also because we are concentrating here on the thematic aspects of the poem.) There are two themes here, interwoven with each other. One is the mythical mutations of living beings: here the blood splatter of Pyramus and Thisbe on the fruits of the tree changes their color forever, so that nature will remember the purity of their devoted love. This theme of *metamorphosis* is not a very popular one nowadays. But think of Shakespeare's comedy *A Midsummer Night's Dream*, in which a bunch of amateur actors attempt to perform a play based on Ovid's poem about Pyramus and Thisbe. They are workmen, called 'mechanics,' not professional actors, so their performance is crude and clumsy, and thereby funny. But it does make use of the story of Pyramus and Thisbe. Shakespeare's play has been turned into musicals and movies innumerable times, and this shows how persistent themes may be over long stretches of time. Why was the theme so popular before the seventeenth century? The reason is not very difficult to guess: because this notion of metamorphoses was rooted in an animistic world view, which was largely shattered by the scientific revolution. At the same time recent adaptations show that the comedy—and with it, the theme—is still enjoyed by large numbers of people, albeit in an amusing, not serious, form, as with Ovid.

The other theme that persistently stays in poetry is that of forbidden love—one of the most widespread motifs around the globe. In the case of 'Pyramus and Thisbe,' it is the parents' prohibition, similar to the feud between the lovers' families in Shakespeare's *Romeo and Juliet*. But lovers may find other impediments on their way: ethnocentrism, racism, different world views or different religions. An early example of the latter is a medieval French romance in verse *Floire et Blancheflor* (*Floris and Blancheflour*), composed around 1160 by an unknown author. The two protagonists are born on the same day: he as the son of a Muslim queen, and she as the daughter of a Christian slave. The two develop a liking for each other, reason why the father sells the girl and she ends up in the harem of an emir. After countless exciting adventures, Floire finds her in the tower of the harem and manages to get to her by means of a ruse. The two are discovered, however. Instead of killing them on the spot, the emir holds a council with his advisers, who are so impressed by the love of Floire and Blancheflor that they convince the emir to spare their lives. The rest is a bit predictable: the two marry, return to Floire's homeland where he becomes the king after his father's death and converts to Christianity. In the Middle Ages, this was one of the most popular verse stories, translated at the time in nearly all European languages. But there are also echoes in the story from the tales of *Arabian Nights* (the twelfth century) and of the Indian *Jakatas* (early fifth century).

In the same way the theme of forbidden love may involve the violation of social boundaries that are accepted by the perpetrators themselves. One such powerful motif is the *Lancelot* theme. It first emerges in a long poem by Chrétien de Troyes, *Lancelot, le Chevalier de la Charrette* (*Lancelot, the Knight of the Cart*) in the twelfth century, but builds upon earlier versions that have disappeared in the mist of history. Not so, however, in the version by Chrétien, which became a blueprint and a source of inspiration for dozens of similar *Arthurian romances* (tales about a legendary British king, Arthur) in the Middle Ages and after. But if we look at contemporary interpretations of the theme, it is striking that all have wandered away from poetry into either narratives, such as T. H. White's *The Once and Future King* (1958), or dozens of novels that deal with this theme. And the theme has wandered into film, with countless variations upon Lancelot's adventures, most of the time including his secret and forbidden affair with Guinevere, King Arthur's wife. One needs to think only of titles such as *First Knight*, *King Arthur*, or *Camelot* to get a feel of the popularity of these movies. And in all of them, just like in the medieval romances, the theme of forbidden love is heavily intertwined with all sorts of adventures by Lancelot and other knights of the Round Table.

A similar theme that pops up also in the works of Chrétien is that of *Tristan and Isolde*—he mentions it, but the work has been lost. The earliest versions that we have are by Thomas of Britain, some 3,300 verses, written in 1155–60, and the twelfth-century version by Gottfried von Strassburg, considered one of the masterpieces of medieval literature. In it Tristan, nephew of king Mark of Cornwall, travels to Ireland, to fetch Iseult (the spellings vary somewhat), the future bride of the king. On the ship, however, they accidentally drink a magic love potion which makes them fall hopelessly in love. Sex occurs, and the couple undergoes many trials of their secret love before they both tragically die. So love that is forbidden, secret, or otherwise impeded is a widespread theme in poetry. Denis de Rougemont, in his book *Love in the Western World* (1983), has suggested that it is precisely such hurdles that make up the great love stories like *Romeo and Juliet* or *Orpheus and Eurydice* (another famous theme in literature and music). Without obstruction, no great love. And no great love, no poetry.

An additional theme contained in the theme of 'Tristan and Isolde' is that of the magic love potion, which we also see in *A Midsummer Night's Dream* and even in *Harry Potter and the Half-Blood Prince* when Ron Weasley is so much affected by drinking a magic substance, which makes him fall in love with Romilda Vane, that he needs an antidote.

The study of such themes reveals their extreme persistence over time, often also their distribution over wide geographic areas. We have already mentioned, in Chapter 2, the theme of madness, and referred to a wide array of literary works that dealt with it. Some themes lend themselves better to narratives, such as the theme of the *double* (sometimes also called the *Amphitryon* theme). In poetry, these are especially emotional themes that are worked on. For instance, the theme of the *Swan*, symbolizing purity, faithfulness, grace, love, and beauty, but sometimes also melancholy, as in Baudelaire's 'Le Cygne' (The Swan) or in Yeats's 'The Wild Swans at Coole.' And then there are the great musical works in which swans are central figures, such as the Swan Knight in Wagner's opera *Lohengrin* and Tchaikovsky's ballet music *Swan Lake*.

Literary scholars have done great work by developing the field of thematics, so that—if you are not familiar with some of the themes mentioned in the previous paragraphs—there are dictionaries of motifs and themes that you can have recourse to. To name only a few:

- *The Motif-Index of Folk-Literature*, often also called Thompson's Motif Index;

- Horst and Ingrid Daemmrich: *Themes and Motifs in Western Literature*;

- *Motif Index of the Thousand and One Nights*;

- *An Index of Themes and Motifs in Twelfth-Century French Arthurian Poetry*, etc.

At the same time, however, literary scholars have totally neglected the study of the psychopoetic dimension, while there are at least two very fundamental questions in this respect. The first relates to the *emergence* of particular themes. Some are age-old crystallizations of deep-seated emotions, such as fear of death, or romantic love. Others, however, turn up at particular historical moments and in specific places, from where they are suddenly disseminated. A clear example of the latter is the theme of *Don Juan* (alternatively known as Dom Juan in Spanish or Don Giovanni in Italian), a male libertine who devotes all his energies to seducing as many women as possible. It was first written as a play by a Spanish Catholic monk, Tirso de Molina, in 1630, under the title *El burlador de Sevilla* (The Trickster of Seville). It literally introduced this theme in literature and become highly popular, from Moliere's *Dom Juan* and Mozart's opera *Don Giovanni* to Byron's long poem *Don Juan* or Pushkin's *The Stone Guest*, to name only a few.

But why does this theme suddenly turn up in the seventeenth century— and not before? And why does it immediately rise to such popularity? To frame the question differently: what does the emergence and distribution of the theme tell us about human psychology—and human societies? Note, by the way, that the story is heavily foregrounded, in that it utterly deviates from courtship, even from common seduction, by its sheer quantity. Mozart pushes it even beyond the boundaries of credibility. Leparello, Don Giovanni's servant, tells Dona Elvira that his boss's erotic conquests number 640 women and girls in Italy, 231 in Germany, 100 in France, 91 in Turkey, and in Spain, 1,003, adding that she should not waste her feelings: *Madamina, il catalogo è questo* (My dear lady, this is the catalogue). Obviously, the theme concerns a male fantasy, but is that all? Then why do we not find it everywhere?

A second question relating to themes from a psychopoetics point of view is their *effect*. Time and again we have immersed ourselves into the question what effects the reading of poetry has on people. We repeat the question here: what are the effects of themes, both individual and on society as a whole? This is a question that has been totally neglected by literary studies, and one has to turn to the field of psychology to find the beginning of an answer, also a clear example of a methodology to tackle the question. The psychologist who has done most in this respect is David McClelland (1961, 1975). Over his lifetime, he developed a motivation theory based on human needs. Three such needs he singled out: *n Power*, the need for power (to be influential), *n Affiliation*, the need for affiliation (to have affective relations), and *n Achievement*, the need for achievement (to succeed). Each of these we can portray as *themes* when they turn up in literary texts. And that is exactly what McClelland investigated: the amount of representation of the three needs in stories, hymns, and plays. He had a large number of popular literary texts scored for each of the three needs. One hypothesis in his research is that violent conflict is the result of a generally high *n* Power combined with a low *n* Affiliation. The result of the investigation can be seen in Figure 17:

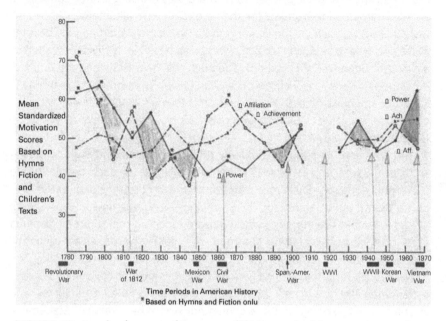

FIGURE 17 *Levels of concern for power, affiliation and achievement in popular literature in the United States in 1780–1970 (McClelland 1975: 316). Reproduced with the permission of Wiley.*

The vertical axis represents the mean scores for each of the three needs, and the horizontal axis represents time, in ten-year intervals, from 1780 through 1970. The shaded areas in the graph are historical periods in which *n* Power was high, and higher than *n* Affiliation, in popular literature. Studying historical events related to this graph reveals something rather spectacular. With only few exceptions, the black shaded areas in the graph precede war, and the white areas precede peace (ibid.: 335). In other words, the occurrence of themes in popular literature predicts that a country (the United States in this case) goes to war *subsequently*.

Another remarkable insight ensuing from this research regards *n* Achievement and Other-directness in children's literature, and its relation to economic growth. Other-directedness refers to a shift away from impersonal traditions, and instead an orientation toward 'the specific needs or demands of particular others, especially peers' (ibid.: 192). Together with his co-workers, McClelland collected a total of 1,300 children's stories from twenty-three countries for the period 1920–9, and from forty countries for the period 1946–55. These stories were then scored for the theme of Achievement by people trained to rate the theme. At the same time the total amount of electricity generated was chosen as a measure of economic growth.[3] This measure was calculated for each country and subsequently related to the measure of Achievement themes in the stories. The results are visualized in Figure 18:

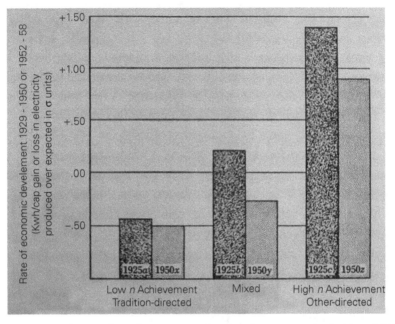

FIGURE 18 *Relation of* n *Achievement and Other-direction in the 1925 and 1950 readers to subsequent economic development (McClelland 1961: 201) © The Free Press 1961. Reproduced with the permission of Martino Fine Books.*

The bars represent the amount of electricity produced for the two periods, 1925 and 1950, split out according to the degree to which the themes of Achievement and Other-directness occurred in children's books. The graph speaks for itself: there is a very strong relationship between both variables. In the words of McClelland himself: 'Obviously the countries which were high in *n* Achievement and Other-directedness greatly outperformed those which were low in both variables, both in 1925 and in 1950, whereas those that were high on one and low on the other showed an average gain somewhere in between' (1961: 202). So a high occurrence of the need for Achievement in children's literature predicts strong economic growth when these children have become adults. Of course, the values in the children's books were inserted there (presumably unconsciously) by adult writers, but apparently the children internalized these values. To summarize: themes in popular literature relate to economic and social/political events of a society. The consequences of this finding are so far-reaching that this kind of thematic study should be a vital complement to what literary studies have been involved in so far. The research by McClelland was carried out in the 1960s, at a time when all the work had still to be done by hand. Today such studies would profit enormously from the use of technology: content analysis, text mining, and artificial intelligence could greatly facilitate but also enhance the power of such investigations.

We now return to the beginning of this chapter: the *Epic of Gilgamesh*, containing the story of the flood. We then pointed out that it is basically the same as the biblical story of Noah in the book of Genesis. That recurrence already makes it into a literary *theme*. But it also turns up in *Hindu* mythology. Similarly, in Plato's 'Timaeus', Zeus, the Greek supreme god, intends to punish humanity with a flood. But Prometheus tells Deucalion of Zeus's plan and advises him to build an ark to save himself and his family. After nine days and nights of rain, the water recedes, and the ark lands on a mountain. Similarities between stories within a thematic strand may be extremely high. But from *Gilgamesh* and Plato the theme of the flood reaches into the twentieth century. Witness this visionary poem by Edna St. Vincent Millay, with which we conclude this chapter, inviting you to look at it in detail, using the knowledge you have gathered from the previous chapters, and especially, enjoy the way it tells one of the oldest stories of humanity to us, some 4,000 years later:

The broken dike, the levee washed away,
The good fields flooded and the cattle drowned,
Estranged and treacherous all the faithful ground,
And nothing left but floating disarray
Of tree and home uprooted,—was this the day
Man dropped upon his shadow without a sound
And died, having laboured well and having found
His burden heavier than a quilt of clay?
No, no. I saw him when the sun had set
In water, leaning on his single oar
Above his garden faintly glimmering yet ...
There bulked the plough, here washed the updrifted weeds ...
And scull across his roof and make for shore,
With twisted face and pocket full of seeds.

Core issues

- In psychopoetics, as a universal theory of general understanding of the workings of poetry, it is mandatory to also investigate texts outside a Western context.

- Likewise, a historical dimension is required to develop psychopoetics into a general theory.

- One of the major issues in psychopoetics lies in the emotional area of the human psyche.

- Oral texts are mental phenomena, belonging to a person's memory. They are learned by heart and then recited.

- Transmission of texts in oral cultures is not stable, but subject to various influences.

- Persistence of poetry can be seen in the endurance of themes, recurrent content that makes up the true significance of the poem.

- The theme of forbidden or impeded love is one of the most widespread motifs in world literature.

- Research (by David McClelland) has revealed the effects of the themes of achievement and power in literature upon society as a whole.

Further reading

Bremond, C., J. Landy and Th. Pavel, (eds) (1994), *Thematics. New Approaches.* New York: SUNY Press.

Charpin, D. (2010), *Reading and Writing in Babylon.* Cambridge: Harvard University Press.

Foley, J. M. (1993), *Traditional Oral Epic: The Odyssey, Beowulf, and the Serbo-Croatian Return Song.* Berkeley: University of California Press.

George, A. R. (2003), *The Babylonian Gilgamesh Epic, Introduction, Critical Edition and Cuneiform Texts.* Oxford: Oxford University Press.

Kanigel, R. (2021), *Hearing Homer's Song: The Brief Life and Big Idea of Milman Parry.* New York: Knopf.

Louwerse, M. and W. van Peer, (eds) (2002), *Thematics. Interdisciplinary Studies.* Amsterdam: John Benjamins.

Oatley, K. (1992), *Best Laid Schemes. The Psychology of Emotions.* Cambridge: Cambridge University Press.

Schmidt, M. (2019), *Gilgamesh: The Life of a Poem.* Princeton: Princeton University Press.

8

Methods to Study Psychopoetics

Keywords

research methodology

context of discovery / justification

independent variable

dependent variable

confounding variable

between-subjects design

within-subjects design

pre-test

post-test

randomization

operationalization

All throughout this volume, we have been discussing poetry and its *effect* on readers—emotional, cognitive, behavioral, and more. And we have persistently emphasized that we are involved in an effort to develop an *evidence-based* study of poetry. But what *is* evidence? This chapter will summarize the basics of the methodology that we have already partially demonstrated in previous parts of this book.

But let us first think why we wish to engage ourselves in research at all. The first reason, we believe, is that we are ignorant about certain things, and without systematic inquiry we are running a risk of remaining uninformed. Second, we need research because often we think we know, but are wrong in our assumptions. Research will help us eliminate the errors caused by intuition, like the belief that the sun rises in the east, while it is instead the earth rotating. The third reason is: mere curiosity, as the world is full of highly interesting 'whys' and 'hows.' Finally, there are cases when there is no other way to find out the truth (see, for instance, the remarks about researching experiences of revelation in Chapter 5). Of course, you can continue the list with your own ideas.

We are quite adamant in our insistence on an evidence-driven approach to poetic texts. Without it, assertions lack persuasive force, not binding in any sense. This does not mean that they are meaningless or unexciting. Only, in order to be trustworthy, they need more (and better) underpinning. The philosopher Hans Reichenbach ([1938] 2018) has made an interesting distinction in this respect, between the *context of discovery* and the *context of justification*, which was made more popular through the works of the philosopher of science Karl Popper ([1959] 2002). The distinction is necessary to clarify where theories come from. Indeed: if we are after evidence in favor of a particular view, a question is whither this view originates. Previous chapters have regularly referred to theories about poetry. But where do these theories come from? This is the context of discovering things.

The difference is between, on the one hand, developing, generating, producing, proposing new knowledge or insight, and, on the other hand, validating, verifying, corroborating or substantiating such knowledge or insight. The former Popper called *discovery*, the latter *justification*. But how do you make 'discoveries'? Popper is a bit frisky about the matter, arguing that it does not matter how, as long as you do make them. Nevertheless, we know from research into creativity that some things help. One, maybe the most important one, is: *loving* problems! Imagination in trying to solve them helps, too, but in order to sieve through a mass of ideas, one needs to have a grasp of previous work that has already been done, so as to avoid having to re-invent the wheel.

But generating new ideas is only half of the work in research: one also wants to know the value of these ideas. This brings you out of the discovery process into efforts at 'proving' your ideas. Within this context, that of *justification*, we are at the heart of what we have loosely called 'evidence' so far. Basically, evidence comes in two forms: *arguments* and *observations*. Arguing in favor of a particular theory compels you to make sure that your arguments are clearly formulated and that they are logical, i.e., avoiding both tautologies and contradictions. Most of what we have been discussing in this book, however, concerns evidence of the other kind, namely, observations. And, of course, we are looking for observations that support (or reject) a particular claim.

It is here that traditional literary studies run into their self-inflicted helplessness. The field simply *lacks* a serious methodology to investigate claims about the workings of literature in the real world, while such a methodology *is* available, and the Social Sciences have been practicing it for over a hundred years. Psychopoetics applies this methodology to furnish evidence for/against claims made by theories of poetry.

There are two major types of methods in this respect: *quantitative* and *qualitative*. The terms are supposedly clear enough in themselves, and you have encountered both in previous chapters. Qualitative methods are in place when there is not yet much information about a particular topic, so that it is difficult to formulate specific hypotheses. Typical qualitative methods are, for instance, interviews, think-aloud protocols, diaries or focus groups. These methods are used as preparation and as tools for interpretation of data at a deeper level—to generate insights that can lead to testable insights. Quantitative methods, by contrast, are used in the alternative situation, where some work has been done, allowing one to test specific hypotheses, turning emotions, attitudes or behavior into numbers. There are, of course, certain dangers of quantifying psychological processes, but do not worry: social scientists have a hundred years of experience with it, and they have developed tricks to avoid pitfalls. Moreover, such quantitative methods may also be complemented by qualitative ones in order to further explore hitherto less well-understood aspects of the hypotheses.

In questionnaires, which we frequently use in evidence-based studies, we often combine both, and in Ancillary Resources at the end of this book you will find a number of samples that may be helpful in your own research.

Qualitative and quantitative methods in combination: Reading Shakespeare

Both types of methods have their own advantages and limitations. That is why they are often used in combination, so as to complement each other and to offset the other's deficits. Let us give an illustration of such a combination. One problem in studying the effects of poetry is that one has little or no control over readers' amount or depth of engagement with the text. Obviously it makes a lot of difference if someone reads a text superficially or engages profoundly with it. So we wanted to study what different effects would be caused by these two modes of reading. To this end we chose a text which is not too easy, but still accessible without much background, namely, Shakespeare's 'Sonnet 18':

Shall I compare thee to a summer's day?
Thou art more lovely and more temperate:
Rough winds do shake the darling buds of May,
And summer's lease hath all too short a date:
Sometime too hot the eye of heaven shines,
And often is his gold complexion dimm'd;

And every fair from fair sometime declines,
By chance, or nature's changing course, untrimm'd;
But thy eternal summer shall not fade
Nor lose possession of that fair thou ow'st;
Nor shall Death brag thou wander'st in his shade,
When in eternal lines to time thou grow'st;
So long as men can breathe or eyes can see,
So long lives this, and this gives life to thee.

The data we collected were by two groups of students (almost exclusively female) from my university. No information was given about the author or the background of the poem. The only extra information supplied was that the meaning of the pronouns 'thee' and 'thou' is equivalent to 'you.' One group, the *control* group ($N = 22$) just read the text and gave us their reactions immediately after reading. It took them approximately ten minutes. The other, *experimental*, group ($N = 23$) also read the sonnet, but before getting their reaction, we made the respondents ponder over a number of issues in the poem. Here are the instructions we gave them (in participants' native or second language, Ukrainian):

Questionnaire sample

1) The first line speaks of an 'I' and a 'you' ('thee'). Who do you think they are? (Please tick your preference):
The 'I' is
        ( ) a woman
        ( ) a man
        ( ) a child
        ( ) an unknown person
        ( ) a God
The 'thee' ('you') is
        ( ) a child
        ( ) a God
        ( ) a woman
        ( ) an unknown person
        ( ) a man
2) Why are there apostrophes in 'ow'st,' 'wand'rest,' and 'grow'st'?

_____

_____

3) There is a marked change of tone in the poem. Do you see where? (And why a change?)

_____

_____

4) What do you think is implied in the line 'in eternal lines to time thou grow'st'?
    ( ) Time will overwhelm you.
    ( ) Time is eternal.
    ( ) Time grows over you.
5) What does 'this' in the final line refer to?
    ( ) beauty
    ( ) the sonnet
    ( ) the 'thee' ('you')
    ( ) the first 'this' refers to beauty, and the second one to the 'I'
6) In the final line the phrase 'gives life' means
    ( ) makes you like a summer's day
    ( ) it will make you eternal
    ( ) that the person will soften the hardships of life
    ( ) nature's never-ending cycle.

The *independent variable* in this research takes two forms: reading the text of the sonnet (in the control group) or (in the experimental group) reading the text of the sonnet plus pondering over the six questions above. The *dependent variables* were: their reactions, on 7-point Likert scales, to six statements about the poem (some of which you will no doubt recognize):

1 I find the text very striking.

2 It is an interesting text for discussion.

3 The text has important things to communicate.

4 I would recommend this poem to a friend.

5 It is an example of high quality literature.

6 The text made me see things in a new light.

The participants also indicated what they found difficult/impossible to understand in the text and what they found most moving/gripping in the poem. Additionally, they answered an open question as to the central message of the text and were invited to give comments on the poem. They also evaluated the poem's beauty. All in all, this took respondents about half an hour to complete the questionnaire, so roughly three times as long as the control group.

You can see that the dependent variables contained both quantitative data (the reactions on the 7-point Likert scales) and qualitative answers (the open-ended questions). Let us first look at the quantitative data. An ANOVA, comparing the reactions of the two groups to the six Likert scales, showed, much to our surprise, no significant differences. So apparently spending twenty more minutes examining the text did not bring about different reactions. But when we then looked at the qualitative data, a completely distinct picture emerged. Thus, the control group, who just read the poem and gave us their reaction on the spot, saw the poem first and foremost as a love poem, while the experimental group had much more elaborate answers on time, eternity and the like—in fact, their reactions were much closer to the central idea of the Shakespeare sonnet. It is indeed a love poem, but there is a much deeper dimension to it, having to do with time and immortality, that apparently escaped readers in the control group.

Here we have a clear example of the differences that both methods allow. In all likelihood, the 7-point Likert scales did not make available enough mental 'space' to express the fine-tuned views of the group that had concentrated on the text. This is perhaps not wholly surprising: such scales compress meanings in a rather primitive space of seven points on a line—something that may go against the grain of multifaceted emotional experiences. What one could do, of course, is extending the scale, for instance, to 100 points. It would be quite interesting to see whether the two groups would show differences on such a fine-grained scale. In any case, the experiment shows that in the study of psychopoetics, qualitative methods should not be neglected.

Nevertheless, you will no doubt have noticed that previous chapters provided many more examples of studies that employed *quantitative* methods. Why? There is a good reason for this: contrary to what you might expect, qualitative methods are more difficult for beginners, in spite of them looking so simple. What could be difficult about interviewing someone—asking people for their reactions? At first sight it sounds counterintuitive to label such a method more difficult. Yet this is indeed so. There are two major quandaries. The first one is that asking questions is much more hazardous than it seems at first sight. Not any question will yield the information you are after in your research. So this aspect requires training, to be agile in a conversation in order to elicit precisely *that* information that you are after. But even if you would be able to surmount this difficulty, there is a second snag: how to deal with the information extracted in the interview? Are you going to transcribe all the answers? This is often done, because that is the value of qualitative data, that they provide very fine-shaded and subtle meanings. But it is a very time-consuming process. And then, the major question becomes: how to cast all these fine-tuned meanings into a general conclusion to your research? Such problems do not arise in the case of quantitative methods: there are usually rather clear and (relatively) simple ways to deal with the data you have collected. Those are the reasons why we have given some priority to quantitative methods in the previous chapters, and why we would also recommend you to use these in your research if you are a beginner. But let us now turn to the way in which to deal with quantitative methods in general.

Research of poetry:
General principles and guidelines

Let us now look at what we propose as the methodological line of inquiry:

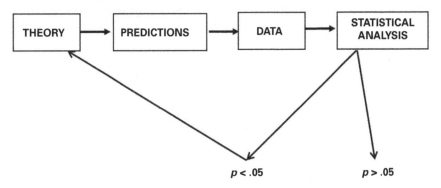

FIGURE 19 *Theory testing model.*

As in any kind of research, if we wish to understand the psychological processes involved in poetry, it must start with the identification of a problem, to which a tentative *theory* is put forward as its solution. That theory must allow *predictions* to be derived from it. In the absence of this possibility, we are not dealing with a real theory, which demands that it can be *falsified*. The next step is to collect independent *data* that correspond to what the predictions outline, but which may also contradict them. (That is the meaning of 'independent.') In order to understand in what way the data bear on the theory, a thorough *analysis* of them is necessary. Such work will in many cases require a *statistical* analysis. The analysis involves, on the one hand, the question of whether the results are in the direction the theory predicted, and at the same time how far you may generalize them. This leads to the famous *p-values,* which reflect how high the chances are that the results came about by mere accident; *p*-values indicate an *error probability*. This is indicated in Figure 19 by the arrow pointing back to the theory. In contrast, the arrow pointing to *p*-values higher than .05 (in other words, higher than 5 percent) is relegated to the domain of *non-significance*: in these cases, we do not accept the data as confirmation of the theory, which is therefore *rejected*, or at least in need of modification.

Two basic concepts are used to clarify this: the *null hypothesis* and the *alternative hypothesis*, two concepts we already briefly encountered in Chapter 4. These are terms used in hypothesis testing of the kind represented in Figure 19, i.e. comparing collected data to a prediction. In collecting data, all kinds of random influences and/or errors of measurement may creep in. The hypothesis that these factors are the cause of the observed results is called the null hypothesis. We accept this null hypothesis as long as we do not have enough good evidence that speaks against it. That is stated by the alternative hypothesis, namely, that the results we obtained are *not* due to chance or error, but due to some structural characteristic. Since both hypotheses are each other's logical opposites, we weigh the amount of evidence in favor of each of them. And in doing this, we use a strict criterion: the *p*-value.

Within quantitative methods, the most usual one is the *experiment*. In our case this most often involves *reading* some poetry and collecting reactions afterward. We, as experimenters, want to control the (kind of) reading, for instance, through manipulating the text—as we have seen in a number of examples in previous chapters. Or we can compare reactions to particular parts of the text, as we saw in the experiments on foregrounding. We are, after all, interested in learning what influence particular poetic structures have on readers' minds and feelings. So we work with (at least) two alternatives: foregrounding vs. background stretches of a text, manipulated vs. original texts, reading with specific instructions or without, etc. Afterward we compare the results under those two (or more) *experimental conditions*.

This can be done in basically two different ways. The first one employs two (or more) groups of readers, one for each experimental condition. This is why the method is called *between-subjects*: we compare reactions 'between' the two groups. ('Subjects' is another word, in this context, for participants.) One fundamental requirement for doing this—one can see this immediately—is that the two groups are highly comparable. It will not work if one group consists of children and the other of adults, or one group of highly educated and the other of untrained readers, or one group consisting of prison inmates and the other of politicians. Except, of course, if we are interested in the typical reading processes of these specific groups. But if we are interested in the effect of poetic devices, we must guarantee that the two groups are, if not identical, then at least comparable. This can be done in two ways.

The first one is simple: the experimenter controls most characteristics of the participants. In concrete terms this may mean to take care that both groups consist of:

- an almost equal number of every gender;

- participants in the same age group;

- a more or less equal educational level;

- etc.

Moreover, one has to take care not to over- (or under-) represent particular skills or interests in one group, especially when such skills or interests are of special importance to the hypothesis under consideration. Suppose you are interested in the musical effects of meter, and in one of the groups musicians are over-represented. That is not a good *design*. This is indeed called the *design*: which (aspects of) texts to use, which groups of participants, and which dependent variables to choose. All of these belong to the planning and preparation of an experiment. Sometimes arranging for the groups to be comparable can be tricky, especially when possible hidden interests may come into play. That is why ultimately *random* allocation to either group is of paramount importance.

If such an interest comes into play, it may confound your data and your conclusions. That is why it is called a *confounding* (or intervening) variable. Confounding variables are invisible to the researcher, but may be the cause of relations between observations. One such (funny) relation is between the murder rate and the sales of ice cream: the more murders, the more ice cream. But also the other way round: the more ice cream is sold, the more murders. Does one cause the other? Unlikely. But the relation exists! This is a clear example of a (hidden) confounding variable: the weather. When it is freezing cold, little ice cream is sold, and people stay more inside, so there is less interaction, and lower chances of fights and of murders. Conversely, however, if temperatures are agreeable, people go out more, so there are more encounters, and thus a higher chance of quarrels and ensuing murders—while at the same time more ice cream is sold.

One method to take care of this kind of *confounding* variables is *restriction*: in a research on musical effects of meter, musicians are excluded from participation. But how do I know about participants' personal interests? There is a simple way to find out: ask them. And subsequently exclude any participants who have a more than usual interest in the topic. Another method to be used is *randomization*: allocation to either the experimental or control group is done at random. For instance, if you have two versions of one text and you have the possibility to collect reactions to both in a class, then make a pile of the two versions so that they alternate each other. Or just allocate odd and even numbers to the questionnaires. Then distribute them in the group. In this case no two neighboring participants will read the same version. If you are sending out the links to online questionnaires, make sure you are sending version 1 and version 2 to odd- and even-numbered participants on your list. That way, the chances are low that the two groups will differ from each other. Randomization is an indispensable precaution to take in experimental research. Without it, the results are open to legitimate criticism. With randomization the danger that one of the groups differs in some important aspect from the other is not completely ruled out, but it is unlikely.

To counter this danger, that through accident the two groups are not really comparable, a second method can be applied. This is called the *within-subjects* method, also called *repeated measures* design. It is a form of experiment in which things are repeated, and they are repeated in the same group of participants. Imagine that you would like to know whether reading poetry about love changes readers' sensibility. You would have to decide how to *operationalize* the notion of sensibility, of course: that is your dependent variable, and you want to know whether the independent variable, i.e., reading love poetry, exerts an influence on it. Suppose that, after having studied the literature on love sensitivity, you have drawn up a number of statements that should gauge such feelings. In this design, you use those statements twice: first before they have read any poetry, and a second time after they have read the poems. These are called a *pre-test* and *post-test* respectively. In the pre-test you actually measure their general sensibility in the area of romantic relationships. Then you expose them to what is often called a *treatment* (or *experimental condition*, sometimes also called *stimulus*); in this case, you request them to read some love poems that you have selected. (And you selected them for a reason, because your hypothesis is that it is something in particular in those poems that may make people aware of the importance and fragility of romantic love.) If your hypothesis is correct, then participants will give different reactions to your statements in the post-test.

It is clear that by using this method you have dispensed with the problem of non-equal groups of the *between-subjects* design because the participants are the same in the pre- and post-tests. But there are now other problems facing you: participants may see the similarity between the statements in the pre- and post-tests and thus guess your intention. If they do, they may want to comply with what they believe are your aims—and so give answers that are *socially desirable*. Or they may thwart your design and give irrelevant answers. In both cases, their reactions are not authentic, and the experiment becomes worthless. The solution is to choose different order and especially also different formulations for the statements in the pre- and post-test. This may be tricky, though, because you want them to mean basically the same thing.

As you can see, every choice in research has its (dis)advantages. But there is one particular design that is, so to say, ideal, in that it combines as many advantages as possible. Its name may sound a bit off-putting, so let us look at it in somewhat detail. The method is called a *pre-test post-test control group design*. It becomes clear in Figure 20 on the next page.

The design makes use of two groups of participants, like in a *between-subjects* design. And you know by now that allocation to either group is done *randomly*, so as to diminish the chances that the groups would be different in their composition of participants. In Figure 20, the two groups are separated by the dotted line. Horizontally, the figure represents time. So we first have a parallel session in both groups, called O_1 and O_3: this is a *pre-test*. Then in Group 1, the *experimental* one, subjects are exposed to an experimental condition, X, while this is omitted in Group 2, which is therefore the *control*

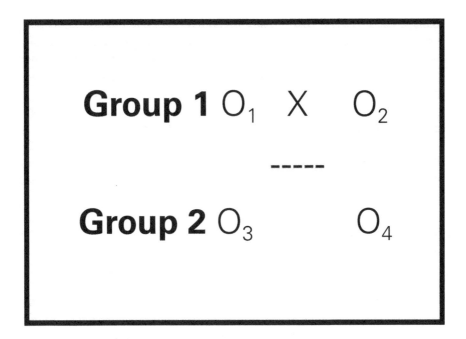

FIGURE 20 *Pre-test post-test control group experimental design.*

group. Finally, then, comes a *post-test* in both groups: O_2 and O_4 in Figure 20. This part you will no doubt have recognized as the *within-subjects* design. So in this method we combine both designs, and thus hope to avoid the shortcomings of each.

The major advantage of this design is that you can control for *extra experimental factors*. For the sake of illustration, suppose that during the experiment a rather dramatic event occurs and that participants hear about it on their mobile phones. Needless to say that this event may influence the results. But it will influence both groups in the same way, so that the comparison between O_2 and O_4 still allows us to isolate the influence of the experimental factor, X. As you can see, this design gives you the best possible combination of methods. However, it is not always possible to use this design. For instance, if your hypothesis has to do with the surprise effect of X, you cannot possibly have a pre-test, because that would impair the surprise. So in practice, one often has to choose a design that is adapted to the concrete situation.

A last remark here concerns a question that necessarily turns up: how many participants does one need? We limit ourselves here to quantitative methods. For qualitative research, the number of participants is mostly irrelevant, since the aim is not to generalize, but to gain insight into processes (which can, if necessary, be tested quantitatively later). With quantitative methods, the question about the number of participants takes a double answer, depending on whether you are testing a concrete hypothesis, derived from predictions that are distilled from theory. In that case you ideally need thirty participants for each condition. If you look back at Figure 20, then it is clear that you will need sixty participants, since there are two conditions: in one group there is the experimental factor X, in the other group not. That is the ideal number, thirty. Would more be better? Yes, more is always better in this sense, but it is not necessary. But what if I can only find twenty or twenty-five participants? Could I still run the experiment? In one sense, yes. You can, and if you find statistically significant support for the hypothesis, you are fine. But what if you do not? There is the rub, because in that situation you are unable to decide whether the results are non-significant because the hypothesis is wrong, OR because there were not enough participants in the *sample*, so that the statistical tests did not reach the conventional value of $p < .05$. You simply do not know, which is why it is advised to go for a number of participants that is close to thirty.

But what if you are *not* testing a hypothesis, but are just interested in, for instance, how many people regularly read poetry? In that case, if you want reliable answers, one needs a *representative* sample of the *population*. That means that everyone in that society must have an equal chance to be included in the sample. In practice this entails (assuming we are thinking of adults) that men and women must be equally represented, people from urban areas as well as from the countryside, people from all (adult) age groups, from all educational levels, etc. It will be clear that such research can only be carried out by specialized research institutes. So we will not deal with it any further.

To demonstrate how the above is at work in psychopoetics, in Chapter 4 we gave you the example of testing Shklovsky's assertions about foregrounding. The prediction was that foregrounded passages in a poem would be experienced by readers as (1) more striking, (2) more worthy of discussion, and (3) more important. This is the alternative hypothesis, and we will use the data (i.e., reader responses) to assess its weight in contrast to the null hypothesis that there is no difference in reader reactions between foregrounded stretches of text as compared to parts of the poem that contain little or no foregrounding. The three types of reader reactions that we collected are called, as you already know, *dependent variables*: they are, according to the hypothesis, caused by the textual characteristics, which go by the name of *independent variable*(s).

The described method applied by van Peer (2020) was later followed by numerous replications that used finer-grained methodology. The first—and maybe most inspiring one—was the study by Miall and Kuiken (1994b), and later there were other investigations, with different respondents and materials, in different countries, in different circumstances and under different conditions. All in all, one can now say that in most of these studies the claims made by the foregrounding theory have been corroborated by the data, though in reality we have come a long way from Shklovsky's initial formulation, and also a long way from the first empirical studies that established the validity of his claims.

But in a series of more recent experiments (Chesnokova and van Peer 2016; van Peer and Chesnokova 2017) the predictions discussed above were *not* confirmed, which is puzzling, as most efforts at corroborating the foregrounding theory so far had been successful. This only means that no theory is immune. Theories are made by people, thus they are bound to be imperfect, and any of them is subject to new efforts at falsification, all the time. No theory has holiness. This is the hallmark of scientific research, that it never stops, but through repeated testing of our theories we arrive at ever better insight into ourselves as human beings.

Perhaps much of what we have said so far may sound unfamiliar, intimidating even. You may have the impression that this is all for advanced researchers, nothing that you yourself could participate in. That, however, would be a wrong conclusion. It is the express goal of the present book to familiarize you with these research methods, so that you can apply them yourself. So we will now present an example of a piece of research that is extremely simple in itself, of a kind that you could set up yourself, and yet yielded very insightful results.

Basic steps: From hypothesis to interpreting the results

Is foregrounding what makes poetry poetic? It is also a central piece of Shklovsky's theory, namely that literary texts generally function by the grace of foregrounding. As he claims:

[i]n our phonetic and lexical investigations into poetic speech, involving both the arrangement of words and the semantic structures based on them, we discover everywhere the very hallmark of the artistic: that is, an artefact that has been intentionally removed from the domain of automatized perception. It is 'artificially' created by an artist in such a way that the perceiver, pausing in his reading, dwells on the text. This is when the literary work attains its greatest and most long-lasting impact. The object is perceived not spatially but, as it were, in its temporary continuity.

(in Shklovsky [1929] 1990: 12)

In order to investigate this claim, a reading experiment was set up.[1] The experiment was triggered by the following *hypothesis*: deviation in poetry increases the aesthetic appreciation of the text. To this end, readers were presented with nine lines of a poem (specifically designed for the purpose), offered to the participants (in fact, projected on to a screen) one by one. After each line appeared, subjects were requested to rate the text they had read so far in terms of its beauty. No definition of beauty was given—participants were told to judge the poem by what they themselves considered as beautiful (or not). Respondents marked their reactions on a scale from 0 through 10. Prior to the experiment readers were given the following instructions:

> We are interested in your reaction to poetry. Therefore, we are going to ask you to tell us how beautiful you find a particular poem. We will show this poem to you line by line, and will ask you to give us your impression of how beautiful it is after each added line.

> Your appreciation of its beauty is to be indicated on a scale from 0 to 10. The former means that you find the poem absolutely NOT beautiful, while the latter means that you find it absolutely beautiful. And, of course, you can pick any values between those two extremes. Thus, for instance, if you find the poem only marginally beautiful, you could indicate this by circling the number 3, and if you find it very beautiful, but not to the extreme, then you could circle the number 8. Or if you find it rather lacking in beauty, then circle 1.

The poem consisted of eight consecutive lines that ran

I love you not.

In other words, readers encountered the same identical line eight times. The ninth line *deviated* from this pattern, and ran:

I love you notwithstanding.

The case may be described in terms of *internal deviation*, which we discussed in Chapter 4. This is also how Shklovsky himself saw it:

> a general rule: a work of art is perceived against a background ... Whenever we experience anything as a *deviation* from the ordinary, from the normal, ... we feel within us an emotion of a special nature, which is not distinguished in its kind from the emotions aroused in us by sensuous forms, with the single difference being that its 'referent' may be said to be a perception of a discrepancy ... This is a field of inexhaustible richness because these differential perceptions are qualitatively distinguished from each other by their point of departure, by their forcefulness and by their line of divergence.
>
> (Shklovsky [1929] 1990: 20–1)

In our case, we *hypothesized* that—since the experience of beauty is an important aim in poetry—the ninth line would be judged considerably more 'beautiful' than the eight preceding lines. In order to submit this hypothesis to the test of universality, we decided to run it with *participants* in different countries: Belgium, Brazil, China, Egypt, Finland, Germany, the Netherlands, New Zealand, Poland, Slovenia, Tunisia, and Ukraine. The total number of respondents (predominantly university students) in this investigation is 675.

The data were collected and processed with the help of *statistical* analysis by way of *within-subjects* comparison, in the sense that we checked how each individual respondent reacted to the nine lines of the poem. The analysis demonstrated that the results are, in statistical terms, *highly significant* ($p < .000$), so the *error probability* is lower than 1 in 10,000, revealing a highly reliable result across multiple cultures, diverse by default. In other words, if we repeat this experiment with similar participants 10,000 times, we will get the same result 9,999 times. Thus we can state that the results of the experiment can be *generalized* beyond the experimental *sample*, and that the foregrounded poetic elements (internally deviant in our case) indeed increase appreciated beauty of the text by its readers.

As results of evidence-based research could be better presented through visualization, Figure 21 summarizes the results of these experiments, showing the responses of over 600 readers in different countries (more about them in an instant).

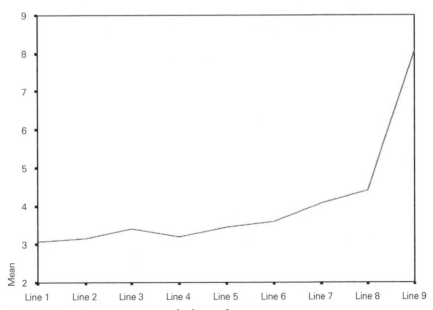

FIGURE 21 *Mean responses to the lines of poetry.*

The horizontal axis represents the nine lines of the poem. The vertical axis indicates the *mean* response for each line. As can be seen from the graph, the final line of the poem ('I love you notwithstanding') is evaluated dramatically higher than the eight initial lines ('I love you not'). Of course, there are individual variations (both within and between cultures), but taken together, in all cultures the predictions derived from Shklovsky's theory hold.

Of course, it is too early to ascribe universal *validity* to the theory, but a systematic effort at *falsifying* it did not succeed. This is no final proof, but it does indicate a serious strength of the theory. In order to further underpin this strength, we ran the experiment, as mentioned earlier, in many different countries. Figure 22 represents the results for some of the countries involved.

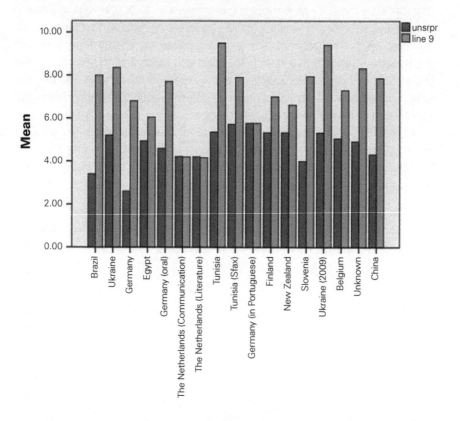

Nationality

FIGURE 22 *Mean responses across the countries.*

Figure 22 demonstrates the average response to line 9 (the light bar) and the average response to the preceding eight lines (the dark bar, marked as 'unsrpr' for 'unsurprised'). As you can see, the bar for line 9 is nearly always higher than the average eight lines before. We take it that these eight initial lines are 'background,' while line 9, because it contains an internal deviation, is foregrounded.

Thus this foregrounded line is almost always experienced as more beautiful—with two exceptions. One is an experiment in which German students read the poem in Portuguese, a language none of them understood. The fact that in this situation the foregrounding prediction was not borne out is nothing remarkable. That leaves only one case, the two groups of Dutch students, in which results showed identical estimates of beauty for the two categories, background lines and the foregrounded line. It is a case we cannot explain. But apart from this, it very much looks as if foregrounding effects are predictable in many countries, some of which are very different from each other. Maybe the theory does point to a universal feature of poetry, and one that is—following the previous research—predictable. To the best of our knowledge, no other theory in literary studies can claim the same, or even a similar, strength of evidence.

Is empirical research in poetry for specialists only? Worries quelled

This chapter has bombarded you with a mass of new concepts and terms that you may not have heard of before. Maybe you found it all rather daunting and very much removed from your personal life. Even if the final example we gave may not have convinced you that doing research is within your reach, you draw the wrong conclusion: because we both have supervised scores of studies carried out by our own students (graduates and undergraduates). Partly this was also done in cooperation between the students themselves, over the internet. The project was called REDES (for Research and Development of Empirical Studies). The word *redes* means 'network,' but also a 'hammock' in Portuguese. Students from the universities of Kyiv, Munich, Utrecht, and Rio de Janeiro took part in it over a period of ten years. The project set up the investigation of literature, culture, and media from a multicultural perspective. In doing so students 'acquired the necessary methodological techniques, were able to analyze the data they themselves collected, and were capable of presenting the results both in writing and orally, in several cases to a forum of specialists at international conferences. All this was done in a spirit of intellectual curiosity often lacking in the standardized courses that are taught in many departments' (Chesnokova, Zyngier, and van Peer 2017: 198).

Functioning as a source of cultural education and international exchange, where cooperation, respect and mutual friendships developed, the project produced several publications (for the full outline see van Peer, Zyngier, and Chesnokova 2010; Viana et al. 2010; Chesnokova, Zyngier, and van Peer 2016). You may be surprised to hear it, but a volume that consisted exclusively of articles by students was published (Zyngier, Chesnokova, and Viana 2007), while in the *Festschrift* by Zyngier et al. (2008) a whole section was produced by students. Does this not sound like an argument for you to stop worrying, and start some research of your own? After all, evidence-based research is not reserved for high-brow academicians only.

We thus would like to close this chapter by encouraging you to go away from blindly believing what you read in books (remember: there are no immune theories) and go out in the world to design and conduct your own experiments in search of evidence for the effects of poetry in people's lives—and for the evidence of psychopoetics in general.

Core issues

- Literary experience and the effects poetry creates are best investigated when one's intuitions are confronted with independent data.

- Psychopoetics applies empirical methodology to furnish evidence for/ against claims made by theories of poetry.

- No theory is immune, and any of them is open to continuing attempts at falsification.

- Research in psychopoetics involves deriving predictions from a theory, collecting independent data and submitting them to a thorough (often statistical) analysis.

- An advantageous design of an experiment is pre-test post-test controlgroup.

- In quantitative research, the ideal number of participants is thirty per condition. In qualitative research, the number of participants is mostly irrelevant.

- The theory of foregrounding is so far the only literary theory that has been subjected to serious falsification procedures.

Further reading

Field, A. (2002), *Discovering Statistics Using SPSS for Windows*. London: Sage.

Fricke, H. (2008), 'How Scientific Can Literary Evaluation Be? Arguments and Experiments,' in W. van Peer (ed), *The Quality of Literature: Linguistic Studies in Literary Evaluation*, 191–207, Amsterdam: John Benjamins.

Kuiken, D. and A.M. Jacobs (eds) (2021), *Handbook of Empirical Literary Studies*. Berlin: De Gruyter.

van Peer, W., F. Hakemulder and S. Zyngier (2012), *Scientific Methods for the Humanities*. Amsterdam: John Benjamins.

9

Toward a General Theory of Psychopoetics

Keywords

effects of poetry

theory of psychopoetics

emotion

internationalism of poetry

catharsis

vulnerability

Sapphic meter

sublime

embodied emotion

Poetry travels

Psychopoetics, then, is the study of how poetry lives. That is: how it lives in us, individuals and groups, societies, cultures. And how we live in poetry when we go through it. There is even a movie about it: *Il Postino* (*The Postman*), a 1994 film by Michael Radford that is pure poetry in itself—not surprisingly, because it is partly about the poet Pablo Neruda (in exile from the colonels in Chile, on a small island off the coast of Naples in Italy), starring Philippe Noiret, Massimo Troisi, and Maria Grazia Cucinotta. Troisi was seriously ill during the shooting, postponing heart surgery so that the movie could be completed. The day the filming was done, he tragically suffered a fatal heart attack, and the movie was released posthumously.

Now please watch the following scene from the movie: in it Mario, the poor and uneducated postman of the island, has just brought Neruda some letters that had arrived. They sit together on the beach—listen to their conversation (if you know Spanish or Italian, try to follow the gist of what they are saying): Link 9.1 on the Companion Website.

Without warning, Neruda starts reciting one of his poems, called 'Oda al Mar' (Ode to the Sea). Here it is, in its original Spanish with an English translation:

Aqui en la isla	Here surrounding the island
el mar	the sea
y cuánto mar	and how much sea
se sale de sí mismo	out of itself[1]
a cada rato,	at every turn,
dice que sí, que no,	says yes, then no,
que no, que no, que no,	then no, then no, then no,
dice que si, en azul,	says yes, in blue,
en espuma, en galope,	in foam, in gallop,
dice que no, que no.	says no, then no.
No puede estarse quieto,	It cannot stay still,
me llamo mar, repite	my name is sea, it repeats
pegando en una piedra	hitting a rock
sin lograr convencerla	without convincing it
entonces	then
con siete lenguas verdes	with seven green tongues
de siete perros verdes,	of seven green dogs,
de siete tigres verdes,	of seven green tigers,
de siete mares verdes,	of seven green seas,
la recorre, la besa	it runs over it, kisses it
la humedece	moistens it
y se golpea el pecho	and beats its chest
repitiendo su nombre.	repeating its name.

This is only the beginning of a much longer poem, which goes on and on, like the rolling waves of the sea, endlessly repetitive, indeed, *repitiendo su nombre*. But here comes Neruda's question: *Allora*? ('Well? What do you think?'). And then—what does the postman answer? If you have not understood, listen again, there is one word that sums up his experience, and also much of the experience of poetry in general, as we have time and again demonstrated in this book. The word in question is the Italian *strano*. It is subtitled as 'weird,' but in fact it is the same word as the English 'strange.' You can see the relationship between the words in these different languages if you check it in an *etymological* dictionary, e.g., the *Online Etymology Dictionary*. Mario then explains that he means that it is not the poem in itself that is 'strano,' but rather his experience of it. He feels uncertain because of the words used in the poem, so the word refers to his psychological impression that is caused by the choice of words in the text: *strano*.

And yes, the Russian word *strannyi* also belongs to this field of meanings. So you may recognize that the word that Mario, the postman, uses to describe his reaction to Neruda's poem brings us back straightaway to Shklovsky's notion of *ostranenie*, of foregrounding: *strano*, strange. It is the ultimate foundation of poetry, making things strange. Mario is living on a small island, surrounded by the sea, and his father is a fisherman, as are nearly all other men on the island. And Neruda's poem evokes the sea, ever present in Mario's head, but it does so in a completely new way. The postman then goes on to say that he cannot really describe his feelings, but that he felt seasick because of the words of the poem, as if he was in a boat (*una barca*). At this point, Neruda interrupts Mario, congratulating him on having invented a metaphor (*una metáfora*). The word is known to Mario, after Neruda has (previously in the movie) explained to him what it means. And now he is after inventing more metaphors, like when he is saying that the whole world, with its sea, rain, and clouds, is a metaphor for something else.

Mark that the situation is also multilingual and multicultural: Neruda, played by a French actor, would normally speak Spanish, and the postman, Italian—albeit with a strong regional accent. In the movie, Philippe Noiret's French is dubbed in Italian, but with a Spanish accent. And the poet is not at home, but in exile, 7,000 miles from Chile. At the same time Mario, the one who *is* at home on the island, does *not* feel at home there, longing for another kind of life. But the endless movement of the waves in Neruda's *Ode* brings home to him his own surroundings in a new, estranged, way. Here we notice an expressive potential of poetry that we have not spoken about yet in this book: the possibility of 'echoing' nature and thus bringing homage to its power and beauty. If you wish, here is another rendering of the poem: Link 9.2 on the Companion Website.

So poetry travels. Not just through time, as Chapter 7 demonstrated, but also through space. Around the world. It is *international*, and it may pop up anywhere. Really anywhere. It is not bound, often not even by the borders of languages. Remember the beginning of Chapter 6? We, schoolboys, did not understand anything at all, and yet, we fell dead silent.

This brings me to my experience as a tourist in a country in Eastern Europe, Ukraine. Once when walking the streets of downtown Kyiv, I saw some kind of graffiti on a wall (see Figure 23 on the next page).

As you see, it is in a Cyrillic script, but even if you do not know the script or the language, it does look like a poem: it has lines, and the first letter of every line is capitalized. Moreover, notice that some words repeated in line 1 (Быть), and so did the final letters of concluding words in lines 1 and 3 (сталь, печаль). So they rhyme, I thought. Later my friends told me that indeed this was a

FIGURE 23 *Graffiti poem.*

stanza from a poem, written in 1915 by the Russian poet Marina Tsvetaeva—
written by someone on a wall more than 100 years later. Here is the stanza
with a loose English translation:

Быть, как стебель, и быть, как сталь,	To be as a stem and to be as steel,
В жизни, где мы так мало можем …	In life where we can do so little …
— Шоколадом лечить печаль	—To cure [your] sorrows with chocolate,
И смеяться в лицо прохожим!	And to laugh in the face of passers-by!

Who put it there, I thought? Why? What drove the person? And—if you
look at the stanza in more detail, you will see that it contains every aspect
we have been discussing in the previous chapters of this book. It clearly has a
structure: lines, rhyme, rhythm, etc. It has some *madness* about it (why would
you laugh at passers-by?). It is *pretty*, and parallelism in the text is abundant. It
has *surprise* about it in the form of semantic deviation (can you cure sorrows
with chocolate?). It might provoke *revelation* in readers: the poem is written on
a wall of a residential block, and many people read it every day when passing
by. Similarly, it may have a *power* of inspiring them to take life problems easier.
It definitely displays *persistence*: the poem was written more than a hundred

years ago, but still today someone put it there in a graffiti. And finally—it travels: a poem written by a Russian author (who lived—in great poverty—in Berlin, Prague, and Paris) was put on a wall in the Ukrainian capital, read by a Belgian tourist, and now mentioned in a book published in English and aimed at an international audience. What more would you need to demonstrate that poetry lives in us?

Why do people read poetry?

If *psychopoetics* should account for the place of poetry in life, the first question is, therefore, *why* is poetry there in the first place? And why do we read (or listen to) it? In other words, the field has to describe and explain the *effects* of poetry. Such effects can be individual, how a person's ideas, emotions, attitudes, or behavior are influenced by exposure to poetry. But they can also be of a social nature: how poetry can bind groups of people, even whole nations—or even supra-nations together. The anthems of most nations are poems; the one of the EU is perhaps one of the most famous poems, Schiller's 'Ode an die Freude' (Ode to Joy), put to music by Beethoven. The efforts to elucidate these effects of poetry could be called a *theory* of psychopoetics. But does such a theory exist? No. Not yet.

In their *Psychonarratology*, Bortolussi and Dixon (2003) laid down the methodology for investigating the mental processes readers go through when encountering narratives. This was the first effort to investigate one particular genre from an evidence-oriented perspective. We believe that this work should be complemented by extending the approach to the other two genres: poetry and drama (in performance). There are some elements that have been gathered in the course of history that may cast light on the form a theory of *psychopoetics* could take. In this chapter we name some of the candidates that we believe are of foremost importance in developing such a theory.

So why do some people read poetry, and enjoy it, while others do not? One could easily brush the question away by saying that it is a matter of preference. Some people like biking, others like swimming while still others do not like either. But is it that simple? One obvious alternative could be that people like to read poetry because they have *learned* so at an early age. Another would be that (maybe as a result of this learning process) they are *good at* it, and people generally like doing what they are good at. And so, the more you do it, the better you become at it. We have here in a kernel a view that handling poetry is the result of a *learning process*. This involves learning what it means that language is poetic; it involves learning about conventions and traditions; it also involves the readiness to be initiated and to upgrade one's knowledge of these. It requires a willingness to be confronted with *strano* experiences, with what feels strange. These processes certainly play a predominant role in the acquisition of poetry, and of one's inclination toward it. About those who do not possess this inclination, one could surmise that the learning processes concerned might not have been inviting. Or might not have been accessible (or available) at an earlier time, as for Mario—until his acquaintance with Pablo Neruda opens up the possibility. And not just the possibility: a whole new *world* opens up for him, one he considers to be a metaphor now.

But all this still does not fully explain the *motivation* why people are ready to undergo such learning processes. So what is it that poetry brings its readers? In our view, the first and foremost motivational force is: *emotion*. When a person falls in love, or when a breakup happens and they suffer, you read poetry, not narrative or drama. In many cultures adolescent girls keep 'poetry diaries' where they would write (by hand to that) poems they like. (Actually, one of the authors of this book did this.) Ultimately, it is poems that great writers address to their beloved ones when they are overwhelmed with feelings—both positive and negative. Next to narrative and drama (theater, opera, or movies), poetry is a highly powerful carrier of emotional experiences. It is *interest* in emotions that drives us toward art, music, and literature, including, and especially, poetry. We experience emotions in real life, of course. We also witness the emotions of other people. Or we may hear people talk about things emotional. But all these are apparently no substitute for poetry, music, and the arts. Or should one turn things around and say that poetry is a substitute for real-life emotions? Whatever direction one takes, the question remains why real-life emotions are not enough for humans, and why they feel this need to experience emotions about events that are not their own. Maybe they want to compare their own emotional states with those of some characters. Or they wish to experience powerful emotions (like life-threatening adventures) that they may never experience in reality.

There may also be another, very pragmatic, but perhaps quite unexpected, reason for people to read poetry. A sample of 3,635 participants in the nationally representative Health and Retirement Study provided information about their reading habits (Bavishi, Slade, and Levy 2016). After adjusting for covariates (age, gender, race, education, commodities, self-rated health, wealth, marital status, and depression) the study found that 'book readers experienced a 20% reduction in risk of mortality over the 12 years of follow up compared to non-book readers' (ibid.: 44). And reading books contributed significantly more than reading newspapers or magazines. Obviously, poetry was there. So—if you want to secure yourself of a long life, read literature (including poetry, as we shall see).

Catharsis

In the previous sections, we offered you some possible explanations of an urge to confront poetry, but one may still wonder why we do it. Why, in other words, do artists like Mariza get involved in all this, placing herself outside society, making people view her as mad (*loucura*), which leads to sadness (*dolorida*), even to her endless weeping (*chorai, chorai*) and, paradoxically, asking for our help (*E se vocês, não estivessem a meu lado*) in order for her to remain mad? Why?

At the same time: why do people go and watch this pitiful spectacle? You may balk at such questions, but they are at the heart of what we are trying to do in this book: describe and explain why poetry is there in the first place. Could we do without it? Individually, apparently yes: there are enough people around you who will have little or no affinity with poetry. But generally, not, in the sense that there are no human societies that eschew it. Ethnographers have been studying a wide range of human groups, and groups without some form of poetry they have not found so far, which means there is something crucial behind it. So what is it?

We will propose two answers: one superficial (but the most popular one), and the other more profound (but less likely to be overheard). The first answer is simple. Why does Mariza go to all this trouble? First, because like all (successful) artists, actors, writers, or musicians, she gets well paid for it. And once you are popular, you do not have to worry about an income any more. Moreover, there is the applause by the audience, the admiration of your fans, the laudatory reviews in the papers, the media appearances, and the interviews that flatter your ego. In other words, investing energy in your performances yields both material and immaterial wealth and mental gratification, social esteem, appealing benefits and pleasant privileges. A similar advantage works for the audience: they share in the glitter. Something of the aura of the artist spills over on the spectators—we were there, and we were part of it! Moreover, a concert is also a kind of entertainment, going out with friends and enjoying a pleasurable evening.

All these are good reasons to pay for a ticket, maybe even an expensive one. But then they do not explain why people will go and listen to *this* artist or performance. One could as well go out drinking with friends, go to a club or a football match, or just watch a movie on television. So we must explain why people want to watch a performance of *this* kind: of someone who declares herself mad, who conjures up sad emotions and even tries to draw you in to participate in her madness and sadness. Is that not a strange thing? And you have to pay her on top of that! So we must delve deeper for an explanation.

Here the second explanation and the theory of *catharsis* (which we have already mentioned in Chapter 6) come in. It was proposed by Aristotle, one of the major Greek philosophers, in his book *Poetics* (which were actually his students' notes) somewhere around 335 BCE. It is the earliest treatment of literary theory and contains several passages that have to do with the experience of poetry. Poetry, in a sense, since the work is mainly about tragedy, so theatrical dialogue performed on stage. But Greek tragedy was written (and performed) partly in verse: considerable portions of the dialogue were *iambic*. So the *Poetics* is about two *genres* in one: drama and poetry. Essential for us here is what Aristotle says about the emotional experience of drama, which he describes as 'purification' or 'cleansing', particularly of the emotions of pity (*éleos*) and fear (*phóbos*), resulting in a renewal of vital energies. It is easy to imagine how spectators underwent the emotion of *fear* when watching Greek tragedy. It is an emotion we all know when watching a movie scene in which the hero/heroine is in grave danger. And when they succumb to evil forces, we do indeed feel *pity* for them. What Aristotle proposes is that we actively seek such emotions because they (psychologically) liberate us and soothe us. Fear is neutralized, and the pity we feel makes us share our humanity with each other. In this sense, *catharsis* is also a regulator of social balance. We are cured, so to say, of negative emotions, emotions we have in common with our fellow citizens. And this process is never-ending.

Let us look at this never-ending process in somewhat more detail. Fitch, von Graevenitz, and Nicolas (2009) propose a three-stage route for aesthetic experiences: (1) recognizing familiar elements; (2) surprise/ambiguity/ tension brought forth by unfamiliar elements such as foregrounding; and (3) resolution of the tension. Jacobs (2015b) makes an interesting remark on the model, namely that the '*sine qua non* of the aesthetic experience is the non-achievement of a final reading' (151). Reading a poem, therefore, is never finished, but perpetually open to new interpretations, new vistas, new applications, and new reflections. It is this openness of poetry that speaks for its cognitive, emotional, and cultural richness. That is what happens when we watch a theater play or a movie. But how does that apply to Mariza's performance? First, there is *fear* of madness. Like suffering, injustice, death, or the unknown, madness is something that frightens people, as it means the ultimate loss of control over oneself. Therefore, we *pity* Mariza. But then she draws us into her madness, so we have to fear for ourselves, and to grieve for ourselves. At least, if we take her words seriously. And certainly her whole performance makes us believe she wants to induce those feelings into us.

Vulnerability

The notion of catharsis, then, exposes our emotional vulnerability. In daily life we may forget about it, or in any case not pay attention to our fragility. Poetry often reminds us of it. One good example of this is the following poem by the Ancient Greek poet Sappho (*Σαπφώ* in Greek). She lived *c.* 630–*c.* 570 BCE on

FIGURE 24 *Earliest known picture of Sappho, photograph by Renate Kühling © State Collection of Antiquities and Glyptothek Munich. Reproduced with the permission of State Collection of Antiquities and Glyptothek Munich.*

the island of Lesbos. One of the earliest pictures of her (see Figure 24), on a red-figure vase, from around 470 BCE, shows her with a lyre in her left and a plectrum in her right hand, listening to the poet Alcaeus.

She wrote mainly lyric poems, in a form she developed herself, and which is still called a *Sapphic meter*. Most of her poetry is lost, however, and some of it we only know through its quotations in other works. Here is one such text, preserved in a first-century treatise on aesthetics and literary criticism called Περὶ Ὕψους (Perì Hýpsous, *On the Sublime*)[2] by an unknown author, who is usually called Longinus—although we do not know who he was. The essay had an enormous influence on poetics over 2,000 years, up to our time. One of the issues the author deals with is the *sublime*, which he characterizes by two major factors, the first of which being a style of writing that is elevated 'above the ordinary,' a 'grandeur of thought,' but also through thoughts in their 'naked simplicity' (Longinus 2018: 2). The second characteristic is a 'vigorous and spirited treatment of the passions' (VIII: 1). To illustrate this, he singles out a poem by Sappho, one of the very few ones by her that has come down to us almost complete: only the final part is missing. Let us look at it in somewhat detail as we present the poem in the Greek original, in transliteration as well as supply an English translation next to it.

φαίνεταί μοι κῆνος ἶσος θέοισιν *phaínetaí moi kênos ísos théoisin*	That man seems to me to be equal to the gods
ἔμμεν' ὤνηρ, ὅττις ἐνάντιός τοι *émmen' ốnēr, óttis enántiós toi*	who is sitting opposite you
ἰσδάνει καὶ πλάσιον ἆδυ φωνεί- *isdánei kaì plásion âdu phōneí-*	and hears you nearby
σας ὑπακούει. *sas upakoúei.*	speaking sweetly
καὶ γελαίσας ἰμέροεν, τό μ' ἦ μὰν *kai gelaisas imeroen to m' ē man*	and laughing delightfully, which indeed
καρδίαν ἐν στήθεσιν ἐπτόαισεν· *kardian en stēthesin eptoaisen,*	makes my heart flutter in my breast;
ὡς γὰρ ἔς σ' ἴδω βρόχε', ὥς με φώναισ' *ōs gar es s' idō broche', ōs me phōnas*	for when I look at you even for a short time,
οὐδ' ἓν ἔτ' εἴκει, *ouden et' eikei*	it is no longer possible for me to speak
ἀλλ' ἄ καμ μὲν γλῶσσα ἔαγε, λέπτον *alla kam men glōssa eage, lepton*	but it is as if my tongue is broken
δ' αὔτικα χρῷ πῦρ ὐπαδεδρόμηκεν, *d' autika chrō pyr ypadedromēken,*	and immediately a subtle fire has run over my skin,
ὀππάτεσσι δ' οὐδ' ἓν ὄρημμ', ἐπιρρόμ- *oppatessi d' oud en orēmm', epirrom-*	I cannot see anything with my eyes,
βεισι δ' ἄκουαι, *beisi d' akouei*	and my ears are buzzing
α δε μ' ἴδρως ψῦχρος κακχέεται, τρόμος δὲ *a de m' idrōs kakcheetai, tromos de*	a cold sweat comes over me, trembling
παῖσαν ἄγρει, χλωροτέρα δὲ ποίας *paisan agrei, chlōrotera de poias*	seizes me all over, I am paler
ἔμμι, τεθνάκην δ' ὀλίγω 'πιδεύης *emmi tethnakēn d' oligō 'pideuēs*	than grass, and I seem nearly
φαίνομ' ἔμ' αὔται· *phainom' em' autai*	to have died.
ἀλλὰ πὰν τόλματον ἐπεὶ καὶ πένητα *alla pan tolmaton epei kai penēta*	but everything must be dared/endured, since (?)[3]

It is clearly a love poem. But who is in love with whom? It is a female speaker (some projection of Sappho herself) who is in love with the girl sitting opposite her. So is this a lesbian poem? No doubt about it, and no one seems to have taken offense at it in Antiquity. The word 'lesbian,' note, derives from Lesbos, the island where Sappho lived. But beware: categories as 'gay,' 'homo-,' or 'heterosexual' are present-day notions that did *not* exist in Antiquity. So calling Sappho a 'lesbian poet' is an anachronism. She herself would not have understood what we mean by it. Yet the feelings expressed in the poem are doubtlessly for another woman—we know this because of the gendered endings of Greek words. Does that mean that lesbian relations were permitted then? We do not know, for the simple reason that explicit sexuality is not expressed in poetry at the time of the ancient Greeks or Romans. In painting we do find overt sexual scenes, but hardly any of a lesbian nature. There is one location in Sappho's poems that could be an open expression of sexual activity. It is in the poem numbered 94 (in Voigt's catalogue), where the eighth stanza runs:

καὶ στρώμναν ἐπὶ μολθάκαν	And lying on a soft bed
ἀπάλαν παρ ὀπαυόνοων	tenderly ....
ἐξίης πόθον αἶψα νεανίδων	you have given satisfied desire ...

The work *Searching for Sappho* by the classical scholar Philip Freeman (2016) comments: 'The climax of the encounter is clear enough for any but the most prudish of interpreters' (ibid.: 127).

Now to the poem at hand, number 31 in Voigt's numbering. You can hear it sung in the following video—the music is, of course, an effort at reconstruction, but it gives a good impression of how Sappho's poem must have sounded: Link 9.3 on the Companion Website. Here is another interpretation, now with German and English translations: Link 9.4 on the Companion Website.

In the case of *Gilgamesh* in Chapter 7 we were dealing with the oldest expression of universal themes of humanity: friendship, belonging, and (fear of) death. In the case of Sappho, we are already more than a thousand years later in human history, but it is still the oldest poetic description of erotic love. Longinus comments:

Is it not amazing how at the same moment her senses abandon her, how she loses soul, body, ears, tongue, eyes, colour, as if they were something outside her, how she freezes and burns at the same time, she is going mad and beyond herself. And this affirms that she is overcome, not by one particular emotion, but by a hassle of emotions come together, trashing her. All these are signs of passionate love, but it is in her choice of words, as I said, of the most forceful features and their fusion into one picture that the sublimity of this Ode by Sappho resides.

(Longinus X: 3)

The intense physical manifestations of love (loss of voice, cold sweat, fire over skin, trembling, blindness, and buzzing ears) are immediately recognized by anyone who has passionately fallen in love. And this builds the power of the poem, what Snyder (1997) has called its 'raw physicality.' But how do we come to recognize these manifestations as such? Because the person in love experiences the same 'symptoms,' you may answer. But that is only part of the story. Another part of the explanation is that Sappho gave these physical sensations a name. She invented, just like Mario in *Il Postino*, a metaphor—several metaphors, that since then have been reiterated thousands of times in slightly different variations by lovers and poets all over the Western world. Without such metaphors, we would have the sensations, but would only half understand them, by lack of words to identify them. Without Sappho's descriptions, we would hardly be able to communicate about these emotions. Sappho gave a name to the vulnerability of lovers. As Jenkyns (2016) pointed out:

> [v]ulnerability is the spur of love poetry.... The best love poet [i.e., Sappho] of all was doubly vulnerable, being both homosexual and a woman: not only can the girl say no, but she will in due course go off to get married.

> (ibid.: 32–3)

Adaptations as exploration

Some 600 years later, the first great Roman poet, Catullus (84–54 BCE), wrote a translation of Sappho's poem in his own language, Latin, the third stanza of which runs:

lingua sed torpet, tenuis sub artus	but my tongue becomes heavy, down my limbs run
flamma demanat, sonitu suopte	flames, their own sounds
tintinant aures, gemina teguntur	roar in my ears, and both my eyes
lumina nocte.	are wrapped in nightly darkness.

Of course, now the gender of the speaker has changed: now it is a male voice addressing a woman. But the poem shows the status Sappho clearly enjoyed. The speaker in the poem even addresses the woman he loves by the name of *Lesbia*—not the real name of Catullus's lover, but another clear reference to Sappho.

By the way, as in Chapter 7 before, we again refrain from discussing the structural characteristics of Greek and Latin poetry here because they are very different from what we have referred to in previous parts of this book, partly owing to the very different phonological structure of the classical languages. If you wish to get an impression how such Latin poems sound, convince yourself of this recitation of poem 64. Even if you do not understand it, clearly the form of the text is gripping, and you can listen to it, swept along on the waves of Catullus's rhythms: Link 9.5 on the Companion Website. Surprising, perhaps: this is not that much different from some forms of slam poetry nowadays. Poetry is persistent!

Now consider the following. Some 150 years later Plutarch writes in his *Parallel Lives* about Antiochus, the son of a Macedonian king (who lived 337–283 BCE), who fell severely ill, would not eat, and suffered from sudden sweats, irregular palpitations of the heart, fiery flushes, stammering speech, stupor, and pallor. Slowly, the young man was weaning away. But his doctor spent day after day in the boy's room, observing attentively his countenance, and soon noticed that some sudden change came over him when Stratonicé, his stepmother, entered the room. The doctor continued his observations, and no such changes occurred in Antiochus when other people came into his chamber, beautiful male or female persons. So the conclusion drawn by the doctor was clear: the young man was passionately in love with his stepmother, showing 'those tell-tale signs of which Sappho sings' (Plutarch 1920: 4). So already in Antiquity the physical sensations of passionate love, described by Sappho in the poem above, were identified as its certain and typical emanations. We could say that this is a clear example of how poetry has shaped life: it is Sappho's metaphors which are so successful that doctors in Antiquity already made use of them. This is one (very good) reason why we should read the classics, or indeed poetry from earlier ages. Nobody formulated this so aptly and so succinctly as Umberto Eco: 'By the age of seventy, the person who does not read, will have lived only one life: one's own! The person who reads will have lived 5000 years, because reading is immortality … working backwards.'

Well, persistent it is. Catullus and Plutarch, that was some 2,000 years ago. Then in 1930 the German composer Carl Orff set a number of Catullus's poems to music, in what became known as his *Catulli Carmina* (Songs of Catullus), which he later, in 1943, expanded into 'Ludi scaenici' (Scenic games). He gave it the provocative subtitle from the fifth song:

Vivamus, mea Lesbia, atque amemus,	Let us live, my Lesbia, and love,
rumoresque senum severiorum	And the blather of overly strict old guys
omnes unius aestimemus assis!	We do not find worth a cent!

And in 2021, Angel Bloom made an artistic video production of a dance performance to Orff's music, performed by Eugene Ormandy. Here is the opening scene, the homage to love, *eis aeina*, forever. Have a look, if you want—but beware, you may find this erotically provocative, so if you think you may be disturbed by eroticism, then do not watch: Link 9.6 on the Companion Website.

The above adaptations and echoes of Sappho's poetry are all instances of what we have previously (in Chapter 5) called *intertextuality*, another form of persistence of poetry, in that it links texts to each other in a historical chain of cross-references, so that one text in the chain reverberates with meanings and emotions attached to all the other texts. This is by no means typical of Western literature. As a clear example,[4] consider the following *waka* (poem) by Saigyo, another famous Japanese poet, who lived in 1118–90. It is addressed to his friend Nishizumi, while he was traveling:

松が根の 岩田の 岸の 夕涼み 君があれなと おもほゆるかな

Have a good look at the characters that are highlighted. Don't you recognize them? You have seen them before, namely, in Chapter 3, when we introduced you to the haiku by Basho. Browse back, and you will see the highlighted passage in that poem, exactly the same albeit in reverse order (in the poem by Basho the first three characters come after the other ones): *yusuzumi kimiga arenato*, meaning: a cool evening, wish you were here. Does that mean that Basho repeated the verse line from Saigyo? Indeed, he did: the former had a profound influence on him, so that he made the quotation a remembrance of a dear poet. The reverberation is similar to that of Sappho in later Western poetry.

Emotions in poetry reading

Emotions, so psychological theory tells us, mirror goals we have— which may be central to our life plans. And which may be obstructed or facilitated by events. Central to reading poetry is our capacity to *imagine* such emotional processes. We may know them partly from daily life, but in poetry they may be intensified by devices such as *foregrounding*. In that sense, emotions experienced in reading can function as a *(re-)orientation* on our deepest life projects and life values. That is where empathy and sympathy for the situations depicted come in—and may be generalized beyond the reading of the text to real social life. These emotional processes are not noncommittal: we do feel the emotions at hand, our bodies are involved, especially when the emotions are strong, so that we may shiver, get goose flesh, or even cry.

A personal example can illustrate that. When the book you are reading now was still in the process of preparation, I told my secretary about the decision to include the 'Wait for Me' poem (see Chapter 6) in it. We started discussing the poem itself, and in a couple of minutes the secretary, who was completely unaware of the theoretic implications of the volume, said, 'Oh my God, I am having goose flesh!' This is the sense in which the word 'embodied' is used to describe our personal involvement. The emotions during poetry reading are *embodied*. And this offers various forms of *gratification* to the reader.

And the encounter with poetry may atone for it. In highly technological societies in the West we may forget that we are often defenseless against calamities. At the same time our health may break down, we may lose our dearest relatives and friends, and love is often a worry. Cultures everywhere around the globe develop measures to protect ourselves from doom or to alleviate the pain. There are many such measures: religion, nature, friendships, sports, humor, travels, hobbies, work, etc. Amid all of these the arts, music and literature, poetry in particular, occupy a very special place. They do not dodge the distress, but confront it head-on, taking us through the deepest layers of human misery (and elation!), engage us emotionally and vigorously, then bring our emotional household again in order. Fate may shatter our cozy, comfortable everyday life—and very often it does so. Or it may lift us to the pinnacles of human exaltation. Poetry (and the arts and music in general) may clarify our emotions, and regulate them, piloting us through the muddy or turbulent waters that often surround them.

Can you do this without poetry? Maybe there are other ways. But we do know what difference poetry makes. To be sure, poetry cannot prevent disasters. But the arts may take the bite out of the suffering, if only because it becomes objectified: in reading poetry we realize there were/are other people who had to go through such calamities likewise, sometimes under much worse conditions. Suffering may be mitigated and the poetry may make peace with the world again. As to the opposite emotion, the celebration of our exultant joy, the rapture experienced in evocations of ecstasy, being of the erotic or mystic kind, may further expand the delight and wonder of the experience. Do not forget that poetry has its own deep and mysterious resources for augmenting and amplifying feelings, as we have seen on different occasions in this book. All in all, even if the arts can neither prevent unhappiness nor turn the world into paradise, our hypothesis is that they will bring a genuine and indisputable enrichment to life: definitely a richer tapestry of emotions across the spectrum, not only wider, but also deeper. Resorting to a *metaphor* (think of Mario, the postman): someone who has never swum does not know the all-enveloping gulf of water around one's body like a velvet sheet. Can one live without this sensation? No doubt: many people do. But is the sensation an increase in experience? No doubt. It is an enrichment, both as expansion and as deepening of one's experiences, one very difficult to explain to someone who has never been in the water. Being immersed in poetry is like being in the water, an uncommon element to be in.

Is there any hard evidence for what we have been discussing? Not so much for poetry. But when narrative—as another genre of literature—is concerned, there is indeed good evidence for the influence of reading on people's lives. The evidence is not overwhelming, but that is not what one would expect in any case. Reading is but one of many activities people may be involved in, next to sports, hobbies, going out, meeting friends, family life, travels, etc. And then there is a multitude of other factors that may shape a person's existence: one's medical and financial situation, the political and social circumstances in the country, housing, and the safety of one's neighborhood, relations with parents, siblings, and partners, one's educational background, one's personal disposition, and so forth. Why would reading poetry override all these essentials of life? At the same time, people (including many literary scholars) tend to negate, or minimize the effects of reading. Or is it mere ignorance of the evidence that *is* there? For this reason, we shall now go into this matter somewhat deeper, because it seems so fundamental to a theory of psychopoetics: why would you study the effects of poetry if there are none? The good news, however, is that the effects, as uncovered by evidence-based research, are both *real* and *consequential*. In what follows, we will outline some of the major findings. We begin by looking at general effects of reading literature *per se*, and will then look at some evidence concerning poetry.

Evidence for effects of reading literature

Some of the general effects of being exposed to literature are quite obvious, such as readers' vocabulary size. One would expect that frequent reading would increase one's word-stock, but the interesting thing is that it is especially reading *literature* (usually called 'fiction' in this kind of research) that augments one's inventory of words—reading non-fiction contributes considerably less to vocabulary enhancement (Reading Habits 2013). Note also that the data are not dependent on the respondents' intelligence, or on educational level. These are factors that have been controlled, so in Figure 25 on the next page, you see differences that are caused by reading literature alone. And the differences are rather spectacular.

Spectacular, we said in the previous sentence? Yes! Because fifteen-year-old youngsters who read a lot of 'fiction' (the top curve) have a trove of words 2.5 as large as their non-reading peers (the bottom line). The gap closes somewhat with increasing age, but it is still remarkably wide in old age: more than 10,000 words (which is about one-third of an adult's vocabulary). And the direct consequence of this is not just your academic ability. Having more words at one's disposal means having more ready access to the world and the information about it, a greater ability to understand texts as descriptions of the world—and being more fluent in expressing one's own ideas and feelings. This higher verbal ability has been attested in several studies: Stanovich and Cunningham (1992); Stanovich, West, and Harrison (1995); Mar, Oatley, and

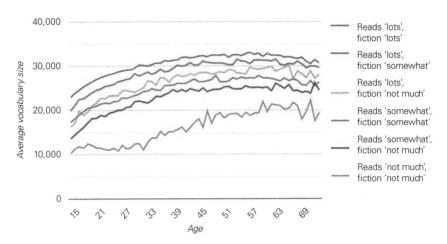

FIGURE 25 *Average English native speaker vocabulary, by age and reading habits (Reading Habits 2013).*

Peterson (2009); and Mar and Rain (2015). In their turn, Mol and Bus (2011) carried out a *meta-analysis* (a summary of a number of individual studies in the field) of ninety-nine empirical studies, involving a total of 7,669 participants, and found a very strong relationship between print exposure (i.e., reading fiction) and all aspects of reading comprehension.

But it is not just academic skills that are enhanced by reading fiction. One major effect that has been found is on so-called Theory of Mind (TOM), the capacity to ascribe mental states to other people, involving their thoughts, beliefs, emotions, and intentions. It is a skill that develops in infancy and is crucial in dealing with others in social interaction. A developed TOM is a prerequisite for smooth interaction with others. In a famous article, Kidd and Castano (2013) found, in a series of five experiments, that reading literary fiction led to better performance on both cognitive and affective TOM, compared to reading popular fiction, no-fiction, or not reading at all.

One measure by which TOM is investigated is the RME test (**R**eading the **M**ind in the **E**yes), in which participants are shown (only) the eyes of a person. They then are requested to identify the emotion of that person at the moment the picture was taken. Thus, for instance, a photograph of a man's eyes has to be identified as jealous, panicked, arrogant, or hateful. There are thirty-six items in the test, leading to a total score of thirty-six if one gives a correct answer to each item. Mar et al. (2006) showed that the amount of literary reading in prior life predicted one's performance on the RME test: the more literature you had read, the better you were at this test—which is a measure of your social skills. Similar results were obtained by Bal and Veltkamp (2013), Black and Barnes (2015), and Pino and Mazza (2016). So if you read a lot, you become more sensitive to human emotions, which is a helpful thing in life. These studies are of a general nature, looking at how much fiction people are exposed to, while Koopman (2016) concentrated on *the* literary characteristic *par excellence*, foregrounding. She sums up the situation, saying that 'foregrounding (…) has a modest but significant and robust effect on empathic understanding' (ibid.: 91).

A special mention is reserved in this respect for so-called *sleeper* effects: this occurs when the influence of a stimulus is not visible immediately in a study, but manifests itself over time (see Kumkale and Albarracín 2004). Thus an argument may not persuade you right away as you get it, but it may work subconsciously and make you change your mind (only) after some time. The work of Paluck (2009) is highly informative in this respect, showing the substantial power of literature to reduce human prejudice and conflict. Her research was carried out in Rwanda, a country in East Africa that experienced mass slaughter (up to 1 million people killed in 1994 in the genocide against the social class of Tutsi). The experiment, which ran over a year, tested the effects of a radio soap opera that featured intergroup prejudice, violence, and trauma in two fictional villages in the country. That was the experimental group. A control group listened to a health radio soap opera. Comparison of the two samples demonstrated that the fictional stories markedly changed the social norms and behavior of its listeners (but not those of the control group) with respect to: intermarriage, open dissent, trust, empathy, cooperation, and trauma healing. And importantly, those effects lasted and only *increased* over time! Apparently the way information about outgroups is organized in stories makes them to be more intensely processed, and—after an incubation time—bolsters listeners' tendency for empathy. Thus Paluck's research (ibid.) is one of the most powerful evidence-based demonstrations of the deep social effects that literature can create.

A third type of effect of reading fiction is the influence exerted by literature on people's concrete behavior, i.e., pro-social conduct. Besides Hakemulder (2000), we will mention two studies on social skills, which are somewhat between attitudes and behavior. Such abilities clearly go beyond attitudes (which may not be sufficient for pro-social behavior), but they also do not necessarily lead to behavior (one may have the skills and not use them).

The two studies in question are both valuable for another reason: just like Mol and Bus (2011) mentioned above, they are meta-analyses. Thus Mumper and Gerrig (2017) analyzed twenty-two studies that found some effect of reading literary narratives on empathy and TOM. They conclude that there is an association (weak, but significant) between reading fiction and these two psychological processes. An even stronger conclusion was drawn by Dodell-Feder and Tamir (2018) who looked at whether reading fiction *causally* improves social cognition. After meta-analyzing fourteen studies, their answer is a clear positive: 'compared to nonfiction reading and no reading, fiction reading leads to a small, statistically significant improvement in social-cognitive performance … This effect is robust across sensitivity analyses and does not appear to be the result of publication bias' (ibid.: 1713). In fact, only Koopman (2016) demonstrated an effect of literature on pro-social conduct. She concluded that exposure to literature was *the only* variable to have an impact on pro-social behavior, namely on donating to a charity. This effect remained in place when controlling for being a student or a parent and for the respondents' education level, which is relevant, since people who read tend to be older and better educated (ibid.: 278).

An even more powerful effect of a popular form of literature has been uncovered by economists. La Ferrara, Chong, and Duryea (2012) found a dramatic influence of watching television soap operas on fertility rates. They identified the so-called *telenovelas* in Brazil as a major source for the considerable drop in the number of children born since 1960, when the rate was still 6.3 per woman, gradually diminishing to 5.8 in 1970, 4.4 in 1980, 2.9 in 1991, and only 2.3 in 2000—a drop by nearly 65 percent. Researchers studied the areas in the country where *novelas* were broadcast and compared them with the regions where they were not on air. The findings indicated that women living in the former parts of Brazil had significantly fewer children, and the researchers interpreted the development as due to the *novelas* portraying small families. Figure 26 gives an indication of the startling shift in the number of children (by age group of the mother).

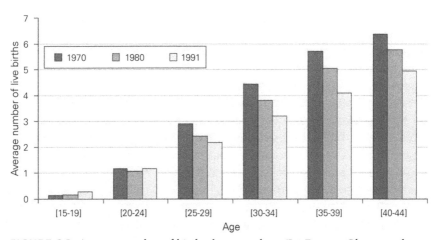

FIGURE 26 *Average number of births, by age cohort (La Ferrera, Chong, and Duryea 2012: 31). Reproduced with the permission of the American Economic Journal: Applied Economics.*

Additionally, there are evidence-based studies on the influence of literature on the quality of life in old age. We have already referred to Bavishi, Slade, and Levy (2016) who conducted a twelve-year longitudinal research. As compared with people who did not read books, those who did so lived on average two years longer. And the difference remained substantial even when factors such as education and wealth had been subtracted out.

The influence on one's cognitive outcomes is attested as well. In a series of studies, Stanovich and colleagues (e.g., Stanovich, West, and Harrison 1995) have found that the amount people read predicts not only their vocabulary size, but also skills of reasoning and general knowledge, even when such factors as IQ and level of education have been subtracted out. In a follow-up study, Mar and Rain (2015) found that by far the largest effect on such outcomes came from reading literature, as a study by the National Endowment for the Arts (2009) indicated that 87 percent of book readers are exposed to fiction.

How beneficial reading literature can be also emerges from the research by Bartolucci and Batini (2019), who conducted another longitudinal study examining the effects of listening to, and discussing, literary texts. Participants suffering from dementia were assigned to either the experimental group or a control one. The participants first completed a set of neuropsychological tests, and then the experimental sample was read aloud to for twenty minutes, five days per week, for fourteen weeks. In contrast, the control group followed their usual schedule. Initially, participants in the experimental group were read very simple texts, short in length and only consisting of short sentences. As time went on, longer texts were included, and the duration of the session also became longer, so that the stories could not be completed in one meeting, requiring participants to remember what occurred during the previous sitting. After forty sessions, both groups completed the same set of neuropsychological tests. In one month, the experimental group participated in additional thirty sessions, after which both groups again completed the same set of neuropsychological tests. Researchers found that scores for the experimental group increased for measures of immediate and delayed memory, visuospatial skills, and attention. It also performed better on some subtests of their language measure, including prose memory and word learning. These results clearly demonstrate the power that reading and engaging with stories have with respect to our cognitive abilities.

Admittedly, all the studies referred to focus on the influence of narratives, sometimes also in the form of fictional radio or television programs, not on poetry. There is one research, however, that may cast light on what poetry does in comparison to prose. In it, Hanauer (2018) offered readers a soldier's story about service in the US Army in Iraq in two linguistic forms (poetry vs. narrative) under two conditions: the text was presented either as fictional or as factual. Two hundred fifteen participants were allocated randomly to one of these four conditions. After reading they reacted to scales relating to their perception of textual features, to empathy, sympathy, and cognitive perspective-taking. The highest ratings were obtained for the *poetic* texts when they were presented as *factual* information. So the tendency of literary texts to enhance empathy and TOM (theory of mind) that we outlined in the previous paragraphs may even be considerably stronger in the case of reading poetry. Of course, one study is not enough to prove this point, but it is a highly interesting avenue to pursue. Also, the results concur with Koopman's (2016) finding that it was the foregrounded features of the text which caused the strongest empathy reactions—and foregrounding, as we have seen, is a typical literary device found in its most outspoken form in poetry. Moreover, in the research by Kidd and Castano (2013), it was predominantly *literary* stories, and not popular narratives, that elicited the strongest TOM reactions. Together these studies allow for the hypothesis that the cluster of effects of reading narrative texts allows equally well, if not stronger, for poetic texts.

But what about the specification that the information in the poem was presented to participants as factually accurate? Hanauer (2018) interprets this finding as an indication of a dual model of processing. On the one hand, poetic form clearly enhances readers' inclination toward empathy, while at the same time the knowledge that the text refers to real events further strengthens this tendency. The interpretation is dovetailed into the NCPM (Neuro-Cognitive Poetics Model) by Jacobs (2015a, 2015b) that we discussed in Chapter 6. We doubt, however, whether it is necessary to invoke Jacobs's model here in order to explain Hanauer's (ibid.) findings.

It is possible, namely, that the results display—apart from, or on top of the dual model—something else which may be very fundamental to poetry, what we will call *factuality*. What we mean by this is that when something is presented in a poetic form, people take it, well, seriously. In reading a novel or a story, you basically rely on fictionality: this is a story, it may have happened, but in all probability did not, and whether it happened or not, does not really matter. You expect it to be entertaining, suspenseful, or funny. But in reading poetry, things are more serious and sincere. If there is indeed, as we hypothesize, an association between poetry and factuality, then Hanauer's (ibid.) findings may be explained rather straightforwardly. There is no need for a dual route model, as poetry automatically enhances typical characteristics of factuality: sincerity, authenticity, thoughtfulness, honesty, and so forth.

As said before, Hanauer's experiment (ibid.) needs further follow-up, though it opens a perspective that has not been suggested so far. Our interpretation of its findings needs validation, of course, but thanks to research on poetry carried out over the past half century, we now know much more about its effects. This work will no doubt go on and increase our understanding of the arts' contribution to human well-being.

Toward a theory of psychopoetics: General principles of experiencing poetry

Let us now, at the end of this book, take stock and project all we have seen into some theory of poetic experience. In what follows, we outline some general principles that are at play. They are hypotheses, but earnest ones, and hypotheses, as we have tried to convince you in this book, make a starting point in an evidence-based search for truth. We consider these principles as main strains of psychopoetics and submit them in the hope that they will soon be subject to further research. Thus on the basis of the previous chapters, we hold that confronting poetry involves the following strands of experience:

1 **EMOTIONALITY**. In reading poetry, one of the central aims is the seeking and exploration of emotions. And the emotions in the text spill over into the emotional realm of the reader. These emotions may be so powerful that they are embodied (felt in chills, weeping, or a lump in the throat) and lead to revelation.

2 **UNIVERSALITY**. Poetry is less concerned with particular things (which is more the realm of narrative), but rather aims at universal human values and concerns (mortality, suffering, justice, relations, nature, or spirituality). It does this through an emotional appeal that promises insight and satisfaction.

3 **FACTUALITY**. In contrast to narratives, which we take mostly as fiction, poetry is taken at its face value. There is an aura of sincerity and authenticity surrounding poetry, which is partly responsible for the strong emotional impact it may have.

4 **OTHERNESS**. Poetry's factuality confronts readers with the Other, the not-me. It also deviates from readers' entrenched world view and their communicative expectations. In essence, this is a form of alienation from everyday experience. The confrontation may cause surprise, but also stronger reactions, something like dismay, for instance. This may turn some readers away from poetry.

5 **DIFFICULTY**. With the presence of numerous superordinate structures and its challenge of everyday concepts and schemata, the reading of poetry poses challenges beyond regular comprehension strategies. Readers may refrain from the additional effort or rejoice in it. Repeatedly going through such poetic sense-making greatly contributes to gains in adroit and rich reading skills.

6 **SOOTHING**. The coping potential of poetic texts, together with their often musical character, creates a soothing atmosphere in which the reader experiences consolation and relief. Even ditties do this. Soothing may generate reassurance in the reader, a readiness to confront the challenges life presents.

7 **PLAYFULNESS**. Poetic texts are a kind of emotional and intellectual game, governed by manifold rules, which, however, have to be broken.

Thus the experience of reading poems resembles solving a kind of puzzle that does not stand still. The multifarious double meanings and the superimposed repetitions and symmetries present readers with a challenge they have to face alone.

8 INTIMACY. In reading poetry, readers are thrown back on their *own* resources, their *own* intelligence and skills. The reader is alone with the text, immersed in it. A poem reveals itself to the reader in intimacy. And the intimacy reveals the reader to him-/herself, forthright and frank.

9 SLOWNESS. Poetry reading takes you into a lower gear. This is the famous retardation of which Shklovsky spoke, and strong experimental evidence has substantiated this claim. Poetry slows the reader down, bringing with it a meditative mind-set. Poetry is the realm of (powerful) gentleness; it is *largo*, *adagio*, or *andante*, almost never *presto*.

10 MEANINGFULNESS. Poetry is about finding meaning in things, in nature, in encounters, in thoughts or in feelings. And events are brimming with singular significance. Most of the topics dealt with in poetry are about the meaning of life—or the search for it. In this sense poetry is pensive, contemplative, and thoughtful.

11 INCANTATION. Poetry involves a listening experience independent of its meaning. This is fundamentally different from narrative, which needs meaning to become significant. Poetry can be meaningful without meaning, like a spell, a mantra, or a hymn.

12 RESTLESSNESS. A poem does not offer any definite insight or final solutions, as it remains fundamentally open to new interpretations. It is never really finished, but permanently unfolds new explorations of experience, physical, mental, or spiritual. Living with poetry is living with openness.

13 VISION. Through imagination, poetry conjures up another world, a reality distinct from everyday life, where readers have to find their own way, with little or no guidance. Poetic texts explore a hitherto unknown territory, which makes for adventure, for discovery, but also for anxiety. It may be a bird's-eye view or a descent into a maelstrom, an Inferno or a Paradise.

14 STILLNESS. The effects of poetry may not be immediately tangible; they may be discernible only later (sleeper effects). One sign of this is also poetry's persistence over long historical stretches of time. This inner stillness breeds a ripening of ideas and emotions.

15 AN END IN ITSELF.

I Each of these processes has a weighting, say from 1 through 100. Different combinations of weightings of individual aspects create different types of poetry, e.g., the *Iliad*, DADA, introvert emotional expression, dramatic ballads, or anthems.

II Readers can (sub)consciously choose a particular mixture of poetic characteristics to enter their lives at specific moments, for reasons they judge relevant. The mix may change over time, depending on mood or misery, seasons or circumstances, love or lethargy.

III There are different types of readers, who will embrace options of their own preference. There is considerable divergence in devotion to poetic forms between social groups, (sub)cultures, or nations.

IV These are a number of topics that need to be studied further. We hope that by studying this book you will be able to contribute to their current and future development.

It is time to finish this book. In the spirit of all that has been said before, we conclude with a poem by Shakespeare. It is one in which the forms, feelings, and functions are, we believe, epitomized in an unforgettable way:

Sonnet 27

Weary with toil, I haste me to my bed,
The dear repose for limbs with travel tired;
But then begins a journey in my head,
To work my mind, when body's work's expired:
For then my thoughts (from far where I abide)
Intend a zealous pilgrimage to thee,
And keep my drooping eyelids open wide,
Looking on darkness which the blind do see:
Save that my soul's imaginary sight
Presents thy shadow to my sightless view,
Which, like a jewel hung in ghastly night,
Makes black night beauteous and her old face new.
Lo, thus, by day my limbs, by night my mind,
For thee, and for myself, no quiet find.

* * * *

Core issues

- Psychopoetics accounts for how poetry lives in us, individuals and groups, in societies and cultures.

- The field describes and explains the experiences and effects of poetry.

- Such effects can be individual (how a person's ideas, emotions, attitudes, or behavior are changed by exposure to poetry) or social (how poetry binds groups of people or even whole nations together).

- The motivation to deal with poetry is mostly of an emotional kind, and emotions are often embodied, offering various forms of gratification to the reader.

- Adaptations demonstrate the resilience of poetry through time and space.

- There is good evidence for the effects of literature on several domains: vocabulary and cognitive abilities, empathy, theory of mind, and pro-social behavior, even on reduced mortality.

- Many of these effects are so-called sleeper effects: they work in the long run.

Further reading

Bloom, H. (2005), *The Art of Reading Poetry*. New York: Harper Perennial.

Calvino, I. (2009), *Why Read the Classics?* London: Penguin Classics.

Elliott, K. (2020), *Theorizing Adaptation*. Oxford: Oxford University Press.

Hanauer, D. (2010), *Poetry as Research: Exploring Second Language Poetry Writing*. Amsterdam: John Benjamins.

Hurley, M. D. (2012), *Poetic Form: An Introduction*. Cambridge: Cambridge University Press.

Lakoff, G. and M. Johnson (2003 [1980]), *Metaphors We Live by*. Chicago: University of Chicago Press.

McCrum, R. (2020), *Shakespearean. On Life and Language in Times of Disruption*. London: Picador.

Nussbaum, M. (1990), *Love's Knowledge. Essays on Philosophy and Literature*. Oxford: Oxford University Press.

Roberts, Ph. (2000), *How Poetry Works*. London: Penguin.

Semino, E. (2020), *The Routledge Handbook of Metaphor and Language*. London: Routledge.

Steiner, G. (2012), *The Poetry of Thought: From Hellenism to Celan*. New York: New Directions.

van Peer, W. (2007), 'The Not-Me in Thee. Negative Identification through Literature,' in I. Baş and D. Freeman (eds), *Challenging the Boundaries*, 37–53, Amsterdam/Atlanta: Rodopi.

Notes

Preface

1   We will not go into these here, because they are irrelevant for our current purposes. For those interested, refer to Bal (1984), Knapp (1987), Etkind (2005), and García (2021).

Chapter 1

1   If you have no inkling about musical harmony, you may skip this part, but for those who are familiar with music, we believe that this analysis is revealing.
2   I will marry you to.
3   But all the time she let the tears fall down.
4   Hall.
5   Gold.
6   Comb.
7   Church.

Chapter 2

1   The song is written by Júlio Campos Sousa and Joaquim Frederico De Brito (see Elliott 2017).
2   This book has two authors, so when we use 'I,' 'me,' or 'my,' it refers to one of us. Often we will not specify which of us—because it is usually irrelevant.

Chapter 3

1   'thee' = 'you';
    'ere' = 'before.'
2   We have been greatly helped in the following analysis by Akiko Hirose, for which we express our deep gratitude.

3   Edward Estlin Cummings (1894–1962) is one of the most important, albeit
     often highly idiosyncratic, poets in American twentieth-century literature.
     As one sign of his idiosyncratic traits, he preferred to spell his name *e e
     cummings* (without capitals or punctuation).

4   For those interested, the performance by Mark Padmore is more historically
     accurate than many others because the tuning of the instrument, a
     fortepiano, not a present-day piano, is set to *A* = 430 Hz (or thereabouts),
     instead of the common tuning of *A* at 440 Hz nowadays. The lower register
     was the one in use during Mozart's time, so that in this performance you are
     actually hearing the song the way it sounded to Mozart himself. (We owe
     this, and various other musical observations, to the late Sonja Moortgat and
     to Elisa Soster, for which we are extremely grateful.)

Chapter 4

1   This is his Russian name. In English, it is usually rendered as Eugene.

Chapter 5

1   Keats makes a mistake here. The first explorer from Europe to view the
     Pacific Ocean was Balboa (with the stress on the second syllable). The friend
     who was with Keats when he was writing his poem, Charles Cowden Clark,
     who was also his teacher, actually pointed out the mistake to Keats, but the
     latter nevertheless kept Cortez in the line. For one thing, 'Balboa' would not
     fit into the meter, but a much more interesting interpretation can be found
     on the site of 'The Nature of Writing,' especially from minute 13:00 onward:
     Link 5.1 on the Companion Website.

2   He is also the 'inventor' of tourism, after his famous ascent of Mount
     Ventoux in southern France, in 1336. Every year, more than 100,000 bikers
     climb to the top—though perhaps not many realize they are imitating the
     inventor of the sonnet.

Chapter 6

1   We do not have sufficient room to discuss his own works, but his *Song of
     Hiawatha* (1855), a long narrative poem about a Native American, Hiawatha,
     who lived in the sixteenth century, is one of the most popular poems in
     American culture.

2   Our translation.

Chapter 7

1   Do not take offense at the word 'savage' in the title: it is a reference to the work of the anthropologist Claude Lévi-Strauss, who used it in a neutral, descriptive sense. The title of his book *The Savage Mind* is a translation of the original French title *La Pensée Sauvage*—but 'pensée' in French can also mean 'pansy,' i.e., a violet. Lévi-Strauss was also close to Roman Jakobson. Together they wrote a famous essay containing an analysis of Baudelaire's poem 'Les Chats,' which became quite famous in the 1970s.

2   There is now an extensive literature on the musical traditions and forms in Mande culture; see especially Charry (2000) for an in-depth study. On the performance aspect of *Sunjata*, see Austen (1999); on the role of singers (*jaliw* and *jalimusow*) in general, see Hale (1998).

3   There is insufficient room here to discuss the methodological issues involved. Suffice to say that the book is full of such considerations, and all choices made during the process of research are meticulously discussed and motivated.

Chapter 8

1   In addition to the authors, Frank Hakemulder and Sonia Zyngier were involved. We are grateful to all colleagues who helped us collect data from their respective students.

Chapter 9

1   This is a rather literal translation. A more poetic one could run: 'but what a sea / it's always / overflowing.' We have rendered the sea a neutral 'it,' but in Spanish it is masculine: 'el mar.' Depending on your native language, any pronoun ('it' or 'he') may sound stilted. We would personally render the sea feminine, so 'out of *her*self,' and similarly in the rest of the poem. But that is a matter of personal preference.

2   Although the treatise dates from Roman times, it is written in Greek, the language of culture at that time. Even the Roman emperor Marcus Aurelius (121–180 CE), then the mightiest man on earth, wrote his philosophical *Meditations* not in his own language, Latin, but in Greek: Τὰ εἰς ἑαυτόν, *Ta eis he'auton* (literally 'things to one's self'). It is also the reason why the whole *New Testament* is written in Greek.

3   The text fragment breaks off here.

4   We owe this information, as well as guidance with the earlier poem by Basho, to Akiko Hirose, for which we are extremely grateful.

Bibliography

Austen, R. A., (eds) (1999), *In Search of Sunjata: The Mande Epic as History, Literature and Performance*. Bloomington: Indiana University Press.

Bal, M. (1984), 'Introduction: Delimiting Psychopoetics,' *Poetics*, 13 (4–5): 279–98.

Bal, M. and M. Veltkamp (2013), 'How Does Fiction Reading Influence Empathy? An Experimental Investigation on the Role of Emotional Transportation,' *PLOS ONE*, 8 (1): e55341.

Bartolucci, M. and F. Batini (2019), 'Long Term Narrative Training Can Enhance Cognitive Performances in Patients Living with Cognitive Decline,' *Educational Gerontology*, 45 (7): 469–75.

Basho, M. (1985), *On Love and Barley – Haiku of Basho*, ed. and trans. L. Stryk, London: Penguin Classics.

Bates, L. (2013), *Shakespeare Saved My Life: Ten Years in Solitary with the Bard*. Naperville: Sourcebooks.

Bavishi, A., M. D. Slade and B. R. Levy (2016), 'A Chapter a Day: Association of Book Reading with Longevity,' *Social Science and Medicine*, 164: 44–8.

Beebe, B., D. Stern and J. Jaffé (1979), 'The Kinesic Rhythm of Mother-Infant Interactions,' in A. W. Siegman and S. Feldstein (eds), *Of Speech and Time: Temporal Speech Patterns in Interpersonal Contexts*, 23–34, Hillsdale: Erlbaum.

Berlina, A. (2016), *Viktor Shklovsky. A Reader*. London: Bloomsbury Academic.

Black, J. E. and J. L. Barnes (2015), 'The effects of Reading Material on Social and Non-Social Cognition,' *Poetics*, 52: 32043.

Bortolussi, M. and P. Dixon (2003), *Psychonarratology. Foundations for the Empirical Study of Literary Response*. Cambridge: Cambridge University Press.

Brone, G. and J. Vandaele, (eds) (2009), *Cognitive Poetics. Goals, Gains and Gaps*. Berlin: Mouton de Gruyter.

Campbell Thompson, R. (2017), *The Epic of Gilgamesh*. Canton: Pinnacle Press.

Charles, R. (2018), 'Poetry Reading by Young People Has Doubled since 2012,' *The Washington Post*, 12 September. Available online: https://www.washingtonpost.com/entertainment/books/poetry-reading-by-young-people-has-doubled-since-2012/2018/09/12/a5724954-b6bd-11e8-94eb-3bd52dfe917b_story.html (accessed June 1, 2022).

Charpin, D. (2010), *Writing, Law, and Kingship in Old Babylonian Mesopotamia*, trans. J. M. Todd, Chicago: University of Chicago Press.

Charry, E. (2000), *Mande Music: Traditional and Modern Music of the Maninka and Mandinka of Western Africa*. Chicago: University of Chicago Press.

Chesnokova, A. and W. van Peer (2016), 'Anyone Came to Live Here Some Time
    Ago: A Cognitive Semiotics Approach to Deviation as a Foregrounding Device,'
    Versus: Quaderni di studi semiotici, 122: 5–22.
Chesnokova, A., S. Zyngier and W. van Peer (2016), 'Long-term Research
    Assessing in the Humanities: A Case Study,' *Advanced Education*, 5: 49–59.
Chesnokova, A., S. Zyngier and W. van Peer (2017), 'Learning through Research:
    Invigorating the Humanities,' *Pedagogika*, 125 (1): 195–210.
De Rougemont, D. (1983), *Love in the Western World*. Princeton: Princeton
    University Press.
Dodell-Feder, D. and D. I. Tamir (2018), 'Fiction Reading Has a Small Positive
    Impact on Social Cognition: A Meta-Analysis,' *Journal of Experimental
    Psychology: General*, 147 (11): 1713–27.
Elliott, R. (2017), *Fado and the Place of Longing: Loss, Memory and the City*.
    London: Routledge.
Etkind, E. G. (2005), *Psychopoetics. 'Internal Man' and External Speech: Papers
    and Studies* [in Russian]. Saint Petersburg: Iskusstvo-SPB.
Fabb, N. (2022), *Thrills, Sublime, Epiphany: How Literature Surprises Us*. London:
    Anthem Press.
Ferguson, D. (2019), 'Poetry Sales Soar as Political Millennials Search for Clarity,'
    The Guardian, 21 January. Available online: https://www.theguardian.com/
    books/2019/jan/21/poetry-sales-soar-as-political-millennials-search-for-clarity
    (accessed June 1, 2022).
Fernald, A. and P. K. Kuhl (1987), 'Acoustic Determinants of Infant Preferences for
    Motherese Speech,' *Infant Behavior and Development*, 10: 279–93.
Finnegan, R. (1992), *Oral Poetry. Its Nature, Significance and Social Context*.
    Bloomington: Indiana University Press.
Fitch, W. T., A. von Graevenitz and E. Nicolas (2009), 'Bio-Aesthetics and the
    Aesthetic Trajectory: A Dynamic Cognitive and Cultural Perspective,' in M.
    Skov and O. Vartanian (eds), *Neuroaesthetics*, 59–102, New York: Routledge.
Freeman, M. H. (2020), *The Poem as Icon: A Study in Aesthetic Cognition*.
    Oxford: Oxford University Press.
Freeman, Ph. (2016), *Searching for Sappho. The Lost Songs and World of the First
    Woman Poet*. New York: W. W. Norton & Company.
Frijda, N. H. (1986), *The Emotions*. Cambridge: Cambridge University Press.
García, R. (2021), *The Event of Psychopoetics. Imagination and the Rupture of
    Psychology*. London: Routledge.
Gavins, J. and G. Steen (2003), *Cognitive Poetics in Practice*. London: Routledge.
Gellner, E. (1988), 'Hochkultur und Niedere Kultur in Europa und Anderswo (High
    Culture and Low Culture in Europe and Elsewhere),' in K. Michalski (ed),
    Europa und die Folgen. Castelgandolfo-Gespräche 1987, 293–304, Stuttgart:
    Klett-Cotta.
Hakemulder, F. (2000), *The Moral Laboratory. Experiments Examining the
    Effects of Reading Literature on Social Perception and Moral Self-Concept*.
    Amsterdam: John Benjamins.
Hale, Th. A. (1998), *Griots and Griottes: Masters of Words and Music*.
    Bloomington: Indiana University Press.
Hamilton, A. (1981), 'A Complex Strategical Situation: Gender and Power in
    Aboriginal Australia,' in N. Grieve and P. Grimshaw (eds), *Australian Women:
    Feminist Perspectives*, 69–85, London: Oxford University Press.

Hanauer, D. (2018), 'Intermediate States of Literariness: Poetic Lining, Sociological Positioning, and the Activation of Literariness,' *Scientific Study of Literature*, 8 (1): 114–34.

Havelock, E. A. (1988), *The Muse Learns to Write: Reflections on Orality and Literacy from Antiquity to the Present*. New Haven: Yale University Press.

Hewlett, B. S. (1991), *Intimate Fathers. The Nature and Context of Aka Pygmy Paternal Infant Care*. Ann Arbor: University of Michigan Press.

Jacobs, A. M. (2015a), 'Neurocognitive Poetics: Methods and Models for Investigating the Neuronal and Cognitive-Affective Bases of Literature Reception,' *Frontiers in Human Neuroscience*, 9: 186.

Jacobs, A. M. (2015b), 'Towards a Neurocognitive Poetics Model of Literary Reading,' in R. M. Willems (ed), *Cognitive Neuroscience of Natural Language Use*, 135–59, Cambridge: Cambridge University Press.

Jakobson, R. (1960), 'Closing Statement: Linguistic and Poetics,' in T. A. Sebeok (ed), *Style in Language*, 350–77, Cambridge: The MIT Press.

Jenkyns, R. (2016), *Classical Literature: An Epic Journey from Homer to Virgil and beyond*. New York: Basic Books.

Johnson, J. W. (1986), *Son-Jara. The Mande Epic*. Bloomington: Indiana University Press.

Jones, D. D. (1998–1999), 'The Pulse of Creation: The Poetics of the Prologue to *Ud-ri-a*,' in *Proceedings of the Red River Conference on World Literature Vol. 1* Fargo: North Dakota State University.

Kawakami, A., K. Furukawa, K. Katahira and K. Okanoya (2013), 'Sad Music Induces Pleasant Emotion,' *Frontiers in Psychology*, 4: 311.

Kawakami, A., K. Furukawa and K. Okanoya (2014), 'Music Evokes Vicarious Emotions in Listeners,' *Frontiers in Psychology*, 5: 431.

Keats, J. (1817), 'Letter to Benjamin Bailey,' November 22. Available online: https://en.wikisource.org/wiki/Letter_to_Benjamin_Bailey,_November_22,_1817 (accessed June 1, 2022).

Kidd, D. C. and E. Castano (2013), 'Reading Literary Fiction Improves Theory of Mind,' *Science*, 342: 377–80.

Knapp, J. V. (1987), 'A Response to Mieke Bal's *Psychopoetics*,' *Style*, 21 (2): 259–80.

Konner, M. (1977), 'Infancy among the Kalihari Desert San,' in P. H. Leiderman et al. (eds), *Culture and Infancy*, 287–328, New York: Academic Press.

Koopman, E. (2011), 'Predictors of Insight and Catharsis among Readers Who Use Literature as a Coping Strategy,' *Scientific Study of Literature*, 1 (2): 241–59.

Koopman, E. (2016), *Reading Suffering. An Empirical Inquiry into Empathic and Reflexive Responses to Literary Narratives*. Rotterdam: Erasmus University Rotterdam.

Kuijpers, M. (2014), *Absorbing Stories. The Effects of Textual Devices on Absorption and Evaluative Responses*. Ridderkerk: Ridderkerk BV.

Kuiken, D. and A.M. Jacobs (eds) (2021), *Handbook of Empirical Literary Studies*. Berlin: De Gruyter.

Kumkale, G. T. and D. Albarracín (2004), 'The Sleeper Effect in Persuasion: A Meta-Analytic Review,' *Psychological Bulletin*, 130 (1): 143–72.

La Ferrara, E., A. Chong and S. Duryea (2012), 'Soap Operas and Fertility: Evidence from Brazil,' *American Economic Journal: Applied Economics*, 4 (4): 1–31.

Leech, G. N. (1969), *A Linguistic Guide to English Poetry*. London: Longman.
Leech, G. N. (1985), 'Stylistics,' in T. A. van Dijk (ed), *Discourse and Literature*, 39–57, Amsterdam: John Benjamins.
Levin, S. R. (1965), 'Internal and External Deviation in Poetry,' *WORD*, 21 (2): 225–37.
Lindauer, M. (2009), *Psyche and the Literary Muses: The Contribution of Literary Content to Scientific Psychology*. Amsterdam: John Benjamins.
Longinus (2018), *Longinus on the Sublime: The Greek Text Edited after the Paris Manuscript, with Introduction, Translation, Facsimiles and Appendices*, ed. A. S. Way, W. R. Roberts and A. S. Longinus, Wolcott: Scholar's Choice.
Lord, A. B. (1960), *The Singer of Tales*. Cambridge: Harvard University Press.
Lüdtke, J., B. Meyer-Sickendieck and A. M. Jacobs (2014), 'Immersing in the Stillness of an Early Morning: Testing the Mood Empathy Hypothesis of Poetry Reception,' *Psychology of Aesthetics, Creativity, and the Arts*, 8 (3): 363–77.
Luzzi, J. (2015), *In a Dark Wood. What Dante Taught Me about Grief, Healing, and the Mysteries of Love*. New York: HarperWave.
Malin, Y. (2014), *Songs in Motion. Rhythm and Meter in the German Lied*. Oxford: Oxford University Press.
Malloch, S. N. (1999), 'Mothers and Infants and Communicative Musicality,' *Musicae Scientiae*, 3 (1): 29–57.
Mar, R. A. and M. Rain (2015), 'Narrative Fiction and Expository Nonfiction Differentially Predict Verbal Ability,' *Scientific Studies of Reading*, 19: 419–33.
Mar, R. A., K. Oatley, J. Hirsh, J. de la Paz and J. Peterson (2006), 'Bookworms versus Nerds: Exposure to Fiction versus Non-Fiction, Divergent Associations with Social Ability, and the Simulation of Fictional Social Worlds,' *Journal of Research in Personality*, 40: 694–712.
Mar, R. A. K. Oatley and J. Peterson (2009), 'Exploring the Link between Reading Fiction and Empathy: Ruling Out Individual Differences and Examining Outcomes,' *Communications*, 34: 407–28.
Mayakovsky, V. V. ([1914] 1955), 'Война и язык,' (War and Language), in *Complete Works* (13 vols.). Vol. 1, 325–8, Moscow: The Academy of Sciences of the Soviet Union. The Gorky Institute of World Literature.
McClelland, D. C. (1961), *The Achieving Society*. New York: Irvington Publishers.
McClelland, D. C. (1975), *Power. The Inner Experience*. New York: Irvington Publishers.
McCrum, R. (2020), *Shakespearean. On Life and Language in Times of Disruption*. London: Picador.
McDonald, M. G. (2008), 'The Nature of Epiphany,' *Journal of Humanistic Psychology*, 48 (1): 89–115.
McNicol, S. and L. Brewster, (eds) (2018), *Bibliotherapy*. London: Facet Publishing.
Menninghaus, W., V. Wagner, J. Hanich, E. Wassiliwizky, Th. Jacobsen and S. Koelsch (2017), 'Negative Emotions in Art Reception: Refining Theoretical Assumptions and Adding Variables to the Distancing-Embracing Model,' *Behavioral and Brain Sciences*, 40: 380.
Merridale, C. (2005), *Ivan's War, the Red Army 1939–1945*, London: Faber and Faber.
Miall, D. S. and E. Dissanayake (2003), 'The Poetics of Babytalk,' *Human Nature*, 14 (4): 337–64.

Miall, D. S. and D. Kuiken (1994a), 'Beyond Text Theory: Understanding Literary Response,' *Discourse Processes*, 17: 337–52.

Miall, D. S. and D. Kuiken (1994b), 'Foregrounding, Defamiliarization, and Affect: Response to Literary Stories,' *Poetics*, 22: 389–407.

Mol, S. E. and A. Bus (2011), 'To Read or Not to Read: A Meta-Analysis of Print Exposure from Infancy to Early Adulthood,' *Psychological Bulletin*, 137 (2): 267–96.

Morson, G. S. (2017), 'Playing Cards with Pushkin,' *The New York Review*, 25 May. Available online: https://www.nybooks.com/articles/2017/05/25/playing-cards-with-pushkin (accessed June 1, 2022).

Moser, R. E. (1974), '*Foregrounding in the Sunjata: The Mande Epic*,' PhD diss. Bloomington: Indiana University.

Mukařovský, J. ([1932] 1964), 'Standard Language and Poetic Language,' in P. L. Garvin (ed), *A Prague School Reader on Esthetics, Literary Structure, and Style*, 17–30, Washington, DC: Georgetown University Press.

Mumper, M. L. and R. J. Gerrig (2017), 'Leisure Reading and Social Cognition: A Meta-Analysis,' *Psychology of Aesthetics, Creativity, and the Arts*, 11 (1): 109–20.

Nabokov, V. (1962), *Pale Fire*. London: Penguin.

National Endowment for the Arts (2009), *Reading on the Rise: A New Chapter in American Literacy*. Washington, DC: National Endowment for the Arts.

Ong, W. J. (1982), *Orality and Literacy*. London: Routledge.

Online Etymology Dictionary. Available online: https://www.etymonline.com (accessed June 1, 2022).

Osgood, C. E. and T. A. Sebeok (1954), 'Psycholinguistics: A Survey of Theory and Research Problems,' *Journal of Abnormal Psychology*, 49 (4): 1–203.

Paluck, E. L. (2009), 'Reducing Intergroup Prejudice and Conflict Using the Media: A Field Experiment in Rwanda,' *Journal of Personality and Social Psychology*, 96 (3): 574–87.

Papoušek, H. and M. Papoušek (1997), 'Preverbal Communication in Humans and the Genesis of Culture,' in U. Segerstrale and P. Molnat (eds), *Nonverbal Communication: Where Nature Meets Culture*, 87–108, Mahwah: Erlbaum.

Parry, A., ed (1988), *The Making of Homeric Verse: The Collected Papers of Milman Parry*. Oxford: Oxford University Press.

Pieters, J. (2021), *Literature and Consolation: Fictions of Comfort*. Edinburgh: Edinburgh University Press.

Pino, M. Ch. and M. Mazza (2016), 'The Use of "Literary Fiction" to Promote Mentalizing Ability,' *PLOS ONE*, 11 (8): e0160254.

Plutarch (1920), *Lives. Demetrius and Antony. Pyrrhus and Gaius Marius*, vol IX, trans. B. Perin, Cambridge: Harvard University Press.

Plutarch (1927), *Moralia*, trans. F. Cole Babbitt, Cambridge: Harvard University Press.

Popper, K. R. ([1959] 2002), *The Logic of Scientific Discovery*. London: Routledge.

Rapp, D. N. and A. G. Samuel (2002), 'A Reason to Rhyme: Phonological and Semantic Influences on Lexical Access,' *Journal of Experimental Psychology: Learning, Memory, and Cognition*, 28 (3): 564–71.

Reading Habits (2013), *Test Your Vocab: The Blog*, 9 May. Available online: http://testyourvocab.com/blog/2013-05-09-Reading-habits (accessed June 1, 2022).

Reichenbach, H. ([1938] 2018), *Experience and Prediction: An Analysis of the Foundations and Structure of Knowledge*. Chicago: University of Chicago Press.

Ribeiro, A. Ch. (2007), 'Intending to Repeat: A Definition of Poetry,' *The Journal of Aesthetics and Art Criticism*, 65 (2): 189–201.

Robinson, M. (2018), *What are We Doing Here?* London: Virago Press.

Rubin, D. C. (1998), *Memory in Oral Traditions. The Cognitive Psychology of Epic, Ballads, and Counting-Out Rhymes*. Oxford: Oxford University Press.

Rubin, J. Sh. (2007), *Songs of Ourselves. The Uses of Poetry in America*. Cambridge and London: The Belknap Press of Harvard University Press.

Rumi (2003), *The Book of Love*, ed. C. Barks, New York: HarperOne.

Sasaki, Y., W. Vanduffel, T. Knutsen, Ch. Tyler and R. Tootell (2005), 'Symmetry Activates Extrastriate Visual Cortex in Human and Non-human Primates,' *Proceedings of the National Academy of Sciences*, 102 (8): 3159–63.

Schwartz, L. K., L. Goble, N. English and R. F. Bailey (2006), *Poetry in America. Review of the Findings*. Chicago: National Opinion Research Centre.

Scott-Douglass, A. (2007), *Shakespeare Inside: The Bard behind Bars*. London: Continuum.

Semino, E. and J. Culpeper, (eds) (2002), *Cognitive Stylistics: Language and Cognition in Text Analysis*. Amsterdam: John Benjamins.

Shklovsky, V. ([1929] 1990), *Theory of Prose*, trans. B. Sher, Elmwood Park: Dalkey Archive Press.

Short, M. (1996), *Exploring the Language of Poems, Plays and Prose*. London and New York: Longman.

Silvia, P. J. (2009), 'Looking Past Pleasure: Anger, Confusion, Disgust, Pride, Surprise, and Other Unusual Aesthetic Emotions,' *Psychology of Aesthetics, Creativity and the Arts*, 3 (1): 48–51.

Snyder, J. M. (1997), *Lesbian Desire in the Lyrics of Sappho*. New York: Columbia University Press.

Stanovich, K. E. and A. E. Cunningham (1992), 'Studying the Consequences of Literacy within a Literate Society: The Cognitive Correlates of Print Exposure,' *Memory and Cognition*, 20 (1): 51–68.

Stanovich, K. E., R. F. West and M. R. Harrison (1995), 'Knowledge Growth and Maintenance across the Life Span: The Role of Print Exposure,' *Developmental Psychology*, 31: 811–26.

Stockwell, P. (2020), *Cognitive Poetics: An Introduction*, 2nd edition. London: Routledge.

Todd, M. L. (ed) (1894), *Letters of Emily Dickinson*. In two volumes. Volume 1. Boston: Roberts Brothers.

Trevarthen, C. (1979), 'Instincts for Human Understanding and for Cultural Cooperation: Their Development in Infancy,' in M. von Cranach, K. Foppa, W. Lepenies and D. Ploog (eds), *Human Ethology*, 530–71, Cambridge: Cambridge University Press.

Tronick, E. Z., G. A. Morelli and S. Winn (1987), 'Multiple Caretaking of Efe (pygmy) Infants,' *American Anthropologist*, 89: 96–106.

Tsoukala, A. D., M. Vogelzang and I. M. Tsimpli (2021), 'The Rhyme Inhibition Task: How Competing Phonological and Semantic Cues Influence Language Production,' Poster session at PALA 2021 Conference. Nottingham University.

Tsur, R. (2008), *Toward a Theory of Cognitive Poetics*. Brighton and Portland: Sussex Academic Press.

van der Starre, K. (2021), 'Poëzie buiten het Boek. De Circulatie en het Gebruik van Poëzie,' (Poetry off the Page. The Circulation and Use of Poetry), PhD diss., University of Utrecht.

van Peer, W. (2020), *Stylistics and Psychology: Investigations of Foregrounding*. London: Routledge.

van Peer, W. (1997), '"High"/"Low" Cultural Products and Their Social Functions,' *Empirical Studies of the Arts*, 15 (1): 29–39.

van Peer, W. (2007), 'Thematic Issue on Foregrounding,' *Language and Literature*, 16 (2): 99–224.

van Peer, W. and A. Chesnokova (2017), 'Literariness in Readers' Experience. Further Developments in Empirical Research and Theory,' *Science and Education*, 11: 5–17.

van Peer, W., A. Chesnokova and M. Springer (2017), 'Distressful Empathy in Reading Literature: The Case for Terror Management Theory?' *Science and Education*, 1: 33–42.

van Peer, W., F. Hakemulder and S. Zyngier (2007), 'Lines on Feeling: Foregrounding, Aesthetic Appreciation, and Meaning,' *Language and Literature*, 16 (2): 197–213.

van Peer, W., F. Hakemulder and S. Zyngier (2012), *Scientific Methods for the Humanities*. Amsterdam: John Benjamins.

van Peer, W., S. Zyngier and A. Chesnokova (2010), 'Learning without Teaching: Literature and the REDES Project,' in L. Jeffries and D. McIntyre (eds), *Teaching Stylistics*, 109–23, Basingstoke: Palgrave.

Vansina, J. (2006), *Oral Tradition: A Study in Historical Methodology*. New York: Routledge.

Viana, V., A. Chesnokova, S. Zyngier and W. van Peer (2010), 'Budding Researchers in the Humanities: An Intercultural Online Project,' in D. Gearhart (ed), *Cases on Distance Delivery and Learning Outcomes: Emerging Trends and Programs*, 231–44, Hershey: IGI Global.

Zijderveld, A. (1982), *Reality in a Looking-Glass: Rationality through an Analysis of Traditional Folly*. London: Routledge & Kegan Paul.

Zyngier, S., A. Chesnokova and V. Viana, (eds) (2007), *Acting and Connecting: Cultural Approaches to Language and Literature*. Munster: LIT Verlag.

Zyngier, S., M. Bortolussi, A. Chesnokova and J. Auracher, (eds) (2008), *Directions in Empirical Literary Studies*. Amsterdam: John Benjamins.

Glossary

A

aesthetic—(sometimes also spelled 'esthetic') refers to the pleasant emotional and sensual experience of beauty.

allegory—a figure of speech inviting the reader to see in the persons and actions of a poem (or story) some more general message about the world.

alliteration—the repetition of the initial consonant sound(s) in two or more succeeding words, e.g.:

> The fair **b**reeze **b**lew, the white **f**oam **f**lew,
> The **f**urrow **f**ollowed **f**ree
> (T. S. Coleridge, 'The Rime of the Ancient Mariner')

alternative hypothesis (often denoted H_a)—the assumption, in testing the difference (usually between the *Experimental* and the *Control group*) that there is indeed a difference between them, thus corroborating the theory. It is the logical opposite of the *Null hypothesis*.

anaphora—deliberate repetition of the same word(s) at the beginning of successive sentences, clauses or lines in a poem, e.g.:

> **What** the hammer? **what** the chain?
> In what furnace was thy brain?
> **What** the anvil? **what** dread grasp
> Dare its deadly terrors clasp?
> (W. Blake, 'The Tyger')

ANOVA (analysis of variance)—a (group of) statistical procedure(s) used to analyze the differences in means in order to examine the effect of one independent variable on more than one dependent variable.

aphorism—a concise and eloquent statement about some general truth.

archaic (word, phrase)—deliberate use of old(-fashioned) words or expressions to evoke the style or spirit of an earlier time, e.g., 'bards,' 'fealty,' or 'demesne' in Keats's 'On First Looking into Chapman's Homer.'

assonance—the repetition, within one or two successive lines of poetry, of similar vowel sounds, e.g.:

> My aspens dear, whose airy cages qu**e**lled,
> Qu**e**lled or qu**e**nched in l**ea**ves the l**ea**ping sun,

All felled, felled, are all felled.
> (G. M. Hopkins, 'Binsey Poplars')

asyndeton (cf. *Polysyndeton*)—the omission of conjunctions in between parts of a sentence to achieve a rhetorical or artistic effect, e.g.:

I have done. You have heard me. The facts are before you. I ask for your judgement.
> (Aristotle, *Rhetoric*, Book III, Chapter 19)

B

ballad—a narrative poem or song that tells a story, often a tragic one, originally in oral folk tradition, but adapted in a written form by literary authors, such as Walter Scott and Edgar Allan Poe.

bar (in musical notation)—a segment of time containing a number of beats having the same duration, so that a bar represents a short section of equal length that a piece of music is divided into. Boundaries of bars are indicated by vertical lines in a musical score.

between-subjects design—a design of an experiment in which reactions of (two or more) groups of comparable participants are tested simultaneously. These groups may differ in gender, age, education level, nationality, or any other characteristic.

C

canto—a longer subdivision of a narrative poem, to be distinguished from a shorter unit such as a stanza. A useful comparison of a *canto* is to a chapter in a novel.

catharsis (from Greek *catharsis*, 'purification, cleansing, clarification')—a feeling of emotional discharge through which one can achieve a state of moral or spiritual renewal, or liberation from negative emotions, usually pity and fear. Aristotle proposes this emotional purification in his *Poetics*, but there is a vast literature on what he meant by it.

chiasmus—a symmetrical repetition in reverse order of otherwise similar phrases, e.g.:

Pleasure's a sin, and sometimes sin's a pleasure.
> (Byron, *Don Juan*)

confounding variable (also *Intervening variable*)—is an invisible and unknown variable that correlates with both the *Independent* and the *Dependent variables*, and may be the real cause of the observed relation between them. Not taking into account confounding variables may befuddle the interpretation of your results. A nice example to ponder: there is a clear correlation between the sales of ice cream and the number of people drowned (for a variation).

control group (cf. *Experimental group*)—a group of respondents who are not affected by the experimental stimulus, but instead serve as the basis for comparison with the experimental sample.

couplet—(1) two successive lines in poetry, usually with the same meter, as in the final two lines of a Shakespearean sonnet; (2) a narrative part of a poem or song, to distinguish it from the *Refrain*.

Cronbach's alpha—a statistical measure of *Reliability*. It is used to gauge whether participants' responses on individual scales are systematically related, e.g., when they consistently score high (or low) on individual variables. In such a case it is meaningful to conflate such variables. Cronbach's alpha tells you whether this is allowed.

cuneiform—a system of writing, used in several ancient languages, including Sumerian and Akkadian in Mesopotamia.

D

data—a technical term for collected empirical observations, either qualitative or quantitative.

de-automatization—see *Foregrounding*.

defamiliarization—see *Foregrounding*.

defeated expectancy—a stylistic device when a lexically, grammatically, semantically, or stylistically unpredictable element appears in the text, enhancing its emotional impact on the reader.

dependent variable (cf. *Independent variable*)—a variable that undergoes the effect of the manipulation of the *Independent variable(s)*. In an experimental design, it is assumed that the *Independent variable* influences the *Dependent variable*.

descriptive statistics (cf. *Inference statistics*)—a set of statistical measures to describe and summarize the data observed. Basically, they consist of averages and measures of dispersion, like *Standard deviation*.

design—a plan for the kind of comparison you want to make in observational research (cf. *Between-subjects design* and *Within-subjects design*).

deviation (poetic license)—a form of *Foregrounding* characterized by violation of language rules or conventions (neologism, metaphor, ungrammatical sentences, oxymoron, etc.).

diction—linguistic choices made by an author; type of individual vocabulary used in the work.

direct speech—a text that reports speech or thought of a character in its original wording.

E

empirical research methods—methodology that is based on independent data, controllable observations, and evidence.

end-stopped line (cf. *Enjambment*)—a line that ends with a major grammatical unit which coincides with the orthographic unit 'line' so that while reading such lines aloud, one can make a pause after each one.

enjambment (cf. *End-stopped line*)—a line of poetry that goes over to the next line without a grammatical pause and terminal punctuation, e.g.:

> Its loveliness increases; it will never
> Pass into nothingness; but still will keep
> A bower quiet for us...
> (Keats, 'Endymion')

epic poetry (epics)—a long narrative poem, usually celebrating heroic deeds of a person of an unusual courage and bravery (used, for example, by Homer, the *Nibelungen, Epic of Gilgamesh, Sunjata, Mahabharata*, and *Ramayana*).

epiphany (from Greek *epiphaneia*, 'appearance, manifestation')—revelation of things hitherto vaguely sensed, but now suddenly enlightened and clarified emotionally, an experience of significant ineffability.

epiphora—repetition of a final component in sentences, clauses or lines in a poem, e.g.:

> I'll have **my bond**; speak not against **my bond**, –
> I have sworn an oath, that I will have **my bond.**
> (Shakespeare, *The Merchant of Venice*)

error probability—see *p-value*.

estrangement—see *Foregrounding*.

experimental group (cf. *Control group*)—the group of respondents affected by the experimental stimulus.

F

factor analysis—a statistical procedure aimed at reducing a large number of variables into fewer 'factors.'

fado—a classic Portuguese urban folk song genre.

falsification (cf. *Verification*)—in the philosophy of science, the procedure to prove a theory false by evidence.

figurative language—a form of language use in which meanings are intended beyond their literal sense, in order to create a special effect, as in a metaphor like 'He is a tower of strength.' In such figurative language, it is quite clear that the person is *not* meant to be a real tower.

filato—a technique a singer can use to slide into *Pianissimo*.

foot—a group of syllables displaying a recurrent alternation between stressed and unstressed syllables.

foregrounding (defamiliarization, de-automatization, estrangement, ostranenie)—a device or a strategy by which authors make some part of their texts stand out either by *Deviation* or by *Parallelism*.

function word—a word indicating grammatical relationships among other words within a sentence (for example, an article, preposition, conjunction, or personal pronoun).

H

haiku—a traditional Japanese poem, usually about nature, containing seventeen syllables only, following a 5-7-5 syllable structure which parallels its contents.

half-rhyme (or pararhyme)—a type of (imperfect) rhyme in which the stressed syllables of ending consonants match while the preceding vowel sounds are different, thus creating the illusion of a rhyme, as in 'hold'/'bald' or 'pun'/ 'pain.'

hypothesis—a claim that can be tested empirically and is thus open to falsification (see *Alternative hypothesis* and *Null hypothesis*).

I

iamb—a metrical foot marked by the repetition of x /, that is first an unstressed, then a stressed syllable, as in 'above' or 'attempt.'

iambic pentameter—a line of verse containing five iambic feet (used, for example, by Pindar, Sappho, Shakespeare and Milton), e.g.:

> When **for**ty **win**ters **shall** be**siege** thy **brow.**
> (Shakespeare, 'Sonnet 2')

iambic tetrameter—a line of verse containing four iambic feet, e.g.:

> Come **live** with **me** and **be** my **love**.
> (Christopher Marlowe, 'The Passionate Shepherd to His Love')

in medias res (Latin for 'into the middle of things')—the practice of starting a story in the middle of the action, without telling the reader what happened before.

independent variable (cf. *Dependent variable*)—a variable manipulated in empirical research to check whether it causes an effect on the *Dependent variable*(s); a condition.

inference statistics (cf. *Descriptive statistics*)—a set of statistical procedures that aim at the possibility of generalizing results from limited observations to a general population.

influence studies—see *Intertextuality*.

internal deviation—a type of *Deviation* when the text establishes a regular pattern and then unexpectedly deviates from it.

internal monologue—see *Soliloquy*.

intertextuality (influence studies)—the study of literary influence, investigating 'echoes' of one text in others.

intervening variable—see *Confounding variable*.

invisible narrator—an instance of telling a story without having a recognizable identity.

L

lexical parallelism—a type of *Parallelism* that involves repetition of words or their meaning.

Lied (pronounced 'leet', plural 'Lieder')—a romantic song originating in German nineteenth-century culture, the German word for 'a song.'

Likert scale—a scale used to investigate participants' emotions, attitudes, or behavior. It has the form of a battery of statements to which respondents are requested to agree or disagree.

literariness—the product of a distinctive mode of writing that is identifiable through occurrence of stylistic features, distinctively associated with literary texts; occurrence of *Defamiliarization* and modification or transformation of a conventional concept or feeling.

lyric poetry—a type of poetry in which the poet, usually in the first person, expresses feelings and emotions.

lyrical I—a conventional literary figure, usually associated with the author of a poem; the voice or person narrating.

M

manipulation—a change in the experimental material (for example, a poem).

mean (arithmetic mean)—a measure of central tendency; the sum of values for data collected in the experiment divided by the number of observations.

meta-analysis—a method of statistical analysis that combines results of several empirical studies addressing the same question.

metamorphosis—stories or poems about supernatural changes of physical form, for instance, of humans turning into animals or plants.

metaphor (see *Figurative language*)—a word or expression referring to something not to be taken literally, but figuratively, implying some similarity.

meter—an abstract pattern of alternating stress in verse lines.

N

N—a symbol indicating the number of participants in an empirical study.

narration—the process of telling a story, recounting a sequence of real or fictional events.

narrative—a story, relating a sequence of events and actions.

null hypothesis (often denoted H_0)—the assumption, in testing a theory, that the *Independent variable* (for instance, reading a poem) will not make a difference (e.g., compared to not reading a poem). It is the logical opposite of the *Alternative hypothesis*.

O

octave (from Latin *octavus*, 'eight')—a group of eight lines, often in a *Sonnet*.

ode—a form of solemn lyrical poetry, in which poets praise or glorify people, events, or abstract ideas (for example, by Pindar and Horace).

operationalization—the attempt to define the concrete characteristics of a fuzzy or diffuse concept or experience, thereby making it empirically measurable. The aesthetic experience may be operationalized by a battery of scales indicating aspects like 'beautiful,' 'sensual,' 'elegant,' or 'pleasing.'

ostranenie—the Russian neologism coined by Shklovsky in 1917 which could be loosely translated as 'making strange'; cf. *Foregrounding*.

outlier—a value that is far removed from most other observations.

P

parallelism—a form of *Foregrounding* characterized by repetitive structures, at various levels: lexical (e.g., chain repetition), syntactic (e.g., *Anaphora*, *Chiasmus*), or phonological (e.g., *Rhyme*, *Assonance*, *Alliteration*).

pentameter (from Greek *penta*, 'five')—a line of verse containing five metrical feet.

personification—a person embodying some general idea or characteristic, for instance, Venus as the embodiment of sexual love and fertility, or Nike, as the winged goddess of victory. It can also be used in the sphere of morality, when a character is seen as the embodiment of good or evil.

Petrarchan sonnet—a *Sonnet* form characterized by the following grouping of lines: 4 – 4 – 3 – 3.

phonological parallelism—a type of *Parallelism* that involves repetition of sounds.

pianissimo (Italian 'very quiet')—a very quiet dynamic marking in music.

plot—sequence of actions or events in a narrative or poem.

poète maudit (French 'accursed poet')—a poet living a life outside the usual pattern of behavior and values, going against the norms of society at large.

poetic license—see *Deviation*.

poetics—the study of linguistic and literary techniques in poetry.

polysyndeton (cf. *Asyndeton*)—a stylistic device which uses several coordinating conjunctions in succession to achieve an artistic effect, e.g.:

> **And** soon it lightly dipped, **and** rose, **and** sank,
> **And** dipped again.
> (Keats, 'Endymion')

population (cf. *Sample*)—all members of a group of people who are the subject of a research project.

post-test (cf. *Pre-test*)—a test administered after participants have been exposed to an experimental condition.

pre-test (cf. *Post-test*)—a test administered prior to the main experimental procedures.

priyom—this Russian word is used by Viktor Shklovsky to refer to specifically literary devices or techniques, especially the ones that are considered as *Foregrounding*. The word is sometimes taken over in Western languages because of its highly specific meaning in foregrounding theory. Its translations to 'technique' or 'device' miss the distinct reference to literature.

prototype—the intuitively 'best' example of a concept. For instance, a sparrow is a more prototypical bird than a penguin. In the same way, some poems (for instance, Marvell's 'To His Coy Mistress') are more typical of poetry than others (e.g., Dante's *Divina Commedia*).

psycholinguistics—the research into the interrelation between language and psychological and neurobiological factors, into cognitive, affective, and social mechanisms by which language is processed and represented in the mind and brain.

***p*-value**—a value, indicating (or not) *Statistical significance* of results, a measure of their generalizability beyond the experimental *Sample*. It is basically an indication of *error probability*, i.e., the probability that the observed group differences were caused by mere chance. Hence *p*-values must be as low as possible, but in any case lower than the conventional .05 (5 percent) level of error.

Q

quatrain—a *Stanza* of four lines.

questionnaire—a specifically designed form with questions probing specific hypotheses.

R

randomization—the allocation of participants to either the *Experimental* or *Control group* based on random assignment; the safest way to ensure that the two groups are composed of highly similar individuals.

refrain (cf. *Couplet*)—a recurring set of lines that is repeated, at regular intervals, in different stanzas of a poem or song.

reliability—the degree to which the participants in an observation respond in systematically the same way to separate items (see *Cronbach's alpha*).

repeated measures—see *Within-subjects* design.

respondent—a participant in empirical research.

retardation—the fact that certain elements of a text may be processed at a lower speed. In literature/poetry this typically occurs in stretches of text that constitute *Foregrounding*.

rhapsode—a performer of *Epic poetry* in classical Greece.

rhyme—the repetition, in two or more words, of the same stressed vowel followed by the same consonant, while the onset consonants differ, e.g.:
'pin' / 'bin', 'killed' / 'spilled', 'malady' / 'banality'.

rhyme scheme—a convention for representing *Rhyme* in poetry, for example, *A A B A/A B B A/A B C*.

rhythm—in poetry reading, the more 'natural' flow of stressed syllables, which may cause a tension to the abstract pattern of *Meter*.

ritardando (Italian 'making slow')— the slowing down of the tempo in music.

S

sample (cf. *Population*)—a group of participants in empirical research, selected from a *Population*; a subset of the *Population*. Statistics is employed to draw conclusions about whether observations in the *Sample* also apply to the total *Population.*

sextet (from Latin *sex*, 'six')—a group of six lines, often in a *Sonnet.*

significance (statistical significance)—an indication of the extent to which one is allowed to generalize the observed results of an experiment to the *Population* to which participants belong.

simile—a poetic comparison, like in Robert Burns's 'My Love Is Like a Red, Red Rose.'

situation model—a mental representation of the 'world in the text,' comprising place, time, characters, relations, and events.

soliloquy (internal monologue)—a type of monologue of the thoughts of a character.

sonnet (cf. *Petrarchan sonnet*)—a poetic form of fourteen lines with strict *Rhyme scheme* and a specific organization of stanzas.

standard deviation (often denoted *SD*)—average deviation from the average.

stanza (strophe)—a group of lines in poetry separated by white from another group of lines.

statistical significance—see *Significance.*

stress—extra prominence or emphasis given to a spoken syllable, relative to its neighboring syllables, mainly through loudness, pitch, or vowel length.

strophe—see *Stanza.*

strophic song—one in which consecutive stanzas are each sung to the same melody. Its structure can be represented abstractly (similarly to the *Rhyme scheme*) as *A A' A'',* etc.

syntactic parallelism—a type of *Parallelism* that involves repetition of syntactic elements, such as phrases, clauses or whole sentences.

T

tercet (from Latin *tertius*, 'third')—a *Stanza* of three lines.

tetrameter (from Greek *tetra*, 'four')—a line of verse containing four metrical feet.

transcription—systematic representation of sounds in written form.

trimeter (from Latin *tri*, 'three')—a line of verse containing three metrical feet.

trochaic trimeter—a line of verse containing three trochaic feet, sometimes (as with the odd-numbered verse lines) with an after-beat.

trochee—a metrical foot marked by the repetition of /x, that is first a stressed, then an unstressed syllable, e.g.:

> **Ne**ver, **ne**ver, **ne**ver, **ne**ver, **ne**ver
> (Shakespeare, *King Lear*).

V

valence—the affective quality of emotions; their degree of positive (pleasant) or negative (unpleasant) tone.

variable (see also *Dependent variable* and *Independent variable*)—a characteristic that is focused on in research. Typical (independent) variables aimed at in research are age, gender, social class, and educational level, or the stimulus to which participants are exposed. Dependent variables are the ones you expect the independent ones to influence, such as emotions, attitudes, and behavior.

verification—an approach (for example, of the Vienna Positivists) to prove a theory by way of finding evidence in the real world through observable data (cf. *Falsification*).

verse (line)—each line in a poem.

volta (from Italian 'turn')—a turn of argument in poetry typically occurring in a sonnet between the octave and the sextet.

W

within-subjects design (also *Repeated measures* design)—the *Design* of an experiment in which reactions within each individual participant are compared, for instance, between a *Pre-test* and a *Post-test*.

Ancillary Resources
Questionnaire Samples

*B*elow you will find some examples of questionnaires that we have developed, and which you can use in your own research.

Sample Questionnaire 1

Dear reader,

Below you will find the opening line of a poem. Please read it attentively, and then circle the number that corresponds best to your opinion. This is not a matter of right or wrong, but solely how *you* feel about it. That is the only thing we are interested in. There are NO right or wrong answers, as your genuine reactions are what are important to us.

Please consider the order of the answers: number **1** means that you do NOT feel that the statement applies, number **7** indicates your absolute agreement. Thus, for instance, if the question is asked whether you find a particular line 'beautiful,' circle **1** if you think it is not beautiful at all, and **7** if you think it is absolutely beautiful. With all positions in between, of course.

Now read the opening line from the poem:

[ADD THE LINE HERE].

I feel that this line:

is musical	1	2	3	4	5	6	7
has a deep meaning	1	2	3	4	5	6	7
makes me more sensitive	1	2	3	4	5	6	7

is beautiful	1	2	3	4	5	6	7
is striking	1	2	3	4	5	6	7
opens up new perspectives	1	2	3	4	5	6	7
diminishes the distance to							
other people	1	2	3	4	5	6	7
is complex	1	2	3	4	5	6	7
introduces a new attitude	1	2	3	4	5	6	7
does not have a							
practical application	1	2	3	4	5	6	7
is elaborate	1	2	3	4	5	6	7
makes me shiver	1	2	3	4	5	6	7
makes me stop and think	1	2	3	4	5	6	7
is written in a very							
special style	1	2	3	4	5	6	7
makes me look at							
things differently	1	2	3	4	5	6	7
is moving	1	2	3	4	5	6	7
could make a change							
to my life	1	2	3	4	5	6	7
gives me gooseflesh	1	2	3	4	5	6	7
probably comes from							
an anthology	1	2	3	4	5	6	7
is the sort of sentence							
discussed in							
a literature class	1	2	3	4	5	6	7
may change something							
in people	1	2	3	4	5	6	7
touches me	1	2	3	4	5	6	7
is the kind of wording that							
gets under my skin	1	2	3	4	5	6	7
makes me want to read it again	1	2	3	4	5	6	7
questions my point of view	1	2	3	4	5	6	7
is so good that I feel							
like memorizing it	1	2	3	4	5	6	7
makes me learn							
something from it	1	2	3	4	5	6	7
is of a kind I would like to							
see more in my							
daily environment	1	2	3	4	5	6	7
has a unique wording	1	2	3	4	5	6	7
is the sort of sentence							
which would inspire							
people to write							

about their
deepest concerns   1   2   3   4   5   6   7

Now please read the following part of the poem, and again answer the questions after it by circling a number on each of the scales:

[ADD THE POEM HERE]

I feel that these lines:

open up new perspectives	1	2	3	4	5	6	7
have a deep meaning	1	2	3	4	5	6	7
are beautiful	1	2	3	4	5	6	7
diminish the distance to other people	1	2	3	4	5	6	7
are complex	1	2	3	4	5	6	7
do not have a practical application	1	2	3	4	5	6	7
introduce a new attitude	1	2	3	4	5	6	7
are elaborate	1	2	3	4	5	6	7
make me shiver	1	2	3	4	5	6	7
are written in a very special style	1	2	3	4	5	6	7
are musical	1	2	3	4	5	6	7
make me look at things differently	1	2	3	4	5	6	7
are moving	1	2	3	4	5	6	7
could make a change to my life	1	2	3	4	5	6	7
give me gooseflesh	1	2	3	4	5	6	7
probably come from an anthology	1	2	3	4	5	6	7
are the sort of sentences discussed in a literature class	1	2	3	4	5	6	7
make me more sensitive	1	2	3	4	5	6	7
may change something in people	1	2	3	4	5	6	7
touch me	1	2	3	4	5	6	7
make me want to read them again	1	2	3	4	5	6	7
are the kind of wording that gets under my skin	1	2	3	4	5	6	7
question my point of view	1	2	3	4	5	6	7

are so good that I feel
> like memorizing them   1 2 3 4 5 6 7

make me learn
> something from them   1 2 3 4 5 6 7

are of a kind I would like to
> see more in my
> daily environment   1 2 3 4 5 6 7

make me stop and think   1 2 3 4 5 6 7

are the sort of sentences
> which would inspire
> people to write
> about their
> deepest concerns   1 2 3 4 5 6 7

have a unique wording   1 2 3 4 5 6 7

are striking   1 2 3 4 5 6 7

Now please read the rest of the poem, and again indicate your feelings by circling a number on each of the scales:

[ADD THE POEM HERE]

According to me the poem as a whole:

is written in a very
> special style   1 2 3 4 5 6 7

has a unique wording   1 2 3 4 5 6 7

is so good that I feel
> like memorizing it   1 2 3 4 5 6 7

has a deep meaning   1 2 3 4 5 6 7

makes me more sensitive   1 2 3 4 5 6 7

questions my point of view   1 2 3 4 5 6 7

is beautiful   1 2 3 4 5 6 7

diminishes the distance to
> other people   1 2 3 4 5 6 7

is complex   1 2 3 4 5 6 7

introduces a new attitude   1 2 3 4 5 6 7

is elaborate   1 2 3 4 5 6 7

makes me shiver   1 2 3 4 5 6 7

is musical   1 2 3 4 5 6 7

does not have a
> practical application   1 2 3 4 5 6 7

makes me stop and think   1 2 3 4 5 6 7

makes me look at
> things differently   1 2 3 4 5 6 7

is moving   1 2 3 4 5 6 7

could make a change

    to my life   1 2 3 4 5 6 7

gives me gooseflesh   1 2 3 4 5 6 7

is striking   1 2 3 4 5 6 7

touches me   1 2 3 4 5 6 7

probably comes from

    an anthology   1 2 3 4 5 6 7

is the sort of text discussed

    in a literature class   1 2 3 4 5 6 7

may change something

    in people   1 2 3 4 5 6 7

is the kind of wording that

    gets under my skin   1 2 3 4 5 6 7

makes me want to

    read it again   1 2 3 4 5 6 7

makes me learn

    something from it   1 2 3 4 5 6 7

is of a kind I would like to

    see more in my

    daily environment   1 2 3 4 5 6 7

opens up new perspectives 1 2 3 4 5 6 7

is the sort of text

    which would inspire

    people to write

    about their

    deepest concerns   1 2 3 4 5 6 7

Finally, please indicate the following:

Gender: male _____   female _____

Age: ____

I hereby give my consent to participate in this experiment _____.

                                Signature

    THANKS AGAIN FOR YOUR PARTICIPATION!

Sample Questionnaire 2
Research on Reading

This questionnaire is part of a study conducted by [ADD THE DETAILS]. It will take approximately [ADD THE TIME] minutes to read the poem and choose the adjectives that describe your reactions to it. This is an anonymous questionnaire, and your identity will be preserved. We thank you for your collaboration.

Please read the following poem.

[ADD THE POEM HERE]

Have you read this poem before?   ☐ YES   ☐ NO

Now, please mark your reactions to the poem. For each line of the table, **choose only ONE of the five options**.

	I think this poem is...					
	Very	A little	Neutral	A little	Very	
sad						happy
dark						light
beautiful						ugly
melancholic						encouraging
nostalgic						not longing for the past
lonely						gregarious
interesting						boring
mysterious						clear
mystical						physical
dreamy						down-to-earth
romantic						realistic
deep						shallow
exciting						dull
solitary						social
gloomy						cheerful

Gender: male _____   female _____   Age: _____

I hereby give my consent to participate in this experiment _____.

Signature

THANKS AGAIN FOR YOUR PARTICIPATION!

Sample Questionnaire 3
Responding to a Text

This questionnaire will be used in empirical research held by [ADD THE INFORMATION]. Your participation is vital to the successful outcome of the investigation. There are no right or wrong answers to the questions below. It will take approximately [ADD THE TIME] minutes to answer them. This is an anonymous questionnaire, so your identity will be preserved.

We *thank* you for your collaboration.

1) Gender: male _____ female _____

2) Age: _____

3) University: _____

4) Major: _____

Please read the following text.

[ADD THE TEXT HERE]

1) How beautiful do you find the text?
   - ( ) Not beautiful at all
   - ( ) Somewhat beautiful
   - ( ) Undecided
   - ( ) Rather beautiful
   - ( ) Very beautiful

2) Which phrase strikes you as the most beautiful one? You may choose up to 3.

_____

_____

3) Would you like to read more works by the author?
   - ( ) Yes
   - ( ) No

4) Do you think the text is contemporary?
   - ( ) Yes
   - ( ) No

5) Do you think the author is a man or a woman?
( ) Man
( ) Woman

6) Do you think these are song lyrics?
( ) Yes
( ) No
Why or why not?

_____

If yes, then what is the music genre? _____

Additional comments:

_____
_____

I hereby give my consent to participate in this experiment _____.

Signature

THANKS AGAIN FOR YOUR PARTICIPATION!

Sample Questionnaire 4
Responding to a Text

This questionnaire will be used in empirical research held by [ADD THE DETAILS]. Your participation is vital to the successful outcome of the investigation. There are no right or wrong answers to the questions below. It will take approximately [ADD THE TIME] minutes to answer them. This is an anonymous questionnaire, so your identity will be preserved.

We *thank* you for your collaboration.

1) Gender: male _____   female _____

2) Age: _____

3) University: _____

4) Major: _____

Now please read the following text. We realize that it is written in a language you are not familiar with.

[ADD THE TEXT HERE]

1) How beautiful do you find the text?

   1 2 3 4 5 6 7

2) What do you think it is about?

   _____
   _____

3) Would you like to read more works by the author?

   1 2 3 4 5 6 7

4) Now tell us how much you agree with the following statements. **1** means that you do not agree with it, and **7** that you fully agree.

I find the text very striking.

1 2 3 4 5 6 7

This is an interesting text to discuss with students in class.

1 2 3 4 5 6 7

The text has important things to communicate.

1 2 3 4 5 6 7

I would recommend this poem to a good friend.

1 2 3 4 5 6 7

This is a good example of high quality literature.

1 2 3 4 5 6 7

The text has made me see things in a new light.

1 2 3 4 5 6 7

I hereby give my consent to participate in this experiment_____.

Signature

THANKS AGAIN FOR YOUR PARTICIPATION!

Sample Questionnaire 5
Responding to Poetry

This questionnaire will be used in empirical research. Your participation is vital to the successful outcome of the investigation. There are no right or wrong answers to the questions below. It will take approximately [ADD THE TIME] minutes to answer them. This is an anonymous questionnaire, so your identity will be preserved.

We *thank* you for your collaboration.

1) Gender: male _____   female _____

2) Age: _____

3) University: _____

4) Major: _____

Please read the following poem.

[ADD THE POEM HERE]

1) Now please <u>underline</u> the parts you find difficult/impossible to understand.

2) What do you think is the central message of the text?

_____

_____

3) How beautiful do you find the text?
  ( ) Not beautiful at all
  ( ) Somewhat beautiful
  ( ) Undecided
  ( ) Rather beautiful
  ( ) Very beautiful

4) Now please circle the phrases that strike you as the most beautiful ones. You may choose up to 3.

5) Finally underline using a dotted line the phrases you consider to be the most moving/gripping in the poem. You may choose up to 3.

Additional comments:

_____

_____

I hereby give my consent to participate in this experiment_____.

Signature

THANKS AGAIN FOR YOUR PARTICIPATION!

Dimensions of Foregrounding Effects

1 Aesthetic appreciation
 - I think this line is musical
 - I think the sentence is beautiful
 - I find it striking

2 Aesthetic structure
 - The sentence has a deep meaning
 - The line is complex
 - The sentence is elaborate

3 Cognitive
 - It makes me stop and think
 - I would like to memorize it
 - I am learning something from it

4 Emotive
 - I find this line moving
 - I am touched by it
 - It makes me sad

5 Social context
 - This is the sort of sentence which would inspire people to write about their love
 - This probably comes from an anthology
 - This is the sort of sentence discussed in a literature class

6 Attitudinal
 - The sentence makes me more sensitive
 - I think it introduces a new perspective
 - It makes me look at things differently

Name Index

Subject Index